EDUCATOR ON AN ELEVATOR

From Chalkboard to Skyward

Dr. S. Ram Kumar M.Sc., B.Ed., PhD
(Science Educator)

Educator on an Elevator
Copyright © 2025 Dr. S. Ram Kumar M.Sc., B.Ed., PhD

All rights reserved. No part of this book may be reproduced, stored in a retrieval system, or transmitted in any form or by any means, electronic, mechanical, photocopying, recording, or otherwise, without the prior written permission of the author.

This book is sold as is, without any warranties, express or implied. The author and publisher are not responsible for any problems that may arise from using this book. If you have a problem with the book, your only option is to return it for a refund. The author agrees to protect the publisher from any legal issues that may arise from the book's content. Any legal disputes about this book will be handled according to the laws of the constitution of India

Publisher: Inkscirbe Publishing Pvt Ltd

ISBN Number: 978-1-966421-72-6

ABOUT THE AUTHOR

Dr. S. Ramkumar, affectionately known as Dr. Ram, is a visionary physics educator and lifelong learner who currently teaches science in California public schools, where he brings the Next Generation Science Standards (NGSS) to life through engaging and meaningful instruction.

His academic foundation is rooted in excellence, having earned a Bachelor of Science in Physics from Alagappa University, followed by a Master's degree in Physics from the esteemed Loyola College, Chennai. He also holds a Bachelor of Education from Vivekananda College, under the Tamil Nadu Teachers Education University, and a Doctorate (Ph.D.) from Sathyabama Institute of Science and Technology, where he specialized in educational and scientific research.

With over a decade of cross-cultural teaching experience, Dr. Ram has served Four years in Indian public schools under the national curriculum, Four years with the Ministry of Education in the Maldives, teaching the Cambridge International Curriculum, and two years in U.S. public schools, where he continues to make an impact through inquiry-based science education.

His passion for teaching and innovation has earned him the Best Teacher Award, celebrating his ability to connect with learners across diverse educational landscapes.

Beyond the classroom, Dr. Ram is a compelling speaker and educational voice, having appeared on numerous leading Indian television channels—including Star Vijay, Zee Tamil, Kalaignar, Podhigai, Jaya, Puthiya Thalaimurai, Tamizhan, and Makkal —where he has shared his insights on education, personal growth, and student empowerment.

His debut book, Educator on an Elevator: From Chalkboard to Skyward, is both a memoir and a mentor's guide. It reflects his journey through the world of education and provides practical, heartfelt strategies for interview preparation, career transitions, and professional growth. Through real-world experiences, he reveals how the skills honed in the classroom can translate into success across a variety of career paths.

With a rare blend of humility, wisdom, and global perspective, Dr. S. Ramkumar continues to inspire and uplift educators and learners alike—transforming classrooms, careers, and communities through the power of purpose-driven teaching.

ABOUT THE BOOK

*Dr. Ram's educational guide focuses on effective teaching practices, classroom management, individualized instruction, and fostering student engagement. The book begins by outlining **classroom management styles**, advocating for the authoritative approach that balances high expectations with warmth and clear communication. The **first day of class** is emphasized as crucial for setting the tone, encouraging early arrival, personal greetings, student-led interactions, and engaging introductions to build a welcoming atmosphere.*

*The author's **teaching goals** centre around student academic and behavioural development through evidence-based strategies, resource availability, emotional support, character education, and promoting a growth mindset. Teachers are encouraged to engage families and communities to build a holistic support system around students.*

*The ideal classroom is described as dynamic, inclusive, and student-centered—where collaboration, respect, and ownership of learning are visibly present. The book offers **organization strategies** for teachers, including time management, delegating tasks, and minimizing distractions.*

*A key theme is the importance of **individualizing instruction** to meet diverse student needs. Techniques like embedded learning, use of multimedia, handouts, and differentiated instruction are detailed to support various learning styles and challenges. **Assessment** is approached through both formal and informal methods to monitor and enhance student progress.*

*The author explores the value of **teamwork** in building social skills, confidence, and reducing bullying. Effective teamwork strategies are shared for both school and home environments.*

***Fairness, active listening, and professionalism** are highlighted as essential teacher traits. Strategies for handling behavioural issues and academic underperformance are shared, stressing reflection and reteaching over blame.*

*Innovative teaching methods such as **flipped classrooms, adaptive learning, and gamification** are also discussed. The book underscores the teacher's role in aligning curriculum objectives with individual student goals and using technology wisely to enhance learning.*

Overall, this book likely provides valuable insights and practical advice for young teachers. If you're interested in becoming a teacher and working abroad, this book might be a great addition to your collection.

ACKNOWLEDGEMENT

*First and foremost, I express my deepest gratitude to **God Almighty** for abundant grace, and strength that have empowered me to walk this journey as an educator and complete this book.*

*I extend my heartfelt thanks to my **beloved mother, Mrs. S. Tamilarasi**, whose sacrifices, and support have been the foundation of my life. To my **family**, your constant encouragement and belief in my vision have meant everything to me.*

*I am profoundly grateful to all my **teachers, tutors, professors, and my research guide**, who have shaped my academic path and instilled in me a passion for learning and teaching. Your dedication and wisdom continue to inspire me every day.*

*To my **friends and colleagues**, thank you for the camaraderie, support, and the many meaningful conversations that have enriched my perspective on education.*

*I also acknowledge the contributions of **motivational speakers, professional trainers**, and the wealth of **internet resources** that have expanded my horizons and helped me grow professionally and personally.*

*A special note of appreciation to the **publishers** who helped bring this book to life with clarity and care.*

*Last but by no means least, I thank my dearest child, **Magizhini**, whose innocence, curiosity, and joyful presence remind me every day why education matters. You are my inspiration and the heart of all I do.*

*This book is dedicated to **all passionate educators** who believe in the power of teaching—not just as a profession, but as a mission to touch lives and transform the future.*

CLASSROOM MANAGEMENT

1. What is your classroom management plan/style? Describe the first day of class

<u>Classroom management style</u>

The *authoritative* style is characterized by behavioral principles, high expectations of appropriate behavior, clear statements about why certain behaviors are acceptable and others not acceptable, and warm student-teacher relationships.

The *authoritarian* style tends to be characterized by numerous behavioral regulations, is often seen as punitive and restrictive, and students have neither a say in their management, nor are they seem to need explanations; the teacher's character is sometimes perceived as being cold, even punishing.

The *permissive* style is characterized by a lack of involvement, the environment is non-punitive, there are few demands on students, and there is a lot of freedom.

The indulgent style presents an environment where there are no demands on the student of any sort, and the students are actively supported in their efforts to seek their own ends using any reasonable means.

2. What are your Teaching Goals?

<u>Student Academic and Behavioral Development</u>

- **Implementing Effective Teaching Strategies** - Use evidence-based teaching methods that cater to diverse learning styles, such as active learning, collaborative learning, and personalized instruction.

- **Providing Adequate Resources** - Ensure that schools have the necessary resources, including books, technology, and facilities, to support student learning Creating a Positive Learning Environment.

- **Offering Support Services** - Provide academic and emotional support services, such as tutoring, counseling, and mentoring, to help students succeed.

- **Promoting a Growth Mindset** - Encourage students to believe in their ability to learn and improve through effort and perseverance
  -To contribute to the teaching and achieving of core performance standards and outcomes
  To develop well-rounded students: including physically, intellectually, socially and emotionally

- **Professional Development for Teachers** - Provide teachers with ongoing training and support to enhance their teaching skills and stay updated with best practices.

Offer training for teachers and staff on behavior management, conflict resolution, and creating a positive school culture. Ensure that all staff members are equipped with the skills and knowledge to support students' social and emotional development.

- **Engaging Families and Communities** - Involve parents, families, and the community in the education process to create a supportive network around students.

- **School Wide Climate** - Encourage positive

relationships among students, teachers, and staff. Promote empathy, respect, and understanding to create a supportive school community.
- Implement a framework of positive behavior interventions and supports (PBIS) to promote positive behaviors and create a supportive environment for learning.
- Integrate character education and values into the curriculum to teach students about positive behaviors and actions. Highlight the importance of kindness, respect, and responsibility in all aspects of school life.

- **Multilevel Goals: Universal Philosophy and Common Language** - To unify the individual, school, family and community with a universal philosophy and a common language
- To encourage accountability across the social strata
- **Teaching the Philosophy of Positive Actions:** Help students understand that engaging in positive actions leads to a sense of accomplishment and well-being.

Note:
Career Goals for Teachers/Instructors

- Teach a new course
- Teach extracurricular activities
- Explore new teaching methods
- Advance education
- Develop skills
- Improve student grades
- Mentor upcoming teacher
- Integrate technology
- Establish a better work-life balance
- Create a teaching portfolio
- Network with other education

3. I walk into your classroom. What would it look, feel, and sound like?

- you would observe children actively involved in meaningful learning activities.
- They would be collaborating with each other and showing responsibility for their own learning.
- You would see me facilitating group work and having one-on-one discussions with students to offer assistance.
- The classroom would be adorned with student work that highlights their progress and achievements in meeting their learning objectives.
- Conversations would revolve around the learning objectives. You might hear soft background music playing during writing sessions, a teacher reading a story aloud, or students discussing and sharing what they have learned.
- The classroom would be decorated with student work showcasing their progress and accomplishments in meeting their learning goals.
- you would feel safe and comfortable making mistakes, as we understand that making mistakes is a natural part of the learning process.
- Above all, you would feel valued and cared for.

4. Describe the first day of class as a teacher.

- **Arrive Early**: Arrive 5 minutes early for class to show students that you are ready and available to talk with them. Use this time to greet students with a smile, nod, make eye contact, and engage in casual conversation.
- **Shake Hands**: Greet students with a handshake, if appropriate. This simple gesture can make students feel welcomed and respected.
- **Student Introductions**: Have students greet someone else in the class. This can help break the ice and create a more welcoming atmosphere.
- **Social Ice Breakers**: Use ice breakers to help students get to know each other and feel more comfortable in the

classroom. However, be mindful of not overusing or using inappropriate ice breakers.

- **Cultural Greetings**: Encourage students to use greeting rituals from various cultures. This can be a fun and educational way to start the class.

- Student-Led Greetings: Allow students to create and lead the daily greeting. This can empower students and create a sense of ownership in the classroom.

- **Attention Grabber**: Start your class with an attention-grabbing problem or demonstration that relates to the material you'll be covering. This can pique students' interest and provide context for the lesson.

- **Make a Strong Beginning**: Instead of using generic phrases like "Let's get started," make a more engaging and personal introduction.

- For example, "Good morning, I'm Professor [Name]. Welcome to [Course Name]." This sets a positive tone for the class and establishes your presence as the instructor.

- **Encourage Participation:** Create a welcoming environment where students feel comfortable asking questions and participating in discussions right from the start.

- **Introduce the Subject**: Provide an overview of the subject you will be teaching. Explain its importance and relevance to the students' academic and professional goals.

- **Discuss the Syllabus and Curriculum**: Go over the syllabus, highlighting key topics, assignments, and due dates. Explain how the curriculum will be structured and how it aligns with the learning goals.

- **Set Learning Goals**: Clearly articulate the learning goals for the course. Explain what Students should expect to achieve by the end of the term.

- your students' trust, foster a spirit of free and open inquiry, display your enthusiasm for the subject, and finally, display a sense of humor.

- Don't run out of time. Have a real ending to the class, especially on the first day. Conclude with something like "I look forward to seeing you on next class."

- Consider handing out a questionnaire, "pre-test," or quiz to get to know your students, and to let them know what they will need to know. (See Sample First Day of Class Questionnaire.)Setting clear expectations with enough notice can help teachers create and meet their set due dates.

5. **Describe your organization management strategies for teachers**

<u>Organizational skills for teachers</u>

Organization in the classroom means preparing ahead of time and always knowing where you can find necessary teachings tools and resources. Here are some important organizational skills for teachers:

- **Creating and meeting due dates:** Teachers frequently create and enforce due dates, making this an important skill to learn.

- In addition to having their own due dates to meet, teachers are also often in charge of setting due dates for students' assignments

- **Delegating tasks:** Delegation can help teachers manage time more efficiently.

- The ability to entrust others to complete

important tasks can help a teacher focus more on educational tasks. Learning to prioritize classroom tasks can also assist with more efficiently managing time and

organizational skills.

- **Making decisions:** An important part of organization is the ability to make decisions. Learning how to compare the pros and cons of each decision and quickly choose one can help teachers manage more tasks each day. In addition to making a decision, the ability to recognize alternative or backup decisions can also help with effective organization.

- **Managing projects:** Teachers frequently have multiple projects at one time, especially if they teach different subjects or classrooms throughout the day. Learning how to efficiently manage projects and break down the requirements of each task helps improve organizational skills. Recognizing barriers that lead to disorganization among different projects can also help with further developing this skill.

- **Managing time:** Time management is an important part of being organized. The ability to divide tasks into time increments can help teachers'

  complete duties throughout the day while staying organized. Some teachers may also find it effective to schedule time to focus on organizational duties.

- **Creating schedules:** Creating schedules is another important task as a teacher, as teachers are often in charge of managing the time in the classroom.

- Preparing schedules ahead of time improves the ability to stay organized, even when unexpected tasks come up.

- This ensures that teachers can fit all topics into the class session

- **Communicating needs and expectations:** The ability to communicate needs and expectations both verbally and written can

- help teachers stay organized. Communication ensures teachers have all the information they need about a task before beginning and allocating resources. Good written communication skills also help teachers take notes to further improve organizational skills.

[Related: Q&A: Why Communication is Important?

- **Solving problems:** Problem-solving skills also correlate with organizational skills. Teache rs who are good at identifying problems and coming up with solutions to them can optimize their time and stay organized in the classroom. Learning how to efficiently solve problems can also help teachers overcome unexpected challenges in the classroom, without affecting their ability to stay organized.

Tips for being an organized teacher:

Becoming organized as an educator may require hands-on practice and the identification of areas of improvement. Here are a few tips you can use to improve your organization as a teacher:

Plan ahead: Planning ahead can help you stay organized while avoiding any barriers to staying organized in the classroom. Preparing your materials and class plans the night before class can help you prepare for lessons.

Use organizational resources: Resources like planners or daily reminder apps can help you stay on track when it comes to organization. You can also use 7 these programs to record reminders of assignments or tasks you want to complete.

Review organizational skills regularly: The specific organizational skills that you excel at may change over time.

Regularly review your organizational skills to identify any areas of improvement, and then create a plan to further develop those skills.

Schedule time for organizational tasks: It can be beneficial to schedule a specific time of your day to catch up on organizational tasks. You can use this time to file papers or create a to-do list.

- **Learn to prioritize tasks:** Learning how to prioritize tasks can also help you stay organized. Create a list of all the assignments you need to complete and then rank them from the most to least important, and focus on the most important tasks first.

- **Reduce distractions:** Reducing distractions can help you focus on the task in front of you.

  When you feel less than organized, aim to identify the distractions and develop a plan to overcome them.

- **Reduce clutter**: Reducing clutter in the classroom and your office can make it easier to find things, which can help you stay organized. Frequently go through class materials and recycle any items you no longer need.

- **Complete one task before moving on to another:** Aim to complete one task before moving on to another assignment. Be sure to complete that task in its entirety before beginning the next.

- **Encourage organization in the classroom:** Students and teachers can work on improving organizational skills together. Teachers can use the classroom to stress the importance of organization and work together with students to improve organization.

- **Use templates:** Templates can be a time-saver for teachers. Create a folder with templates that you can use in the classroom to reduce the time it takes to complete common classroom tasks, like grading assignments.

6. **What does "teamwork" mean to you as a teacher? Give an example.**

Participating in team activities can help students develop essential *communication and collaboration skills* while preparing them for success inside and outside of the classroom.

Four Benefits of Teamwork for Student Development and Success

I. Teaches Essential Social Skills

- Teamwork fosters essential communication and social skills, such as active listening and effective speaking.

- Working as a team, students learn to listen to their leaders and teammates to fulfill their individual roles and function cohesively.

- Teamwork teaches students how to express their ideas and opinions respectfully and confidently in group settings.

- Students should understand that speaking is distinct from mere talking; it involves communicating effectively with an audience.

- The manner in which a student speaks to other group members reflects their level of understanding and respect for others.

II. Improves Self-Confidence

- Teamwork teaches students that their voices are respected and valued.

- Knowing that they will be heard helps build students' self-confidence, encouraging further participation in group activities.

- This creates a self-sustaining cycle: participating in team activities teaches students how to be better communicators, which in turn helps every member of the team feel valued and respected.

- As a result, even the most introverted and quietest members of the team can become active participants and learn to enjoy team activities.

III. Reduces bullying

- Teamwork has the potential to significantly reduce the impact of bullying on students.

- When a student feels valued and respected by others, they can better cope with the hurtful acts or comments of a bully.

- Being part of a team that genuinely cares about its members provides a strong support system for students.

- Team members often stick together outside of formal team settings, such as during sports practice or club activities, allowing them to support each other in challenging situations.

- Additionally, the self-confidence gained from participating in team activities may empower a student to stand up for other victims of bullying who may not have a similar support system.

IV Sets Students Up for Future Success

- The benefits of teamwork almost always translate into *success outside the classroom.*
- There are very few career paths that operate in isolation. As an employee in almost any industry, people are required to work closely with others.
- That's why employers prefer to hire people who have demonstrated their ability to work as a part of a team.
- Introducing students to collaborative environments early in their school experiences presents opportunities for them to more *productive and joyful* as they work with others in a team-based environment.
- This satisfaction will be reflected in their job performance and career advancement.

How to Teach Teamwork Skills to Students

At home

Successful teamwork starts with excellent communication skills.

- To teach these skills to your students, led by example.
- Listen attentively to what they say and communicate with them clearly and respectfully
- Family activities like board games and cooking are excellent for teaching vital social skills such as collaboration, compromise, and respect.

At School

- School is the perfect place to develop your student's teamwork skills.
- She should have plenty of opportunities to develop her listening and speaking skills during partner activities and group projects.
- Team sports, school plays, and debate teams are also great experiences for learning how to be a part of a team.
- Don't underestimate the impact that a qualified, professional instructor or coach can have on your student's enjoyment of team activities.

7. **Given the multitude of material that must be taught what is the optimum way to cover all subjects and still meet individual needs? How does your management of your classroom facilitate this?**

Every teacher must believe and understand that all their learners ought to acquire equal hopes, education and future aspirations from their learning. On the other hand, the teacher must know that they will meet learners with different dynamics during their teaching career.

The main difference is that some students will learn fast, and others will be slower. Again, they will teach learners that are challenged or disabled in some way. In the light of this, it is crucial that a teacher identify and meet the needs of every learner without discrimination.

The five following reasons can identify and meeting individual learner needs is essential for promoting student success, engagement, and well-being in the classroom

1. Enhancing Quality Education: In the classroom, some children face behavioral, emotional, social, or other challenges that may impede their learning abilities. By identifying these challenges and implementing strategies to address them, teachers can help all students access education without barriers. This ensures that students facing challenges do not feel marginalized or discriminated against.

2. Nurturing Talents: Classroom needs are not always negative. Learners, especially young ones, are often in the process of discovering their skills. Teachers, with their experience, can identify when a student has a particular skill or talent. These skills and talents also become needs, as they require nurturing for development. Therefore, when teachers identify and provide essential support to develop these talents, they help students discover and cultivate them.

3. Fostering Interest: Recognizing and addressing individual learner needs can boost their morale and motivation. In some cases, students may not benefit greatly from standardized instruction. Therefore, when teachers provide individually tailored instruction (ITI), it significantly aids many students in comprehending educational concepts. This is particularly relevant in subjects like mathematics and art. When students feel supported by their teachers, they are more likely to develop, rather than lose, interest in learning.

4. Planning Classroom Activities: Once teachers are familiar with the personal needs of their students, they can effectively plan their day-to-day classroom activities to accommodate everyone. For example, teachers can schedule counseling sessions, individual tutoring, group interactions, and general supervision based on each student's needs. In short, each activity is designed to address the specific needs of students so that by the end of the day, every learner's needs are fully met.

5. Organizing the Classroom: The most effective way for teachers to organize their classroom is by first understanding the characteristics and needs of each student.

Students requiring more personalized instruction can be seated closer to the teacher. For students with visual difficulties, seating them closer to the blackboard or near a door or window with ample light can be beneficial. In essence, the needs of students should determine the availability of supplementary materials, accessibility of equipment and supplies, as well as seating arrangements.

Clearly, it is crucial for teachers to identify and address individual learner needs in their teaching. This allows them to go beyond traditional teaching methods and create an educational environment that is supportive and considerate of each learner.

Consequently, students are motivated, supported, empowered, and developed as optimal learning conditions are established.

Resources and methods providing support for learners:

1) Learning Method - Embedded Learning using Computers: Embedded learning using computers allows individuals to conduct their own research, create handouts/posters, and demonstrate/develop their functional skills in ICT.

Learners are hands-on and self-directing their learning, which supports kinesthetic learners. This method also helps learners who are completing the course through online distance learning methods. Electronic materials can be provided for learners who are unable to attend courses due to other commitments, such as having dependent children.

2) Learning Method - Delphi Technique: The Delphi Technique involves using a large quantity of the same colored post-it notes. It allows learners to get up and move around, which supports kinesthetic learners. It also offers support for visual learners and those with low ability or self-esteem, as learners can look at the board and use it as a reference point. The technique itself takes away the fear of making mistakes, creating a more inclusive learning environment.

3) Video/ Film/ Television: The use of video/film/television supports auditory learners by allowing them to absorb information through sound. It also helps visual learners as it provides them with something to watch. Tutors can use chapters in films, YouTube clips, news readings, and general video clips to help explain or demonstrate what they are teaching, catering to different learning styles.

4) Handouts: Handouts are beneficial for supporting visual and read/write learners by providing them with reference points and allowing them to take information away to read and digest at their own pace. This method also supports individual needs, such as learners with dyslexia, as they can review the material beforehand to prevent falling behind during class.

To cater to dyslexic learners, handouts should be in an easy-to-read font and available in larger sizes if needed. Additionally, more detailed handouts can be provided to higher-ability learners without pressuring others to keep up; a "Read this if you are interested" approach can be taken.

Handouts can also include PowerPoint presentations used in class, if necessary, to reinforce key points and provide additional visual support.

5) Newspapers/articles/books - These will help

support the read write learners as they have the opportunity to read through information and make notes on it should they wish to. These can either be available in class or posted to learners who are on distance learning correspondence courses.

Why is it important that resources meet the needs of learners?

It is important that resources meet the needs of learners for several reasons:

1. Engagement: Resources that are tailored to meet the needs of learners are more likely to be engaging. Engaging resources can help maintain learners' interest and motivation, leading to a more effective learning experience.

2. Relevance: Resources that are aligned with learners' needs are more likely to be relevant. Relevant resources help learners see the practical application of what they are learning, making the learning experience more meaningful.

3. Clarity: Resources that are designed with learners' needs in mind are more likely to be clear and easy to understand. Clear resources help learners grasp concepts more easily and reduce confusion.

4. Inclusivity: Resources that cater to a variety of learning styles and needs are more inclusive. Inclusive resources ensure that all learners, regardless of their learning preferences or abilities, have access to the material and can engage with it effectively.

5. Effectiveness: Resources that are well-matched to learners' needs are more likely to be effective. Effective resources help learners achieve their learning goals and objectives more efficiently.

Overall, resources that meet the needs of learners are essential for creating a supportive and effective learning environment that fosters engagement, relevance, clarity, inclusivity, and effectiveness.

What are resources?

Anything that can help aid learning in a classroom selecting the right resources is crucial for effective learning in the classroom. Here are some examples of resources that can aid learning, along with considerations for selecting them:

1. Computers: Computers can be powerful tools for learning, providing access to a wealth of information and educational software. When selecting computers as a resource, consider factors such as the software available, internet access, and the technical support needed to ensure they are used effectively.

2. Interactive Whiteboards: Interactive whiteboards can enhance classroom presentations and allow for more interactive lessons.

Consider the size of the whiteboard, its compatibility with other technology, and the training needed for teachers to use it effectively.

3. Educational Software: There is a wide range of educational software available to support learning in various subjects. When selecting software, consider its compatibility with existing technology, its ability to engage learners, and its alignment with curriculum standards.

4. Textbooks: Textbooks are a traditional but valuable resource for learning. When selecting textbooks, consider their relevance to the curriculum, their readability for students, and whether they include supplementary materials such as study guides or online resources.

5. Supplementary Reading Materials: Additional reading materials can help reinforce learning. When selecting supplementary materials, consider their relevance to the curriculum, their readability for students, and whether they provide diverse perspectives on the subject matter.

6. Manipulatives: Manipulatives, such as blocks or counters, can help make abstract concepts more tangible.

When selecting manipulatives, consider their appropriateness for the age and developmental level of the students, as well as their ability to enhance understanding of the subject matter.

7. Online Resources: The internet offers a vast array of resources for learning, including educational videos, interactive tutorials, and online quizzes. When selecting online resources, consider their accuracy, relevance to the curriculum, and accessibility for all students.

Overall, selecting resources that reflect the needs of the learners and are aligned with the curriculum is essential for creating an effective and inclusive learning environment.

8) How do you evaluate student learning in your classroom (formally and informally)?

Formal Assessment: A formal assessment is an evaluation method that uses a grading system to score a student's level of knowledge. Typically, students respond to the same questions under the same conditions, and the instructor grades them based on the extent to which they satisfied pre-defined requirements. Formal assessments often include exams, quizzes, standardized tests, and graded assignments.

Informal Assessment: An informal assessment measures students' progress and performance with no standard grading criteria. The instructor uses different methods that allow students to show their knowledge while providing feedback on learning gaps.

Informal assessments can include observations, classroom discussions, student self-assessments, and peer assessments. These assessments help teachers understand students' strengths and weaknesses and tailor instruction to meet their needs.

Types of Informal Assessment:

Quizzes: Quizzes are used to improve class engagement and participation. In this type of assessment, the instructor may split the class into groups and have every student attempt the questions. Writing Samples: Writing samples can be used as an informal assessment tool. For example, the teacher may ask students to write a summary of their ideas for a project.
Project-Based Assignments: Project-based assignments can also be used as an informal assessment. For instance, the teacher may ask students to create a science project and then summarize their ideas in writing.

Types of Formal Assessment:

Norm-Referenced Assessments: In norm-referenced assessment, the teacher measures a student's performance based on the average performance in their class or a larger group. This type of assessment is used to compare a student's performance to that of their peers.
Criterion-Referenced Tests: Criterion-referenced tests are used to judge a student's performance individually, based on specific criteria or standards. These tests are often scored using a rubric or other predefined standards.

9) Do you know a person who is a good listener? Describe that person as a listener. How can you tell when you are doing a good job of listening?

Being a good listener means focusing on the person who's speaking, not to interrupt or respond but rather just to hear them out. Good listeners play a more passive speaking role in the conversation, but they actively engage with the other person using body language and follow-up questions. They respect the person who's speaking, even if they disagree with them and react in the moment without expectation. At the end of an interaction with a good listener, the speaker should feel respected and understood

13 qualities of good listeners.

1.They're fully present. Being present means that you're engaged in the current moment.
Instead of harboring on the past (whether your own or the speaker's) or anticipating what they'll say next, you're processing information as it's told to you. You avoid all distractions, including your phone and other people. This means you maintain good eye contact to emphasize and

demonstrate your focus.

2. They don't listen to respond. If you're constantly thinking about how you're supposed to react to what the speaker is saying, you're not being a good listener. Good listeners don't focus on what they're going to contribute to the conversation next. Instead, they listen to process and understand. If you're having trouble with this, try pretending you aren't able to react or respond to the speaker.

What would you do if you wanted to remember and understand the conversation without verbally engaging with it? You'd be listening to comprehend, not respond.

3. They react in the moment. Like not listening to respond, good listeners use their focus in the present to react on the fly. While the planners among us might be made uneasy by this quality, these moment-to-moment responses will be great if they're made with understanding. If you're present, you'll be able to focus and react with your gut, not with a critical (and often wrong or harsh) mind. Your honest responses will produce an organic environment where you're more likely to foster better connections with the speaker.

4. They don't have an agenda. Good listeners go into conversations without any expectations. They're not attached to a certain outcome, so they're not going to steer the conversation any one way purposefully.

Rather, they let the speaker guide the interaction and respond based on how they feel in the current moment. They don't have a higher initiative, but rather let the conversation flow where it needs to go.

5. They don't jump to give advice. While good listeners shouldn't stray from helping someone in need or giving their input, they don't think their goal is to "fix" whatever the speaker needs. Sometimes, the best way to work through a problem is to talk through it—and that might mean no responses from a listener at all. Good listeners know when to offer their assistance and don't rush to add in their thoughts and risk taking attention away from the speaker.

6. They never interrupt. It's frustrating to speak and constantly get interrupted.
 You might lose your argument or train of thought or even get your whole point derailed and forgotten. Good listeners understand this fury and simply listen until the speaker's finished. If they're confused, they follow up after the speaker has made their point. Often, initial confusion will be clarified later. If it's not, good listeners aren't afraid to politely ask — as long as it's after the speaker's finished.

7. They ask follow-up questions. An important part of listening is engaging with the speaker. Good listeners encourage what the speaker has to say and make sure they understand what's been communicated. They ask relevant questions or try to get more detail.

If it's an emotional conversation, they provide support and ask the speaker about their needs. If it's more business-related, they may clarify and reiterate the agenda or ask anything they might not be sure about.

8. They listen as much (or more than) they speak. Good listeners aren't worried about getting their say in. Instead, they're focused on what the speaker's saying and respond when necessary. Because they don't interrupt or have expectations of what to say, they respond organically and appropriately. They don't aim to dominate the conversation, but rather try to listen the same amount or even more than they verbally contribute.

9. They show that they're listening. Although they might not be speaking much during the conversation, good listeners show that they're engaged by using active body language. This may include nodding or leaning in to show agreement or to encourage the speaker to continue.
 One of the best ways to show you're listening is to keep eye contact with the speaker — even if they're looking away, make sure to focus on them instead of letting your eyes constantly wander. These nonverbal cues are especially important during virtual meetings or talks where it may be harder for a speaker to know if you're actively listening.

10. They're patient. While they might want to jump in with a response, good listeners don't interrupt and wait until the speaker's finished with what they have to say. Imagine all that someone has to say fills up an imaginary personal balloon. Listeners don't wait until the speaker pauses but rather until they've emptied "their balloon." This means they encourage them to say all that they have to rather than rushing to finish the conversation.

11. They listen to learn. Good listeners believe they'll learn something new from each conversation.

They actively listen to understand new information or ask open-ended questions to allow the speaker to elaborate. Instead of having similar conversations again and again, they remain interested and invested and try to learn something from everyone.

12. They're interested in what the speaker is interested in. This doesn't mean that every good listener loves basketball and indie movies if their speaker does.

Yet caring and supporting other people means being interested in what they have to say. Good listeners are genuinely curious and want to find out more about what the speaker has had to say. They aren't asking questions to seem polite; they want answers, and they're excited about how the speaker will provide them.

13. They summarize what they've heard. While they don't need to repeat what they've listened to word for word, good listeners respond with a summary that clarifies and processes what the speaker's just said. This typically comes closer to the end of the conversation to help highlight important moments or illuminate any outstanding issues.

Benefits of being a good listener
- You'll be more focused. Good listening requires the listener to pay great attention to what others are saying. This ability to focus is a great tool in any situation, whether you're working with others or trying to accomplish something yourself.

- You build strong relationships. Imagine what it's like to have someone focus on what you're saying, without any distractions, and encourage you and engage with what you've communicate.

- You're likely to feel respected and valued. When you're a good listener, you connect with others more easily by showing you're trustworthy, reliable, and supportive.

- You'll process information better. Because you're not focused on a specific outcome or expecting anything out of the conversation, you'll be present which allows you to focus on the current moment and exactly what the speaker is saying. Instead of letting your head wander elsewhere, you can put all your attention into the interaction and take in all the information you need.

- Learning to be a good listener is a continuous process, one that changes based on the situation, environment and person you're listening to.
- Although there are many listening opportunities to learn from, becoming a better listener means you can apply your skills across the board, whether you're in a business meeting or letting a close friend confide in you.

- Good listening is therefore an invaluable skill, one that not only improves your ability to understand and focus but also your relationships with the world and with others.

10) **When students say they want their teacher to be fair, what do you think they mean?**

Fair describes something as being free of bias or injustice. Fair also describes something as being done according to the rules or as being neither good nor bad. Fair has many other senses as an adjective, adverb, verb, and noun. If something is fair, it does not favor one side or the other.

All students are different. They have different backgrounds, abilities, motivations, moods, coping mechanisms, support structures, habits, responses to stress of different kinds, knowledge, and so on. Making things even more complicated, each student is a different student at different times.

Students have changing schedules, feel different kinds of stress at different times, having various degrees of sleep, are well or sick, and so on. Just as one can't step in the same river twice, we can't teach the same student twice. Fairness is a lot more than we think. It is not only making sure that everyone is treated the same. It encourages, respect, responsibility, leadership, trust and a life that matters. All of these things affect a community. We should not show fairness to anyone.

11. **Describe a situation in your last job when you felt pressure. How did you handle it?**

Challenging behavior can take many forms and it is not always obviously aggressive. For example, many new teachers fall prey to engaging with personal questions such as, "do you have a boyfriend?" "are you gay?" or "do you have a girlfriend?" These questions are not asked out of nosiness but as a way of bullying you in front of the classroom audience.

If you fail to engage and you reprimand your questioner, he or she can act in an aggrieved way, claiming to be only asking a question – switching the blame onto you. If you do respond and answer the questions, expect to have this information thrown back at you constantly, shouted across the playground and posted on social media

Mind games like these are never easy to deal with especially when this is all one way.

Challenging behavior in primary schools is also a major issue. Children may be aggressive, engaging in fighting or biting the other pupils. They may throw tantrums and screaming fits, as well as destructive behaviour such as breaking equipment or spoiling other pupils' work

Sometimes, but not always, this can be classified as attention seeking, but whatever the underlying cause it will need to be managed in the classroom environment.

Reasons:

- Home environment
- Lack of routine and basic care
- Learned behavior
- Changes at home
- Behavioral issues
- Boredom
- Health

Solutions:

• Speak to the pupils calmly and explain what you require them to do. Keep it polite, non-aggressive and in a neutral tone – sometimes this will be enough to manage their behaviour.

• If they fail to respond, repeat the instruction, keeping the tone calm and neutral.

• If your instructions are ignored again, remind the students that failing to follow your instructions puts them at risk of sanctions. Your school should have a behavioral policy in place, so remind them that failing to comply with your instructions could have long-term consequences for them.

• If the student still will not comply, you may need to call in some help from your line manager. If you can issue sanctions such as a detention and calling the child's home, this may be effective. If you can't issue sanctions, report the incident to your line manager who can. You cannot afford to ignore an escalating incident or it sends the message that you can be bullied and pushed around with impunity.

• Speak to the offender privately. Most students will respond on a one-toone basis once they are deprived of their audience. They will be able to climb down without losing face. Sometimes this is all that is needed.

• Don't lose your temper and start screaming and shouting. Do this and you have lost control of the class and have provided some free entertainment as well.

- Remember the names of the people in your class. This can be hard if you teach in a large secondary school, but taking time to remember names is basic good manners and it helps you maintain order far more effectively. Calling someone out by name is far more personal and effective especially if you have to report an incident.
- If there has been an incident in your classroom, follow it up to ensure that any promised sanctions have been issued. If a pupil challenges your authority and gets away with it, it sends a message that the students can do what they like.
- Remember, you are not the only teacher in the school, so any bad behavior in your classroom does tend to reflect the level of behavior that is tolerated. Acting promptly to report issues and to deliver sanctions for challenging behavior is important for everyone's wellbeing. You should be supported by your line manager and other staff members.

12) What would you do if 50% of a class did poorly on a test?

Reason: It's important to show your knowledge of pedagogy. If half the class failed your test, it'd be prudent to look into your test or teaching methods. Chances are, the teaching strategy you used didn't stick with students, the practice wasn't aligned with the test, or students did not have enough time to practice the skill before the test. Whatever you do, do not place the blame on students. Instead, demonstrate your professional competence by giving specific examples of what you would do.

Solution: Motivate instead of shouting. "Clearly, the mark was missed. I'd first look to the test to see how it may have stumped the students in light of the material. If that holds up, then I go to the material and the strategy I used to deploy it. Then I'd have a conversation with the class and gain their feedback, because I can't always see what they see."

RRR- Revise, Reteach, Retest, Item analysis method
It is time to find out the number of students who are kinesiologic learners, and how many are auditory and visual learners. Put them into groups.

If most of the class are visual learners and you prepare them through lecture (auditory) means, without visual preparation, they will fail.

If most of the class are auditory learners and you prepare them through kinesiologic and visual cues without auditory preparation, they will fail.

If most of the class are kinesiologic learners and you prepare them through lecture (auditory) means or just with visuals without kinesiologic preparation, they will fail.

My suggestion is to determine the learning strengths of the class and teach to those strengths. Explain to the class what you are doing and why. That will get you more cooperation. For now, teach to the core concepts.

13. If a student with a significant behavioral concern is disruptive, what strategies would you use?

Stay calm and listen to student concerns – identifying the catalyst for disruption can help you address the situation in the moment or in a later meeting.
- Be steady, consistent and firm
- Acknowledge the feelings of the individual.
- Remember that disruptive behavior is often caused by stress or frustration.
- Address the disruption individually, directly and immediately.
• Be specific about the behavior that is disruptive and set limits.
• Remove the student from that class session if the student does not comply with your actions. If the student does not leave after being asked to do so, you can call UWPD for backup.
• Ask the student to see you after class to address the disruption, explore the causes of the incident and discuss appropriate behavior.
• Pay attention to warning signs that the situation is nearing escalation toward violence.

Be aware of your own limitations – operate within your own scope of comfort:

• Faculty can contact UWPD and have the student removed from class.
• Faculty can bring class to an end for the day.

Faculty can seek out additional resources and coaching to handle the disruptive student.

What to avoid
• Do not allow the behavior to continue.
• Avoid making it a class issue – address only the student who is causing the disruption.
• Avoid an argument or shouting match.
• Do not blame or ridicule the student, or use sarcasm.
• Do not touch the student

Suggestions for intervening in a disruption

These are excellent strategies for intervening in a disruption in a classroom setting.
By focusing on the individual student, being clear about the behavior that needs to change, and referring to the class syllabus for expectations, you can effectively address disruptive behavior while maintaining a positive and respectful learning environment.
Acknowledging and addressing any underlying distress is also important for diffusing the situation.
If it becomes necessary to ask a student to leave the classroom, doing so calmly and directly, and pausing class until the situation is resolved, can help maintain control and respect in the classroom.

14. How would students in "your" class describe you as their teacher? Why?
Students in my class would likely describe me as a fair, supportive, and engaging teacher. They might appreciate my ability to explain complex concepts in an easy-to-understand manner and my enthusiasm for the subject matter.
They might also see me as approachable and empathetic, someone who listens to their concerns and provides guidance when needed.
Overall, I strive to create a positive and inclusive learning environment where students feel motivated and empowered to succeed, and I believe they would recognize and appreciate these efforts in their descriptions of me.

INSTRUCTIONAL SKILLS

1. Describe the best lesson you have delivered. Why was it successful?
How to Answer The interviewer wants to learn more about what your lessons look like and how you engage students. Be specific about a lesson that stood out as meaningful and successful. Share what

you did to plan, how you executed the lesson, and how you knew it was successful for the student.
It will be successful if these factors are identified.
Engage, Explore, Explain, Elaborate, Evaluate

A successful lesson is a lesson where my students are fully involved, listening and interacting with me and each other regarding the material presented.

I plan my lessons to be thought-provoking and fun at the same time because I believe that students want to have fun and that they learn more effectively when learning is a pleasure, not a chore. I try to implement this concept into each lesson to the best of my abilities.

The true measure of a good lesson, however, is when I can look at tests and quizzes on the material and see a good level of understanding and comprehension on the student's part.

There is no easy answer to this question because it depends on many factors including the course you teach (a history course or engineering course) and the level of audience (K-12 or colle). However, I can say, a good lesson will include the following:

1) It provides the big picture behind the concept students have to learn (this answers the question why they study what they study)
2) An understandable, relevant example, preferably from real world or something that students can relate to.
3) Application
4) Perhaps a story (anecdote, incidents, etc.) that ties in with example or helps you remember
5) Practice material
6) Good resources for review and follow up (website links, YouTube videos etc.) Give example from your best lesson.

2) What are the two ways to evaluate learning?

• **Summative assessments** - tests, quizzes, and other graded course activities that are used to measure student performance.
• **Formative assessment** - any means by which students receive input and guiding feedback on their relative performance to help them improve.
• Creating assignments
• Creating exams
• Using classroom assessment techniques
• Using concept maps
• Using concept tests
• Assessing group work
• Creating and using rubrics

3) Describe your typical lesson. What does it include and who participates? how do they participate (what activities occur)?

How to Answer The interviewer would like to know how you organize your lessons. Think back to your student teaching lesson plans or what has worked in your past experiences.
Typically, a good class starts with a game, warm-up activity, or discussion about the topic of the lesson you will be teaching.
Then, you might do homework check or get started on the day's lesson.
For example, include a reading passage, discussion questions, project-based activities, Poster making, riddles making and a short quiz at the end of the assessment. Make sure to include some way to access whether students have understood the material.
In typical lesson will participate and perform some activities which is based on the topic.

4) How important is success in learning? How do you help pupils experience success? Tell us how you assess your students to determine how well they are learning.

Success is the most fundamental outcome for our every action. No one wants to become a failure. Even if you breathe you want to breathe successfully otherwise you will die.
But the definition of success has to be decided by you considering the basic nature of things.
For example, if you take learning then most fundamental criteria for success as per me is I should be able to implement and/or take advantage of that learning in the practical world otherwise it's just a piece of information for me.

Helping students succeed is a multifaceted task that involves more than just delivering lessons. Here are eight things' teachers can do to support their students:

1.Build Relationships: Establishing a positive

relationship with students can foster trust and open communication, making it easier to address their needs and concerns.

2. **Create a Positive Learning Environment**: A classroom environment that is safe, inclusive, and supportive can help students feel comfortable and motivated to learn.

3. Set High Expectations: Setting high, yet achievable, expectations for students can motivate them to strive for success and reach their full potential

4. **Provide Constructive Feedback:** Feedback should be specific, timely, and focused on areas for improvement, helping students understand their strengths and weaknesses.

5. **Differentiate Instruction:** Recognizing that students have diverse learning needs and styles, teachers can tailor their instruction to meet the individual needs of each student.

6. **Encourage Student Engagement**: Engaging students in the learning process can increase their motivation and retention of information.

7. **Promote Collaboration:** Encouraging students to work together can enhance their learning experience and develop important social and teamwork skills.

8. **Support Student Well-being**: Recognizing and addressing the social, emotional, and physical well-being of students can help create a positive and supportive learning environment.

These strategies can help teachers create a more effective and supportive learning environment, ultimately helping students succeed academically and personally.

5) Do you feel that the teacher should be responsible for developing objectives or should they be provided in the curriculum?

Yes. Of course. Another name for the teacher is curriculum implementer.

Both teachers and curriculum designers play important roles in developing objectives for learning. Curriculum designers typically create overarching objectives that align with educational standards and goals. These objectives provide a framework for what students should know and be able to do by the end of a course or grade level.

On the other hand, teachers often have the responsibility of translating these broader objectives into specific, measurable, and achievable learning objectives for their individual lessons or units. Teachers are in the best position to understand their students' needs, abilities, and interests, allowing them to tailor objectives to meet the specific context of their classroom.

In an ideal scenario, curriculum designers provide the broader objectives, while teachers adapt and refine these objectives to suit the needs of their students and the specific learning context.

This collaboration ensures that objectives are both comprehensive and tailored to meet the needs of individual learners.

6) It seems like there is never enough time to cover the curriculum or to get children to master content and skills. Would you comment on that.

The challenge of covering the curriculum and ensuring that students master content and skills is a common concern among educators. Several factors contribute to this issue:

1. Curriculum Overload: In many cases, curricula are designed with ambitious goals that may be difficult to achieve within the available time frame. This can lead to a feeling of constantly being behind and struggling to keep up.

2. Diverse Learning Needs: Students have diverse learning needs and abilities. Some students may grasp concepts quickly, while others may require more time and support. Addressing these diverse needs can be time-consuming.

3. Lack of Flexibility: Some curricula are rigid and leave little room for teachers to adapt instruction based on students' progress and needs. This lack of flexibility can make it challenging to ensure that all

students master the required content and skills.

4. External Pressures: Teachers often face external pressures, such as standardized testing and curriculum mandates, which can further limit the time available for teaching and learning.

To address these challenges, educators can consider the following strategies:

- Prioritize essential content and skills to focus on depth rather than breadth.
- Use formative assessments to monitor student progress and adjust instruction accordingly.
- Implement differentiated instruction to meet the diverse needs of students.
- Collaborate with colleagues to share resources and strategies for more effective teaching.
- Advocate for more flexible curricular frameworks that allow for personalized learning.

While time constraints will always be a challenge in education, strategic planning, collaboration, and a focus on student-centered approaches can help teachers make the most of the time available to them.

How To Improve Students Learning Skills?
It is a fact that some students learn more quickly & easily as compared to others. By studying only for 2 to 3 hours, they score more than those who spend half the time in cramming the subject. Be it a kindergarten child or a high school student, all learn to improve their learning skills. We know that is the important matter of concern for students. Don't worry; this article will help you out with this problem. Therefore, we have jotted down some useful tips to improve the learning skills of students.
1. **Identify Your Learning Style** First of all, try to understand what learning style suits you the most. If the learning technique doesn't yield you good fruits, then it's time to change the one. Or think back to a pleasant work or study experience where you performed well. Think about how you were studying. Learning skills, such as good comprehension & speed reading are useful for the information you want to take in. This can give the most yielded results to students.
2. **Underline the Key Points** Understanding the main key points helps learners effectively. This is a common method used by many students. While learning, highlighting & underlining the main points that help in briefing up the whole topic or concept. These key points provides help during the time of examination as highlighted statements assist us in brushing up the subject before exams or class tests. Highlight or underline important points & be selective just enough to use them as review material.
3. **Clarity Over Concepts** One should have clarity of subjects, topics & concepts while learning. This is of utmost importance as whenever anyone asks you or discuss their queries, you can answer them easily. Whenever you get a doubt, clear it immediately because you don't know how it will affect you in the process of preparation. Be strong in your concepts, take the plunge & discuss all your problems with teachers & intelligent students. Get acquainted with textbooks & other related study material to resolve all your problems over a topic.
4. **Problem Solving Ability** Students must have problem-solving ability to assess all types of information they have processed into their mind. They must be well prepared to solve out any type of study- related issue or can help others with the same.
5. **Use Memory Techniques** to Develop Your Memory Using different Memory tricks will help you in better learning. There are a variety of memory techniques that can make remembering & learn much easier. Active & critical thinking, questioning, reasoning & assumptions, and applying the knowledge practically in the right way helps to develop learning skills.
6. **Study with Others & Collaborate with Them** If you find studying in groups interesting than choosing a couple of study partners with whom you work & study well.
Studying in a group helps to break down the usual habit of sitting alone with your nose in books all throughout the day. Doing a group study with great collaboration with teammates helps in processing the information deeper & quicker. Active engagement with information with your study mates not only helps in good learning but also makes studying more enjoyable & easier. The best way to learn something is to teach it to others to get mastery over the topic.
7. **Give A Try** to New Technologies Though the old handwritten method still has & will be at its place. In the world of technologies, try to adopt newer techniques in studies. There are so many online tools like social media, mobile apps, blogs, YouTube videos, Google & much more. All these modern tech-tools have truly made learning easier & user oriented.
8. **Recall Your Learning** Never forget to recall what you've learned all through your study sessions. Do something else not connected to your studies, at the time when you go for a break after studying for 1 or 2 hours. But don't stop thinking about what you've read, remember it! It's quite important for us to solve & recall the whole piece of information as this is the time when one can realize what topics are in mind & which are forgotten.
At the end of the period, the information you were reading will then be much clearer than it was at the time of beginning.

7) How would you assess your effectiveness as a teacher?

Assessing effectiveness as a teacher can be done through a combination of self-reflection, student feedback, peer evaluation, and observation. Here are some key ways to assess effectiveness:

1. Self-Reflection: Regularly reflect on your teaching practices, lessons, and interactions with students. Consider what worked well, what could be improved, and how you can grow as a teacher.

2. Student Feedback: Seek feedback from students through surveys, evaluations, or informal discussions. Their perspectives can provide valuable insights into your teaching style and effectiveness.

3. Peer Evaluation: Collaborate with colleagues to observe each other's classes and provide constructive feedback. Peer observations can offer fresh perspectives and ideas for improvement.

4. **Administrative Evaluation: Participate in** formal evaluations conducted by school administrators. These evaluations often include criteria such as lesson planning, classroom management, and student engagement.

5. Student Achievement: Assess student learning outcomes to determine if students are meeting the intended learning objectives. This could include analyzing test scores, projects, or other assessments.

6. Professional Development: Engage in ongoing professional development to stay current with best practices in teaching and learning. Attending workshops, conferences, and training sessions can enhance your effectiveness as a teacher.

By using a combination of these methods, teachers can gain a comprehensive understanding of their effectiveness and identify areas for improvement to enhance student learning outcomes.

8) What was your most creative lesson for reading to help the struggling reader?

13 WAYS TO MAKE READING FUN FOR YOUR CHILD

1. **Pick the right books or topics** Making reading fun starts with selecting a book your child will enjoy reading. Ask your child what kinds of stories he or she likes reading best (Adventure? Fantasy?) Make a list of books in these categories and use it to help your child choose what he or she will read next.

2. **Read aloud** Reading aloud with your child can add a bit more excitement to any book. Make the story more fun by using different voices for each character and an expressive voice for dramatic parts. You can also take turns reading aloud together, choosing a character you will each provide a voice for.

3. **Act out the story** Help your child bring some extra excitement to reading by using his or her imagination. Have your child draw pictures of what he or she is reading, act out the scene, put on a character puppet show, or make up alternate endings.

4. **Encourage all forms of reading** Reading doesn't always have to mean picking up a book. Magazines, graphic novels, and newspapers are other great reading materials that feel less like "work" to your child—but they still help your child practice and improve his or her reading skills.

5. **Choose books about his or her interests** Reading something your child enjoys makes reading less of a chore and more of a fun activity he or she will want to do. Help your child choose books that are related to his or her interests—whether it's sports, animals, dinosaurs, or something else.

6. **Create a reading space** Make a reading area or fort where your child can read and relax on his or her own. Add blankets, pillows, and a variety of books, and your child will have a reading corner where he or she can read a book whenever the urge to read hits.

7. **Make connections between books and life** Make connections between what your child is reading and your child's own experience. Read adventure books before you take a camping trip, dinosaur books before you visit a museum, and so on. This will help make reading (and learning) more exciting for your child.

8. **Let your child choose** Let your child choose what book he or she wants to read. Giving him or her a choice helps your child feel like he or she has more control, so your child will be more excited to sit down with the book he or she has chosen.

9. **Listen to audio books** For children who find reading frustrating, audio books are a great alternative to help make reading more enjoyable—while still helping your child improve his or her comprehension skills. 10.Start a series Book series are a great way to keep your child's interest in reading high and eliminate the problem of figuring out what to read next. Another option is reading

multiple, non-series books written by the same author.

11. Have "reading hour" Each day, schedule reading time for your child to sit down and read a chapter of a book. During this time, talk to your child about what is happening in the book, what his or her favorite part was, and what he or she thinks will happen next.

12. Take a trip to the library The library is a great resource where your child can find lots of books to read. Take advantage of the selection at your local library by letting your child pick choose a book (or two!) that catches his or her attention.

13. Teach reading strategies Many children dislike reading simply because they don't have the necessary reading skills. If your child avoids opening a book at all costs, talk to his or her teacher about strategies to help develop reading motivation.

Once you have some tips to try, work with your child to build reading motivation together.

9) What are the most current and effective trends in teaching science and reading? Describe the teaching techniques or strategies that are most effective for you.

Modern Trends in Science Teaching Methods and Strategies

Multiple teaching strategies have recently emerged, based on science education research, which align with the requirements of the current era. Such strategies rely on the use of educational technology to teach science and enhance students' opportunities for self-learning and meaningful learning. Examples include: teaching strategies based on Web 2.0 technologies, integrated learning, and flipped learning; strategies that rely on visual stimuli such as the thinking maps strategy, mind maps, the fishbone strategy, and the circular house shape strategy; and strategies that focus on individual differences, such as differentiated teaching and adaptive education Flipped Learning Flipped learning is a form of combined learning that involves both e-learning and direct learning; it reshapes the educational process, and the roles of both school and home. The learners use technology at home (e.g., video clips, audio clips) to learn the basic concepts and the basic ideas associated with them. Then, s/he goes to school to apply and solve problems associated with these concepts with the help of her/his teacher, and her/his peers participate in carrying out activities related to the lesson. Flipped learning targets teaching in the classroom to make learning easier and more fun and make it possible for the teacher to use the class time to share in learner centered interaction rather than dumping information on students. This type of learning can convert class time into home through recorded videos.

Flipped learning is important in that it ensures an appropriate investment of class time that allows more time for investigation. The teacher spends most of the time in the classroom guiding, motivating and assisting students and building stronger relationships with them. In this way, students are transformed into researchers of information sources, which promotes critical thinking and self-learning. This method also provides freedom for students to choose their own time and speed for learning; students receive feedback from the teacher during class, which provides remedial teaching for late students.

Because flipped learning depends on technology to keep pace with current developments, it's very helpful for science teaching and learning.

Differentiated Education It is clearly one of the goals of science education to take into consideration the individual differences among learners. This is done by searching for teaching strategies that help to achieve meaningful learning and assist science teachers in creating educational situation for learners of different levels. Therefore, new trend as differentiated education has emerged in science education, which calls for the diversification of teaching strategies according to the nature of learners in the classroom.

Differentiated education is defined as an integrating approach in teaching that satisfies the diversity of skill levels and students' abilities in a single classroom. That is the teacher changes and modifies the elements of the curriculum to correspond with the characteristics of the learners, in order to raise the level of all students. The importance of differentiated education is that it helps the teacher to consider differing students abilities and to realize the needs of all students, including those who excel and those with learning difficulties. Moreover, differentiated learning helps to promote students human right to receive a good-quality education without discrimination. A number of studies have focused on differentiated education as a recent trend in teaching science according to the diversity of learners.

Adaptive Learning Many educational institutions around the world rely on e-learning programs. However, students' adaptation to e-learning receives little attention. Therefore, e-learning must be designed according to the needs and capabilities of students. Education must also be adapted to the nature of learners' abilities. An adaptive learning environment is a personal electronic system that supports adaptive interaction; the system receives data, creates a model of its own, and then performs adaptation according to that model . Recent studies in the field of learning technology have focused on the possibility of adapting e-learning to learners according to different learning styles, which introduces a new pedagogical model based on adaptive methodology. The adaptive methodology provides content for learners in a unified way while allowing them to choose from the different learning elements according to various standards that suit each of them separately. Adaptive learning depends on three basic elements: a learner's primary knowledge, the learning objectives, and the learner's preferred learning methods.

Adaptive e-learning is a new approach to education that makes an e-learning system more flexible in displaying information to build links for each learner to fit with their knowledge and capabilities. This type of learning depends on the distinct characteristics of each learner which must be observed within the learning environment. Thus, what is appropriate for one learner may not be appropriate for another. Therefore, adaptive e-learning helps to develop learning processes and thus improve students' results.

Certain considerations were observed when building an adaptive educational system:
1. The educational content should fit the learner's level; thus, a learner's initial level is first identified, and educational activities are then presented that align with their needs and abilities.
2. Content elements should be organized in a specific manner, from easy to difficult.
3. Learners' characteristics previous experiences should be determined.
4. Learners should be given the opportunity to practice the required behavior through repetition, and different methods should be used to provide feedback.

A number of studies have focused on adaptive e-learning as a modern teaching strategy that relies on technology while taking into account the individual differences among learners.

The Current Trends in Education Technology

Education technology, or EdTech, is constantly evolving, with new trends and innovations emerging regularly. Some of the current trends in EdTech include:

1. Personalized Learning: Technology allows for personalized learning experiences tailored to individual student needs, preferences, and pace of learning. This includes adaptive learning platforms, personalized learning paths, and data-driven insights to inform instruction.

2. Blended Learning: Blended learning combines traditional face-to-face instruction with online learning activities and resources. This approach allows for more flexibility and personalized learning experiences.

3. Gamification: Gamification involves using game elements and principles in educational settings to engage students and motivate them to learn. This can include game-based learning platforms, rewards systems, and interactive learning activities.

4. Artificial Intelligence (AI) and Machine Learning: AI and machine learning technologies are being used to analyze data, personalize learning experiences, and provide targeted feedback to students. These technologies can also help educators track student progress and identify areas for improvement.

5 Virtual and Augmented Reality: Virtual reality (VR) and augmented reality (AR) are being used to create immersive learning experiences that can enhance understanding and retention of complex concepts. These technologies are particularly useful for subjects that require visualization, such as science and mathematics.

6. Collaborative Tools: Technology tools that facilitate collaboration, such as video conferencing, collaborative document editing, and online discussion forums, are becoming increasingly popular in education. These tools help students work together, regardless of their location, and develop important teamwork and communication skills.

7. Digital Citizenship and Online Safety: With the increasing use of technology in education, there is a growing focus on teaching students about digital citizenship and online safety. This includes educating students about responsible online behavior, cyberbullying, and protecting their personal information online.

8. Remote and Hybrid Learning: The COVID-19 pandemic has accelerated the adoption of remote and hybrid learning models, leading to increased use of online learning platforms, video conferencing tools, and other technologies to support distance learning.

These trends reflect the ongoing efforts to leverage technology to enhance teaching and learning experiences, improve educational outcomes, and prepare students for success in a rapidly changing world.

10) How would you include cooperative learning in class teaching?

Cooperative learning is a teaching approach that involves students working together in groups to achieve a common goal or complete a task. Here are some ways to include cooperative learning in class teaching:

1. Group Projects: Assign group projects that require students to work together to research a topic, solve a problem, or create a presentation.

This encourages collaboration and helps students develop teamwork skills.

2. Jigsaw Technique: Use the jigsaw technique, where each member of a group becomes an expert on a specific topic and then teaches that topic to the rest of the group. This promotes active learning and ensures that all group members are engaged.

3. Think-Pair-Share: Ask students to think about a question or problem individually, then pair up with a partner to discuss their ideas, and finally share their thoughts with the whole class. This encourages students to articulate their thoughts and listen to others' perspectives.

4. Peer Teaching: Have students take turns teaching a concept or skill to their classmates. This not only reinforces their own understanding but also helps them develop communication skills.

5. Collaborative Problem-Solving: Present students with a complex problem or scenario that requires teamwork to solve. This challenges students to think critically, communicate effectively, and work together to find a solution.

6. Group Discussions: Organize group discussions on a topic related to the lesson. Provide guiding questions to help students stay focused and encourage everyone to participate.

7. Role Play: Use role-playing activities to help students understand different perspectives or practice real-world skills. This can be particularly effective for subjects like history, literature, or social studies.

8. Peer Editing: Have students work in pairs or small groups to review and provide feedback on each other's work. This helps students improve their writing and editing skills while also learning from their peers.

By incorporating cooperative learning activities into your teaching, you can promote active engagement, improve communication and teamwork skills, and create a more interactive and dynamic learning environment for your students.

11) If pupils were having difficulty learning a skill or concept, what would you do? What techniques would you use to be sure that pupils understand?

1. Give Examples and Counter-Examples My 4-year-old daughter went through a phase a few years ago

where she had to clarify everything, she said. "Mommy, that car was blue. It wasn't green. It was blue." "Mommy, this is a circle. It's not a square. It's a circle." Like any mother, I thought it was cute at first, but after a while, it proved to be a challenge. "Mommy, I saw a duck, not a bird, a duck." Try explaining to your 2-year-old that a duck is, in fact, abird, and you quickly realize there is no reasoning with a 2-year-old! However, she was onto something! When students struggle with difficult concepts, start by using examples and counter-examples. For instance, when teaching that a number is divisible by 2 if it ends in an even number (0, 2, 4, 6 or 8), you should give them lots of examples (2, 48, 356) and counter-examples (9, 83, 761).

2. Define Difficult Words If students are stuck on a particular concept or rule, then be sure they understand the relevant vocabulary.
You may need to define words or rephrase using simplified terms. For example, if you are teaching a short vowel spelling rule, and your students get stuck on the word "consonant," be sure to first define the word for them.

If they continue to have a hard time, then consider using a different word (i.e. "letters").

Students often struggle with math concepts when they do not understand vocabulary in word problems. In my resource room, I kept these key words poster on the wall as a reference for students as they worked through word problems.

3. Use Visuals Whenever Possible Visuals can help turn a concept from abstract to concrete. Use models to help students visualize concepts such as the water cycle. Use manipulatives to teach math. For example, in teaching division, you could try to verbally explain to your students how 5 can be divided into 15 equally 3 times, or you could show it using objects as the picture illustrates below. Some spelling rules can also be difficult for students to remember. In an effort to help students visualize the rules, I created a set of short vowel spelling rule posters, where I tried to simplify, define, and illustrate each rule.

On my Rabbit Rule poster, I used images such as two hands to represent two syllables. Since students often clap the syllables, the image of the hands should trigger their memory of the definition of a syllable.

Another strategy is to have students draw what they think when they hear about a particular concept. This will give you further insight into their level of understanding and prior knowledge, which you can then build upon.

Connecting new information to prior knowledge will also help with long-term memory storage and retrieval. For more on this, read my popular blog post called 10 Tips for Teaching Memorization.

4. Break It Down Use task analysis – teach a concept in small chunks until students have gained mastery. When teaching a new rule, be sure your students have a solid understanding of the rule before you teach them the exceptions to the rule. Try to first teach the concept in isolation, and then re-introduce it in context. For example, sequencing is a skill that can be difficult for students to master. In my sequencing sort skill center, students learn to sequence outside of reading by ordering a set of picture cards and then describing the order they chose. For more on this topic, read my blog post called 3 Ways to Help Students Master Sequencing.

5. Know Your Students' Learning Styles and Multiple Intelligences Knowing your students' learning styles and multiple intelligences will help meet the needs of individual learners. If you know the student learns best through music, then put the new rule or concept to a familiar tune to help with recall.

If your student is a kinesthetic learner (which I have found a tendency in struggling students), then use math manipulatives and demonstrate the rule. This will also help your visual learners! There are several quick assessments you can use to learn about your students, including assessments for learning styles and others for multiple intelligences. If you have young learners, then you can use something like my learner profiles (pictured below) to help determine your students' learning styles and multiple intelligences.

6. Give Students Many Opportunities to Practice
Students will need lots of opportunities to practice the new skill or concept they have learned. One great way for students to review a new concept is to have them teach it to someone else. Teaching a concept reinforces the learning process, prompting differentiated and more in depth comprehension.

The process of communicating the new skill or concept also develops learning, as the student must be able to explain using practical application. Finally, the opportunity to answer questions will enhance comprehension specific to the new concept or skill, as well as promoting communication and adaptive thinking skills.

12) What do you include when you write objectives?

Somes points to Writing Clear and Measurable Learning Objectives

Identify the Level of Knowledge Necessary to Achieve Your Objective

Before you begin writing objectives, stop and think about what type of change you want your training to make. In other words, what do you want your participants to do differently when they return to work?

The domains of learning can be categorized as affective (attitude), psychomotor (skills), and cognitive (knowledge).

An easy way to remember this is with the acronym ASK: Attitude — Changes how a learner chooses to act. Compliance training is a good example of when you will have to teach to this domain.

It's usually the hardest to craft objectives for this, since it's dealing with feelings, emotions, and attitudes. Skills —This domain focuses on changing or improving the tasks a learner can perform. Knowledge — This domain focuses on increasing what participants know.

Learning safety rules, troubleshooting, and quoting prices from memory are all examples of this level of learning.

2. Select an Action Verb Now that you've identified what domain you intend to focus on for your objective, it's time to start crafting your objective. To do that, it'll help to have an action verb to describe the behavior at the appropriate level of learning. Here's a list of action verbs, separated by domain. Avoid having more than one action verb for each level of learning, and make sure it's a verb that can be measured. "Understand" is too vague, but "complete," "identify," or "recognize" are specific.

ATTITUDE Advocate • Accept • Agree • Allow • Analyze • Approve • Assess • Believe • Choose • Collaborate • Comply • Conform • Convince • Cooperate • Decide To • Defend • Endorse • Evaluate • Pick • Recommend • Select • Support • Tolerate

KNOWLEDGE Compare • Define • Describe • Designate • Discover • Distinguish • Explain • Identify • Itemize • Label • List • Name • Recite • Recognize • Recount • Relate • Retell • Specify • Spell Out • State • Tell • Term • Write

SKILLS Actuate • Adjust • Administer • Align • Alter • Assemble • Build • Calibrate • Change • Copy • Demonstrate • Design • Develop • Draft • Execute • Form • Handle • Manipulate • Measure • Mend • Perform • Prepare • Process • Record • Regulate • Remove • Repair • Replace • Set • Service

Check Your Objective Make sure your objectives include four pieces: audience, behavior, condition, and degree of mastery. For every one, identify and label the component. Here are the A, B, C, D's every objective should contain:

Audience: It's important that your objective identifies the people that will be doing the learning. Typically, this will involve the word, "learner" or "participant."
Behavior: You'll need to identify what the participants are going to do differently. This component will contain your action verb.
Condition: This part of the objective will describe the situation of the participants.
Degree of Mastery: This part of the objective is closely tied to the change in behavior, as it stipulates the degree of the change.

13) How can individualization actually be practiced in the classroom? How would you put individualization into practice?

Individualization in the classroom involves tailoring instruction to meet the unique needs, interests, and learning styles of each student. Here are some ways to put individualization into practice:

1. Differentiated Instruction: Provide different pathways for students to learn based on their readiness, interests, and learning profiles. This could include offering different reading materials, assignments, or activities that cater to individual learning needs.

2. Flexible Grouping: Group students based on their learning needs for specific activities or projects. This allows students to work with peers who are at a similar level or have similar learning styles.

3. Personalized Learning Plans: Develop personalized learning plans for each student based on their strengths, weaknesses, and learning goals. These plans can outline specific learning objectives and strategies tailored to each student's needs.

4. Student Choice: Provide opportunities for students to choose topics, projects, or assignments that align with their interests. This can increase engagement and motivation.

5. Assessment for Learning: Use formative assessments to gather information about students' understanding and adjust instruction accordingly. Provide timely feedback to help students improve.

6. Flexible Seating: Allow students to choose where they sit in the classroom based on their learning preferences. Some students may prefer to work in groups, while others may work best independently.

7. Technology Integration: Use technology to individualize instruction through adaptive learning software, online resources, and digital tools that allow students to learn at their own pace and receive immediate feedback.

8. Regular Reflection: Encourage students to reflect on their learning and progress. This can help them take ownership of their learning and identify areas for improvement.

By implementing these strategies, teachers can create a more personalized and engaging learning experience for each student, ultimately leading to improved learning outcomes.

14) How do you feel when a student fails?

When a student fails, it can evoke a range of

emotions for teachers, including disappointment, concern, and sometimes even frustration. Teachers often care deeply about their students' success and well-being, so seeing a student struggle or fail to meet expectations can be disheartening. However, many teachers also see failure as a learning opportunity and use it as a chance to provide additional support, guidance, and encouragement to help the student improve.

15) What techniques do you use to keep pupils actively involved during a lesson?

Teaching strategies to ensure student engagement 1. Begin the lesson with an interesting fact Did you know that the brain disengages when it thinks it already knows something?
One way to jump-start the brain out of its slumbering state is to give it startling or interesting information that it knows it …
doesn't know.
Besides waking up the brain and getting it ready to engage in the rest of the lesson, these facts also give the students fun ammunition to use against the adults in their life as a way to show off their smarts.

"Hey, mom," they say, "Did you know that baby camels are born without a hump?"

"They are?" mom replies. "No, I sure didn't! Is that really true?"

"Yep! My teacher told me!"

Education World offers some introductory fun facts that are already formatted into usable templates.

2. Exude enthusiasm and engagement
Enthusiasm is contagious and, at the very least, entertaining to watch. If you're excited and engaged with the topic you're teaching, your students will at least give it a chance.
If you obviously aren't interested in teaching it, then in their minds, why should they be interested in learning it?

3. Encourage connections that are meaningful and relevant

While having your own enthusiasm for a topic is a good start, it isn't enough to keep the students engaged in the long term. Instead, you need a way to bring them into that enthusiasm. One way to do this is to make it relevant and meaningful to them. Ask the students questions: Have you ever …? How would you feel if …? Incorporate areas of student interests into the lessons.

With writing, grammar, spelling, and reading, you can create sentences and other content around things they like. As an example, you could have your students try to find all the nouns in sentences like this: Spider-Man shot out his web and pinned the bad guy against the wall.

4. Plan for short attention spans

Students, especially younger ones, have a relatively short attention span. Studies suggest that:
• **Kindergarteners** (ages five and six) are able to focus on an interesting task for 10–30 minutes.
• **First-grade students** (ages six and seven) can focus for 12–35 minutes.
• **Second-grade students** (ages seven and eight) can focus for 14–40 minutes. And so on. With teaching, it's better to keep the lower number in mind when planning and executing your lessons.
To keep the students engaged, plan several short activities that will aid you in teaching and reinforcing the lesson and will keep the minds of the students moving. Read on for some activity examples.

5. Address different learning styles and multiple intelligences Every student has their own way of learning and their own set of strengths and weaknesses. It's impossible to give each student what they most need at every moment.

However, if you include a variety of activities from some of the categories below, you can ensure that you're giving everyone at least one thing that works for them.

Auditory/linguistic learners with the auditory learning style and linguistic multiple intelligence, students learn best when they are both listening and talking. They think in words and will often be learning as they are speaking.

Good activities for these students include:

• Brief lectures
• Discussions
• Stories
• Word games
• Reading aloud (especially if they're doing the reading)
• Group projects

Visual-spatial learners' Visual learners and those with visual-spatial intelligence learn best by seeing. Visual learners may see in words or pictures. Those with spatial intelligence may enjoy such activities as drawing and reading maps.

Good activities for these students include:

• Reading
• Taking notes
• Looking at charts, organizers, pictures, models, videos, etc,
• Drawing their own charts or models
• Solving puzzles

As a visual learner myself, I also tend to be a more visual teacher. I like to use different colors of markers when I'm giving notes or explaining something on the board.

I use these colors to connect similar concepts or to simply keep my mind awake by providing more visual stimulus

Bodily-kinesthetic learners These students learn best by touching, moving, and doing. They don't want to simply see the model — they want to make the model. They are the first to get antsy during lectures and note-taking. Good activities for this learner include:
• Actions-cues that relate to the information
• Roleplaying
• Hands-on activities

Teaching Tip: Address auditory, visual, and kinesthetic learners at the same time in a lecture by writing the information, reading it out loud, showing a picture of the information, and having the students perform an action that relates to the information.

Musical learners These learners have a heightened awareness of rhythm and sound. They learn best when lessons are presented in song format or when information is given in rhythm.

Good activities include:
• Songs (singing or creating their own)
• Poems (reading or creating their own)

Teaching Tip: Address linguistic, visual-spatial, bodily-kinesthetic, and musical learners by printing out the lyrics to a new song, reading them out loud, teaching the students actions to go with the music, and then singing the song together.

Interpersonal learners These students are your social butterflies. They thrive and learn through interacting with others.

Good activities include: • Group projects • Class discussions • Individual student-teacher conversations • Conducting surveys and interviews

Intrapersonal learners Unlike interpersonal learners, intrapersonal learners are not social learners. Instead, they are very private people who possess a good understanding of their own thoughts, feelings, interests, strengths, and weaknesses. They thrive in independent work environments.

Good activities include: • Any independent work • Written discussion questions that are deep and contemplative in nature.

Teaching Tip: Use think-pair-shares to address both the interpersonal and intrapersonal intelligences. In this activity, the students think about and write down their answer to a particular discussion point, pair up with a partner, and take turns sharing their answers.

Logical-mathematical learners These learners are abstract thinkers, explorers, and debaters. They see, understand, and create patterns and connections. They like to ask questions, experiment, and solve problems.

Good activities include: • Experiments • Logic games • Puzzles • Investigations • Conducting surveys.

6. Converse with students — don't talk at them
Teaching isn't just about what you teach and which activities you lead the students in; it's also about how you teach it — how you speak to the students and present the information. Think about your tone and demeanor when you're having a conversation with someone.
 Is it different than when you're presenting information to your class? It's easy, especially when you're presenting important foundational information, to talk at students instead of talking with them. Students are more likely to check-out when they're passive recipients of information. So, instead of just giving the facts, think of this whole-class presentation time as though you're having a conversation with your students and sharing

something with them that you think is really great.

7. Turn lessons into games Students learn best and are most engaged when they are having fun. With this concept in mind, more attention has been given to the benefits of playing games in the classroom.

8. Turn lessons into stories Storytelling is another highly engaging strategy to use in the classroom. This practice, which has been around since the beginning of history as we know it, engages both the emotional and logical areas of the brain. With multiple areas of the brain being activated, the hearer is better able to engage with and remember the information embedded within the story.

9. Maintain close proximity and eye contact Have you ever noticed that you can "feel" it when someone is looking at you? For whatever reason, something within us seems to know when someone is paying attention to us. The moment we sense this, we snap to a greater state of alertness. This holds true in the classroom.
Students are more likely to be engaged when you make eye contact with them and stand in close proximity. If they know that you are circulating and are making eye contact with them on a regular basis, they will maintain their level of engagement.

10. Offer choices Students, like most people, enjoy the opportunity to have choices. They like knowing they have control over some aspect of their learning. Having choices puts the student in the driver's (or passenger's) seat.
This responsibility means that they're no longer merely recipients who can mindlessly sit back and enjoy the ride.

Instead, they are responsible for sitting up, taking notice, and making intentional decisions about which direction their education will take. Choices can come in the form of deciding which topic they want to learn about, how they want to learn it (which activities they want to do), or how they want to present what they have learned.

A note on choices: Too many choices for students who are not ready to make them can be overwhelming. Be sure to limit how often and how many choices students have. Be sure to also approve all options beforehand and to provide guidance in the process.

A bag of tricks: In teaching, not every strategy will prove effective with every student. For this reason, it is good to carry around a big bag of tricks that you can pull from when student interest starts to waver.

16) What are your beliefs about reinforcement of pupils?

Reinforcement is an important aspect of teaching and learning, and my beliefs align with principles of positive reinforcement. Here are some key beliefs about reinforcement of pupils:

1. Encouragement: Providing positive reinforcement, such as praise, rewards, and recognition, can motivate students to engage in desired behaviors and continue their efforts.

2. Effective Feedback: Constructive feedback that highlights students' strengths and areas for improvement can help them learn and grow. Feedback should be specific, timely, and focused on the task or behavior, not the individual.

3. Consistency: Reinforcement should be consistent and applied fairly to all students. This helps establish clear expectations and promotes a positive classroom environment.

4. Individualization: Recognizing that students have different preferences and motivations, reinforcement strategies should be tailored to meet the needs of each student.

5. Long-term Goals: Reinforcement should be used to help students develop intrinsic motivation and a growth mindset, rather than relying solely on external rewards.

6. Behavioral Expectations: Reinforcement can be used to reinforce positive behavior and encourage students to meet behavioral expectations set by the teacher or school.

Overall, my beliefs about reinforcement are grounded in the idea that positive reinforcement, when used effectively and appropriately, can help create a supportive and motivating learning environment that encourages students to achieve their best.

17) How do you end a lesson?

7 effective ways to end a lesson – because those last minutes matter!

What have you learned today?
It goes without saying that you should never end a lesson by introducing something new, just to leave your students hanging till the next class.

The best way to end a lesson is to give students some kind of review activity, so that they may see the progress they've made in just one lesson. One of the most common and easiest to implement is simply taking the last 5 minutes of class to ask your students, "What have you learned today?" Notice, here, that you're not the one telling them what they've learned.

They may give you a list of new words, or say they learned to speak about what they did in the past or what they will do in the future, etc... Students may pick up something they missed earlier. Also, it's important to speak in functional ways, for example not say they learned to use the "simple present" but rather that they learned to speak about their habits, schedules, and everyday activities.

Performance correction and feedback
Right before the last 5 minutes of class you can have some sort of performance activity, for instance a role play. Usually, we don't correct students during the role play so we don't interrupt the flow, but when they're done you can end the class with corrections of words or expressions they used incorrectly; things they forgot to say, etc...and your students will go home with these corrections fresh on their minds. Students may also give their opinion or feedback on their classmates' performance.

60 seconds Choose a few students and give each 60 seconds to speak about something you've covered that day: what they did yesterday if you worked on simple past; talk about Halloween, professions, or animals; older learners may even give a "how to" lesson; they may also summarize a story they heard, or place themselves in another person's shoes, like a celebrity, profession, or even animal.

But they must speak for a full minute. To motivate students to speak, you may choose to reward the student who says the most, or includes the most information, with a reward sticker.

Write an email

Ask students to imagine they have to write an email to a friend or family member and tell them what they did today in their class. Students have a chance to summarize what they've learned in written form. This writing activity may be tailored to any topic. If you talked about farm animals, ask students to write about their favorite animal and why it's their favorite. And the same goes for foods, sports, celebrities. Adult learners may write a business email with the new vocabulary they've learned.

Say goodbye

For very young ESL learners the best way to wrap up a lesson is with a goodbye song or saying goodbye to a puppet. The puppet may "ask" them questions about something they learned, and even give them a short "review" by asking, "What's this?" or "What's that?" or any other question or expression they may have learned. You may set aside this special time with the puppet every day at the end of the class, so children know what to expect, and even though they may be very young, they will still have this sense of closure.

Tidying up

After a special holiday class, or right after a lesson packed with arts and crafts, ask students to help you tidy up the classroom. Make sure you factor in this tidy up time when you plan crafts. Letting students run off with their art work just to leave you in a classroom littered with papers and art supplies gives them the wrong message.

Sharing with the class

Another great way to end your class is by asking your students to share whatever it is that you worked on that day: a fall collage; a painting; they may read something they've written. The important thing here is to give them a space to share something they've produced with the language elements they've learned. Even adult learners may read a letter or email they've written.

You can do anything you want to wrap up your lesson and be as creative as you want to be. However, it is essential that you provide these three things: • a time for students to cool down after an activity-filled class • some sort of review of what they've learned • the proper closure to the day's tasks

Keep these three essential points in mind, and you'll come up with great, effective ways to end your lessons every time!

18) Is drill and practice important? How and when would you use it?

Drill and practice use repeated exercises and individual feedback to master a specified learning objective. Drill and practice are used to master basic skills and improve speed or accuracy. For example, using flashcards to help a student master basic multiplication fact. Several goals can be attributed to drill and practice exercises. They can be used to build confidence as more answers are correctly provided. They also help to reinforce important materials. Learners are also provided an opportunity to practice critical skills and knowledge sets. Sample objectives are shown next.

During and after performing the activity, students will…

• increase skill at performing the given task…
• increase speed at performing the given task…
• internalize the given information until it is an automatic assumption as determined by successfully attending to 80% of rubric items.

Drill and practice activities offer the benefits of improved learning transfer to the performance context. There are three basic steps to achieve this activity: assigning a task, performing a task, and providing feedback. Drill and practice activities repeatedly exercise a simple or small area of knowledge.

19) What would you do to insure that children understand exactly what is expected of them in a homework assignment?

To ensure that children understand exactly what is expected of them in a homework assignment, you can take several steps:

1. Clear Instructions: Provide clear, concise, and specific instructions for the homework assignment. Use language that is appropriate for the students' age and comprehension level.

2. Modeling: Demonstrate examples of what is expected, especially for new or complex tasks. This can help clarify any confusion and give students a clear understanding of the task.

3. Visual Aids: Use visual aids such as charts, diagrams, or illustrations to supplement written instructions and help students visualize the task.

4. Verbal Instructions: Explain the assignment orally, especially for younger students or those who may struggle with written instructions. Use simple language and repeat key points as needed.

5. Check for Understanding: Ask students to repeat the instructions in their own words or summarize the task to ensure they have understood correctly.

6. Provide Written Instructions: Provide written instructions for students to refer back to while completing the assignment. This can help reinforce understanding and prevent confusion.

7. Use Rubrics: Provide a rubric or grading criteria so that students know how their work will be evaluated. This can help them focus on meeting the specific expectations of the assignment.

8. Encourage Questions: Encourage students to ask questions if they are unsure about any part of the assignment. Be available to clarify instructions and provide additional guidance as needed.

9. Review Together: Before students begin the assignment, review the instructions together as a class. This can help address any common questions or misunderstandings.

10. Provide Feedback: Provide timely feedback on completed assignments, highlighting areas where students have met or exceeded expectations and areas where they may need improvement.

By taking these steps, you can help ensure that children understand exactly what is expected of them in a homework assignment, leading to greater success and learning.

How to solve the problem of monitoring and evaluating homework?

Pedagogical experience teaches us: make sure that you can check and evaluate the homework you give at home. This rule is still not applied everywhere. The teacher does not always check whether the students have completed their homework. Even less often, the completeness, correctness and form of the task is subjected to control. Control, assessment of homework and marking - together with other factors of the pedagogical process - are motivating and mobilizing the forces and abilities of students. If we refuse to control homework or do not take it seriously enough, we disappoint the student, because we ignore his work, his achievements. Negative consequences of this kind should be expected especially when the work is done by the student conscientiously, with full dedication, but the teacher systematically does not pay attention to the completion of homework. The result of doing homework has a double function for the teacher. Firstly, he is an object of control over the activities of students, and secondly, and more importantly, his own activities in the last lesson.

And further a few tips:

Ø with the help of constant monitoring, ensure that students do not have doubts about whether homework is necessary;
Ø use various forms of control depending on the content, type and purpose of homework, as well as the attitude of your students to doing homework;
Ø determine what and how you will evaluate, whether you will put a mark for it, based on specific conditions, and also taking into account the educational impact of the assessment;
Ø if students do not do their homework, look for the reasons and then decide how to eliminate them; Ø Ensure that work not done on time must be completed later.
Ø Remember that checking homework is an inevitable part and a necessary addition to a good lesson Organize the test so that the students do not consider this stage the "most boring" in the lesson.

A harmonious combination of various types, forms and methods of submitting and checking homework will affect the formation of independence among schoolchildren and increase the level of learning motivation, the formation of a positive attitude towards learning in schoolchildren in the process of doing homework is the most important task of a teacher in any In addition to educational, the educational potential of homework is extremely high. After all, the teacher gives knowledge, first of all, in order to educate a person, a creative person, not indifferent. And in this noble cause, homework is an indispensable assistant.

The main thing is that this light of creativity does not go out in the teacher, so that he himself would be interested in all this. If the students see that the teacher is also interested in how the homework is done, in what form it is presented, then they will take a responsible approach to doing the homework.

Federal State Treasury Educational Institution "Secondary school No. 2"

Toolkit "Forms and methods of organizing the stage comprehensive check of homework.

(for OU teachers) The manual was compiled by the primary school teacher Gulchenko Elena Yurievna.

Considered at a meeting of the Methodological Council and recommended for use in the educational process.

Content. Introduction Game methods for checking homework in elementary school.
Literature and Internet resources.
Forms and methods of organizing the stage comprehensive homework check.

Target: generalize pedagogical experience in the organization of checking homework. Help teachers organize a comprehensive check of homework.

Tasks: Describe practical methods for organizing homework checks. Show the relevance of the systematic checking of homework, as well as the importance of using a variety of forms and methods.

Introduction. "In fact, gradually blur the line between classroom and homework with the transition to continuous,individual, independent educational activity of the student." Elkonin - Davydov The problem of organizing homework is very relevant.
Very often, homework assignments are of a random, ill-conceived nature, preparations for their implementation are poorly conducted, and checks are formally built.
The consequence of these shortcomings in the planning, preparation and organization of homework is the overload of students with homework, which negatively affects the activity, efficiency and interest in learning.

Of course, you can work without homework.

But centuries-old practice and pedagogical laws prove that if the knowledge acquired in the lesson is not repeated at home, then they are forgotten.

Refusal from home independent work necessarily entails a decrease in the quality of education, a drop in the level of educational motivation.

New approaches to the modern lesson involve 7 stages of a comprehensive check of homework: For solutions did act task of the stage necessary for to establish the correctness and awareness of the performance of homework by all students; to eliminate the revealed gaps in knowledge during the check, while improving ZUN.

Stage content sets a goal for the teacher in find out the degree of assimilation of the material given at home; identify typical shortcomings in knowledge and their causes; fix any deficiencies found.

Conditions for achieving positive results possibly when the teacher uses a system of techniques that allows you to determine the completion of homework for all students in the class An indicator of the fulfillment of the didactic task of the lesson is the ability of the teacher in a short period of time (5-7 minutes) to establish the level of knowledge of the majority of students and typical shortcomings; the opportunity to update and correct the basic concepts during the verification of homework; eliminate the causes of the identified deficiencies Optimality presented requirements among other stages of the lesson, allows you to take into account the age and individual characteristics of children; at the same time, preference is given to tasks of a search and problematic nature.

The use of various forms and methods of control contributes to activation of mental activity in the lesson. Search, creative, individual tasks for students become dominant Implementation Errors, such as the uniformity of lessons and survey methods; the lack of consideration for the individual characteristics of students and the specifics of the material being studied lead to the use of new approaches to solving this issue.

In view of the variety of forms and types of homework, the methods and ways of checking it are different. New approaches to the modern lesson put the question of organizing homework checks as one of the dominant ones in teaching methods.

The main task of the teacher at the stage of a comprehensive check of homework is to take control not only of the systematic completion of homework by each student, but also the degree of independence of the student in doing it, as well as the level of assimilation of educational material in the process of doing homework.

Innovative Homework Checking Methods

Checking homework is carried out by the teacher constantly and, as a rule, is associated with the material being studied, and this is an obligatory element of each school lesson. Just walking up to the board and telling a rule or writing down an example that has been done can seem boring to students.

That is why I am using innovative verification methods.

These methods include: Asking unexpected questions The unexpected question asked by the teacher is a question that is phrased slightly differently than the assignments after the paragraph. If the children are attentive to the home exercise, then it will not be difficult for them to answer it. For example: - What discoveries did you make for yourself while working? (Question to the author of the presentation about the life and work of V.P. Astafiev.)

Raise your hands to whom the neighbor on the desk helped. How? - Analyze your own text. Reviewing the oral response the students themselves listen carefully to the answer of their classmate and prepare an oral review of it, note the advantages and disadvantages of the answer, supplement and expand it.

- You listened to Vlad's answer. What advice can you give him?

Dictation based on home exercise At the Russian language lessons, the teacher can prepare a selective dictation, a graphic dictation, a dictation grouped by spelling. All material is taken from a familiar home exercise.

For the same purpose, cards and punched cards can be used for verification. Brief written answer to the question

The teacher asks an extremely specific question that can be answered in a nutshell. Such tasks will help to consolidate knowledge and draw students' attention to the main points of a given paragraph. After a written answer, the learned theory will be stored in the memory of students for a longer time.

Checking with new computer technologies The text of the given exercise, example or task is projected on the screen. In this text, accents are placed in color font over the most difficult moments. The guys check the notes in their notebooks with what they see on the screen and correct possible errors.

For example: - Compare your notes with mine. If there is a complete match, give yourself 1 point; if you have more information, add 1 more point. Discussion To conduct it, the class must be divided into groups, each of which will defend its position or view of the problem. One point of view may be stated in a textbook or reference book, and another, different from it, may belong to one of the students or the teacher. In the discussion, the reasoning and arguments of students are important, and the result of it will be a deeper knowledge of the essence of the studied phenomenon.

Question to the author (in the form of an interview) This is an unusual and very interesting way to check homework. The teacher invites the children to come up with a few questions to the author of the discovery, invention, work, in order to better understand its meaning. The most prepared students can answer the questions, and the teacher can answer the most difficult of them. For example, when checking homework in chemistry, you can address questions of interest to Dmitry Ivanovich Mendeleev, in physics - to Isaac Newton, in geometry - to Pythagoras, in literature - to Fyodor Mikhailovich Dostoevsky.

Thematic crossword puzzle Many guys are fond of solving crossword puzzles, while showing enviable perseverance. To make it interesting to check homework, the teacher needs to make a crossword puzzle on the relevant topic and offer it to students

Mutual verification When checking written homework in chemistry, Russian or English, mathematics, students can be invited to exchange notebooks with a classmate, check assignments, grade and talk about the mistakes made, discussing contentious issues.

3. Recommendations for organizing an oral survey. Checking homework by questioning students is the traditional and most popular way. Often it is used to find gaps or shortcomings in knowledge, forgetting about the main task of the survey - to support the student, to help, to teach. In my work, I use the following methods:

poll-traffic light A long cardboard strip of red on one side and green on the other acts as a traffic light. The green side facing the teacher indicates the student's readiness to answer the question posed ("I know!"), The red side indicates that the student is not ready to answer ("I don't know!").

If the student shows the red side to the questions of the basic level, this is an alarm signal for the teacher. This is a deuce, which the student set himself. You can also ask creative questions, while the red signal means "I don't want to answer!", And the green one means "I want to answer!".

Solidarity Poll If the student at the blackboard cannot cope with the task, it is necessary to ask the class for help. Who wants to help? Of those who wish to help, the teacher chooses the strongest student and invites him to give a hint to a friend in a whisper. Alternatively, the student himself chooses the one whose help he needs, and the teacher gives the coach 10-15 minutes to prepare.

Mutual interrogation The teacher instructs the three most prepared students to conduct a survey of those who prepared for "5", "4" or "3". A student who enrolled in the third group and successfully answered the questions in it can try his hand again.

Programmed poll In this case, the student must choose the correct answer from those offered by the teacher. This form of work in oral questioning is rarely used. And absolutely in vain. Indeed, in the clash of different opinions of students, misunderstanding "melts". The teacher can defend the wrong answer to give the children an opportunity to argue.

Silent poll The teacher is talking quietly to one or more students, and the whole class is doing another task.

Poll chain This method of questioning is recommended to be used to obtain a detailed and logically coherent answer. At the same time, one student starts the answer, the teacher interrupts him anywhere with a gesture and invites another student to continue the thought.

"Protection" sheet Created for unprepared students and is always in the same place. A student who is not ready for the lesson writes his name on the protective sheet and can be sure that he will not be asked today. The task of the teacher is to keep the situation under control.

4. Game methods for checking homework in elementary school. For many teachers, the question of how to avoid monotony when checking homework in primary school is relevant. For younger students, the game form of testing acquired knowledge is especially relevant and effective.

I offer several practical ideas that will not only allow you to perform an interesting homework check, but also help to activate the mental activity of students.

Game "Draw the answer" The teacher needs to prepare questions on the topic covered, the answers to which the children can quickly and easily draw. Children should be warned that the answers should not be voiced, but depicted on paper.

The game "Slap-stomp" Checking homework, the teacher asks questions and offers answers to them. If the answer is correct, the task of the children is to clap their hands, but if the answer is incorrect, to stomp their feet. This game is a great warm-up and a good way to de-stress in the classroom.

Team game "What and why?" In the created teams, the captain is appointed as a teacher. The task for each of the teams is to come up with questions on the topic studied and answer them in turn. The right to answer is provided by the captain. It is important that all team members participate in the discussion.

Game "Semitsvetik" The teacher needs to prepare in advance paper flowers with seven colored petals according to the number of teams. For the correct answer on the topic covered, the team receives one petal. They play until one of the teams collects the flower completely.

Game "Catch the ball" The game is played in a circle. The teacher asks a question and tosses the ball. The student who caught him gives the answer. Let's summarize. The degree of effectiveness of homework completion by students largely depends on how interesting and diverse in form and content its verification will be. It should be noted that the above methods of checking homework in a school lesson will be effective if they are applied comprehensively and systematically.

20) Are you constantly searching for things you can show, tell, or demonstrated to pupils? Tell us about some recent discovery, something that you have found.

❖ Artificial intelligence-based teaching,
❖ Virtual reality-based teaching
❖ Augmented reality-based teaching
❖ 3D based teaching

21) How do you deal with the unmotivated student?

No matter how cohesive the class, there's usually one student who just isn't, let's say, feeling it. But what can you do with an unmotivated student?

Turns out, quite a lot. Check out these 12 tips, specifically chosen for language teachers.

1. Identify their "type" Your class is a mix of visual, auditory, and kinesthetic learners; who lean towards extroversion or introversion; and identify with one of nine Enneagram, 16 Myers Briggs, and any number of "types" from other personality frameworks. Whew! Due to all this diversity, it's natural that each student's learning preferences differ. While you can't deliver a personalized lesson to each learner, you can reach them better by committing to using different teaching techniques throughout the semester. And they don't have to be complicated: try mixing up group with individual work time; including moments of hands-on, visual, or aural learning; and offering students chances to lead, choose, compete, or go outside. Or, reach out to your Director of Studies for support in implementing opportunities for blended learning or task-based learning.

2. Stop effusive praise Michael Linsin of Smart Classroom Management recommends giving students specific, honest feedback – and then leaving them alone. Catch your student in the act of good work, no matter how small, he suggests. Tell them (in a normal voice, no exaggerated excitement!) that they are doing well. Use specifics: "Great introduction," "yes, that's exactly right," "spot on description," "great use of the passive tense". Interestingly, he advises that you then simply walk on off without looking back. You see, unmotivated students sometimes expect effusive praise and have grown immune to it. By giving specific feedback and letting students continue their work, this approach aims to plant the seed of pride in a job well done.

3. Highlight the positive Your unmotivated student has probably experienced failure recently. Celebrate their wins and help them see the positives of their studies: increased vocabulary, more fluid speaking, increased reading ability, better pronunciation, leadership skills, grammar—the list goes on. You know that something will apply to your student; but do they?

4. Foster a threat-free classroom Because fear isn't an effective motivator, students who worry about the wrath of their teachers and parents aren't likely to thrive. Support your most anxious students and learn what has grown their anxiety.

Maybe they have an overbearing parent, are having a tough time at work, or are a sleep-deprived new parent? Make your classroom a positive place by being supportive, positive, and enthusiastic.

5. Take the focus off extrinsic motivation Jennifer Gonzalez of Cult of Pedagogy writes that extrinsic rewards can actually hamper motivation when applied to complex or creative activities. Instead, she suggests teachers learn to focus students' attention (and their own classroom approach) on an activity's intrinsic value.

6. Embrace routine Using a series of predictable moments to "hook" your lessons on can be comforting to students, and give a sense of control to the unmotivated. Ideas include starting class by checking homework; playing soft music while students are engaged in individual work; including a "word of the day" moment; or ending class with a familiar warm-down activity.

7. Encourage friendly competition When used well, competition is a powerful motivator. Use games to review grammar points and vocabulary—but always encourage lightheartedness: this will keep students "with you for the ride" and work to keep the atmosphere positive

8. Get out of the classroom Does your academy have a garden, cafeteria, computer room? Hold the occasional class there. However, if physically moving your students isn't possible, try "getting out" of the classroom by including music, films, and podcasts in your lessons, or inviting special guests (such as an expert in a field you're studying) to teach a guest lesson.

9. Allow choice where possible Whether choosing between completing a listening or reading activity; selecting an assignment topic, or which problems to tackle first, some unmotivated students will dig into the chance to own their class experience. This sort of technique is easier to employ when students are involved in creative, longer-term activities, or task-based learning, which naturally provide more opportunities for decision making.

10. Try the 2×10 technique Simple in its effectiveness, the 2×10 technique involves talking for two minutes, each day for ten days, with a student with challenging classroom behavior. But what do you talk about? Anything they want to.

Why? Because you'll learn about your student, create rapport, and perhaps even pinpoint what has been troubling them.

11. Give responsibilities Younger students will enjoy being in charge of a particular classroom job; such as wiping the whiteboard, handing out worksheets, or distributing counters. Older students can help lead games, write homework on the board, or "teach" a five-minute class on a topic of their choice.

12. Track progress When it comes to our progress, human beings are usually quicker to see the negative over the positive. Tracking student progress helps learners uncloud potentially untrue perceptions of their own development. Use diagrams, simple charts, or color-coding and literally show your students how far they've come.

Of course, this habit will come in handy for you when it's time to do your own teacher self-evaluation.

22) Tell me about some specific motivational strategies to get students excited about learning.

Best 11 Strategies Involving Students Interest

In Learning Teachers/Parents often spend a lot of time thinking about how to motivate the students and get them interested in learning. But often, the simplest way is overlooked – involving students in setting up their own learning space from the ground up. One of the biggest mistakes teachers and parents can make when it comes to developing good learners is to limit their learning to the classroom. Often, the school is considered as the primary source of instruction, but the social, intellectual and academic growth should extend beyond the walls of the classroom, which will give them wings to fly and soar to new heights!

In this article let's talk about the Best 11 Strategies To Students Interest In Learning!

Here are some tips for including students in the process –

1. Develop A Reading Atmosphere: It is often observed that students who have a keen interest in reading, develop a love for learning too because they are want to explore endless possibilities and opportunities. Reading not only helps them to develop a rich vocabulary, but it also helps them to process formal communication and concepts.

Reading to the child frequently and having them read aloud will create an atmosphere for reading at home as well as in school. Let children pick their own book and make it fun for them instead of compulsion.

2. Put The Child In Charge As Much As Possible: When it comes to education, some kids experience just domination and instruction. When a child is controlled so much, they often withdraw themselves from learning. Children should be allowed to have their own learning experience instead of being regulated all the time. The more control and input the child has in their own learning, they will become more engaged and motivated to learn.

3. Encourage Open And Sincere Communication: Encouraging open and sincere communication with the child is the key to make him/her feel comfortable and share his/her opinion about everything. When they know that their opinions matter and are taken into consideration, they feel reassured and open up even more.

4. Focus On Your Child's Interest: When learning engages children in what they are interested in, learning becomes fun for them and they look forward to it. Ask the child which topic interests him the most and find books related to that topic.

5. Encourage Different Types Of Learning Styles: Every child has a different style of learning and there is no right or wrong style. Whichever technique the child is comfortable in learning should be encouraged. There are seven fundamental styles of learning, such as Visual, Audio, Verbal, Physical, Mathematical, Social and Solitary.

6. Share Your Enthusiasm For Learning: When it comes to learning new things, enthusiasm definitely rubs off. Children definitely get inspired by you and if he/she sees that parents/teachers are enthusiastic about learning, they follow the same trait. Always tell the child that learning is a journey of exciting new discoveries. Take every opportunity and discover new information and see the child follow your footsteps.

7. Game-Based Learning Is The Key: Game-based learning provides opportunities for deeper learning and development of cognitive skills. It motivates the children to learn more. When a child is engaged in a game, their mind experiences the pleasure of learning something new. This is the biggest factor in team-based learning.

We often see the competitive spirit of the child come out in games and them wat to win it for themselves or the team. They want to perform at a higher level and outshine everyone. It's a great way to introduce new ideas, concepts, and knowledge which motivates the children to learn.

8. Help The Child Stay Organized: Helping the child to remain organized will definitely go a long way in making him feel motivated to learn. Children at a young age are a bit disorganized which leads to being frustrated and worried when they cannot finish their assignment or project on time. When a child is organized, they feel in control, less overwhelmed and are motivated to learn.

9. Always Celebrate Achievements: Celebrating and recognizing their achievements, no matter if they are big or small goes a long way in boosting their morale. It builds a positive environment and keeps them motivated to learn and challenge themselves to do better. It could be as small as getting ice cream or appreciating them in front of the whole class.

10. Focus On Strengths: Children often need that push or nudge which motivates them to perform than the last time that they did. Instead of focussing on the weakness, make them aware about their strength and tell them that if they can perform well in one area, they sure have the potential to shine the brightest.

11. Make Every Day A Learning Day: Turning every day into a learning day will help the child develop the internal motivation to learn something new(no matter how small or simple) in the classroom, at home or wherever he may be. So try these simple but effective ways to engage the children in their learning process and make it a pleasant experience for them too. Children who take charge of their learning, become responsible and are driven to learn and explore new things.

23.What is the most important "thing" a student could learn in your class?

Schools are one of the pillars upon which there stands a strong building called SOCIETY. Our transition from a child to a teenager takes place in schools only that act as guiding light during our next stages in life.

Here, taking cues from my own experiences, I list what one learns in school:

✓ Education is the road to heaven.

✓ Respect elders & teachers
✓ How to socialize & make friends
✓ Friendship is everything.
✓ Teamwork & responsibility
✓ Study>>>other activity
✓ Ethical & moral values are supreme
✓ Marks decide your fate. Bit eerie even today.
✓ Comparison among students
✓ Intelligent is the one who is 'topper'.
✓ Respecting teachers
✓ Working as a team for inter-house or inter-school competitions
✓ Being understanding towards classmates
✓ Moral values like honesty, kindness, empathy
✓ Adjusting with others
✓ Importance of punctuality and self-discipline
✓ The true value of friendship
✓ Presenting our ideas and thoughts
✓ Being open to others' suggestions
✓ Knowledge about the world around us
✓ Basic life skills like finding directions and following instructions.

24) Explain how you have changed your lesson plan preparation and presentation to students as you have gained experience.

What is a lesson plan?
A lesson plan will be the set of subject matter materials you will be teaching during a specific timeframe. The lesson plan should be an index that students can constantly consult to understand better the parts of the learning journey they will go through during each session. Teachers and professors should have a lesson plan template that happens in every session. This is different from a syllabus because, in the latter case, the whole curriculum of the program will be laid out; however, for each lesson, there should be one individual lesson plan example to guide the instructor in the set timeframe.
When building the materials for the class or lesson's attention, it's always essential to share elements like the purpose or rules that guide the learning process.

How to write a lesson plan Education nowadays guides different sorts of students and target specific learning needs. Therefore, it's important and relevant to understand how lesson plans can change and be varied to truly implement the best learning path for your students.

Lesson plans will comprise several different sections that will clarify the first questions students can have: How long will the course be? Will it be an online course? What will be the main objectives? Which subjects will be discussed along with the class?

1. Introduction
As the lesson begins, it's essential to place a brief yet descriptive introduction about what the session will cover. A good practice is to create a catchy title for each lesson to have an overall understanding of the information they will be receiving.
Example: Digital Marketing Basics: Industry background, historical review years 1980-2010. In this session, we will cover the birth of digital marketing, including all the touchpoints that shaped today's industry.

2. Audience
If your class is a one-time-only or recurring session, or even a blended learning journey, it's essential to explain to your students who this class is for; this will allow them to calibrate their expectations about the matter to be taught ahead.
Example: This lesson is directed to professionals who work in traditional marketing, business owners, or communication specialists seeking to have a profound understanding of how digital marketing came to be.

3. Lesson Objectives
This piece is critical because it will allow the students to assess the intention of each lesson. When thinking about the objectives, it's vital to consider the acquired skills we expect our students to have at the end of the class.
Like any other goals in life or business, each one should be actionable and measurable, meaning after each class, students should be able to use what they have learned and put into action the concepts.
Example: Understand and be able to create a timeline framework of reference to explain the story of the Internet.

4. Materials Suppose the lesson requires using any specific materials, physical or not, including any software or hardware necessary. In that case, it´s important to list or include within the lesson plan so students can set clear expectations on what they might require.
This is particularly important if the session you will be delivering requires them beforehand to bring anything.

Example: • Computer • Scratch paper

5. Learning Activities
We´ve covered all the logistics by this point; however, now we need to start sharing the actual activities during the lesson. Ideally, this is a play-by-play of how each activity will guide the lesson towards the already established objectives. To add the list of learning activities that will be helpful for your students, take into account how all of them align with each goal and the requirements students need.

Make sure that you add variety to the activities that you are proposing, go ahead and research trends of how many other teachers or professors, students will appreciate your search to engage them in learning.

Also, consider how much time they will take so that you can note it in the next section.

Example: • Create a timeline on the wall with the most important moments of digital marketing history, including creation of social media, mainstream of email, etc.

Time periods Pairing each learning activity with a specific timeframe will be useful both for instructors and students. Make sure you calculate a reasonable amount of time for each activity and list it within the lesson plan so everyone can set correct expectations. Assigning time slots for each exercise will also help students and teachers stay on track with the lesson and not waste valuable time invested in learning.

Example: Creation of a timeline – 45 min.

Lesson plan adjusting methods

Whether you're adjusting an existing lesson plan or starting from scratch, try the following tips for a productive school year:

1. START WITH THE BIG PICTURE

I believe that starting is the hardest part. If you're struggling in the initial steps of lesson planning, try taking a step back. Connect with other grade level teachers at your school to see how your year can fit into the bigger picture—like a curriculum calendar. From there, break it down to objective-based, shorterterm units. Within each unit, what do you want to accomplish? What do you want your students to know and be able to do by the end? With each lesson, outline a desired outcome or goal for you and your students to work towards.

2. DON'T RELY ON FLUFF

Even after I've planned my lessons, I like to reassess my own strategies. I ask myself what I can improve or make more efficient. What are the structures or systems within my classroom that are working? How can I use these more? Rather than breaking your day into tiny little pieces, focus on the activities that provide richer opportunities for deep thinking. While Pinterest-inspired little activities may keep kids busy, they don't always teach to the rigor and relevance that they need.

3. GET CREATIVE ABOUT YOUR RESOURCES

These days, inspiration is all around us. I use (free!) tools and resources that elevate my lesson plans. One of my favorites is Understanding by Design, which is a template for lesson planning created by Grant Wiggins and Jay McTighe. Their website has articles, webinars, videos and more for online learning. Their method is a way of thinking that's backwards planning—you start by thinking what you want to accomplish, then creating a performance assessment.

4. THINK BACKWARDS AND RELATE THE LESSON PLAN TO REAL LIFE

Step one is to identify the learning standards set out by your state or national standards. In step two, identify what some of the enduring understandings are. Create essential questions that will motivate the student to actually learn that unit. For example, show them how measurement is used in the world and show the different ways people measure and the tools they measure with. Put students in scenarios where they have to select tools and use the lesson in a practical way.

Then step three is the learning activities that you scaffold, which refers to a variety of instructional techniques used to move students progressively toward stronger understanding and, ultimately, greater independence in the learning process. Start with what they already know about measurement. For example, maybe they were measured at the doctor's office.

Try to relate it to their real life. A real-life example I use with my students is the grocery store. I take them on an imaginary tour and ask them where and how they measure their fruit. Soon they start recognizing scales and using this vocabulary in their everyday lives.

5. GET NONTRADITIONAL

Don't be afraid to incorporate something new and different into your curriculum. For example, get your kids out of the classroom to see the lesson from a different perspective.

In my second-grade class, we learn about urban, rural, and suburban communities. I built a field trip for each unit so they could experience each the urban unit, we took a bus ride into a city and took a walk through the historic sections. They were able to observe and experience the community and think through why certain houses were built differently than others. For the rural unit, we went to a dairy farm. For the suburban unit, we walked into the town with clipboards and backpacks. We interviewed business people as they were working in their businesses at the bank and at the bagel shop.

Then they came back, and presented their findings. Let's face it: a good lesson plan is hard to come by. My best advice is to build something that works for you, and is flexible enough to change if needed. As you're building your lesson plan for the year, try my five tips for a unique and fun curriculum your students will enjoy all year long!

25) How do you differentiate instruction?

Differentiated Instruction Defined and How to Implement It
Engage the most students and create the best outcomes for entire classrooms with differentiated instruction. It's a teaching method that helps bring struggling students up to speed, enables gifted students to learn at a faster pace, and makes teacher's lives easier because learning is more effective. When you use differentiated instruction, you're steering all your students toward the same learning objectives, while giving students the freedom to choose how they get there.

What Is Differentiated Instruction and Why Is It Important?
Differentiated instruction is the process of tailoring lessons to meet each student's individual interests, needs, and strengths. Teaching this way gives students choice and flexibility in how they learn, and helps teachers personalize learning. This method also requires instructional clarity and clearly defined goals for learning, better enabling students to meet those goals.

What Are Some Differentiated Instruction Strategies?
You can differentiate instruction across four main areas: content, process, product, and environment. To differentiate content, teachers consider the objective of a lesson, then provide students with flexible options about the content they study to meet the objective, from subject or topic to approach or presentation. With process differentiation, teachers differentiate how students learn. Grouping students based on their individual readiness or to complement each other is one way to accomplish process differentiation.

Another is varying the way concepts are taught: through visual, auditory, or kinesthetic lessons, for example. Product differentiation applies to the types of assignments students create. A teacher might ask students to explain a concept; the product could be a written report, a story, a song, a speech, or an art project. Varying the types of assessments you give students is also an example of product differentiation. The classroom environment also affects learning. Changing physical things in the classroom, like how desks are set up or arranged, or where students can sit (on beanbags, for example), serves as classroom environment differentiation, which can also include changes to routines and habits.

What Are the Benefits of Differentiated Instruction?

Differentiated instruction is beneficial because it helps educators connect with different learning styles. Not all students will respond to a class lecture; a game or a video may work better with other students. Some students may learn better by reading than they do using a computer.
Giving students choices about how they learn enables them to meet learning objectives in the best way for them. In some classrooms, differentiation will be required for students with disabilities and for English language learners.
Differentiating instruction gives all students the opportunity to keep pace with learning objectives. No matter what you're teaching, some students will find certain material engaging, while others won't, and students will learn the same material in varying amounts of time.
Want to make whatever you're teaching more likely to resonate with each one of your students? Differentiated instruction motivates them to learn the material in a way conducive to their own interests and unique learning styles.

What Do Experts Say About Differentiated Instruction?

"We differentiate instruction to honor the reality of the students we teach. They are energetic and outgoing.
They are quiet and curious. They are confident and self-doubting.
They are interested in a thousand things and deeply immersed in a particular topic. They are academically advanced and 'kids in the middle' and struggling due to cognitive, emotional, economic, or sociological challenges. Many of them speak a different language at home. They learn at different

rates and in different ways. And they all come together in our academically diverse classrooms." – Carol Ann Tomlinson (William Clay Parrish, Jr. Professor and Chair of Educational Leadership, Foundations, and Policy) "Differentiating instruction is really a way of thinking, not a preplanned list of strategies. Oftentimes, it is making decisions in the moment based on this mindset. It's recognizing that 'fair' doesn't always mean treating everyone equally.

It's recognizing that all of our students bring different gifts and challenges, and that as educators, we need to recognize those differences and use our professional judgment to flexibly respond to them in our teaching." – Larry Ferlazzo (award-winning teacher at Luther Burbank High School in Sacramento, California, who writes a teacher advice column for Education Week) "All teachers want their students to succeed, and all teachers try to make this happen.

That is all differentiation is. We complicate differentiation by not allowing ourselves to be provisional with how we apply the foundational pieces of differentiated instruction. Instead, if we address these four questions in our instructional planning, differentiation will always be the result: What do my students need? How do I know? What will I do to meet their needs? How do I know if what I'm doing is working?" – Lisa Westman (instructional coaching, differentiation, and standards-based grading consultant and professional development facilitator)

"Differentiated instruction is dynamic and organic. In a differentiated learning space, teachers and students learn together. Students focus on learning the course content, while teachers tailor their instructional strategies to student learning styles." – Alexa Epitropoulous (media and author relations specialist at ASCD).

How to Implement Differentiated Instruction

To ensure that the same objectives are being pursued by all students (though they each take their own path to get there), differentiated instruction must be standards-based. First steps for teachers should include diagnostic testing and learning inventories.

Your goal is to set baselines for individual students. Then you can identify tactics to help each student achieve the objectives and deliver custom tailored content.

Differentiated instruction is evident when teachers:
• Offer students options to choose from in assignments or lesson plans.
• Provide multiple texts and types of learning materials.

• Utilize a variety of personalized learning methods and student assessments.
• Customize teaching to suit multiple forms of intelligence.

For differentiated instruction to be successful, teachers must clearly explain the learning goals and the criteria for success.

Differentiated learning thrives in a classroom environment where students are working toward shared goals with a growth mindset. Teachers must identify and be responsive to student needs, creating a supportive classroom culture where students embrace differentiation for themselves and their peers.

Knowing the unique needs of your students enables you to teach them more effectively, with the goal of improving cognitive and academic outcomes. Learning A-Z provides thousands of differentiated instruction resources for all types of learners. Our products make teaching easier and more effective, giving students more flexibility and learning options.

26) **Many of the children have not acquired successful strategies for problem solving and critical thinking. Where would you begin if this were your classroom? What would you do at your grade level to better prepare students for this challenge?**

Our job is to teach our students HOW to think, not WHAT to think.
In This Post:
• The importance of helping students increase critical thinking skills.
• Ways to promote the essential skills needed to analyze and evaluate.
• Strategies to incorporate critical thinking into your instruction.

We ask our teachers to be "future-ready" or say that we are teaching "for jobs that don't exist yet." These are powerful statements. At the same time, they give teachers the impression that we have to drastically change what we are doing.

So how do we plan education for an unknown job market or unknown needs?

My answer: We can't predict the jobs, but whatever they are, students will need to think critically to do them. So, our job is to teach our students HOW to think, not WHAT to think.

Helping Students Become Critical Thinkers

My answer is rooted in the call to empower our students to be critical thinkers. I believe that to be critical thinkers, educators need to provide students with the strategies they need. And we need to ask more than just surface-level questions. Questions to students must motivate them to dig up background knowledge.

They should inspire them to make connections to real-world scenarios. These make the learning more memorable and meaningful. Critical thinking is a general term. I believe this term means that students effectively identify, analyze, and evaluate content or skills. In this process, they (the students) will discover and present convincing reasons in support of their answers or thinking.

You can look up critical thinking and get many definitions like this one from Wikipedia: "Critical thinking consists of a mental process of analyzing or evaluating information, particularly statements or propositions that people have offered as true."

Essential Skills for Critical Thinking

In my current role as science teacher of 8th grade curriculum and instruction, I work to promote the use of 21st-century tools and, more importantly, thinking skills. Some essential skills that are the basis for critical thinking are:
• Communication and Information skills
• Thinking and Problem-Solving skills
• Interpersonal and Self- Directional skills
• Collaboration skills

These four bullets are skills students are going to need in any field and in all levels of education. Hence my answer to the question. We need to teach our students to think critically and for themselves. One of the goals of education is to prepare students to learn through discovery. Providing opportunities to practice being critical thinkers will assist students in analyzing others' thinking and examining the logic of others.

Understanding others is an essential skill in collaboration and in everyday life. Critical thinking will allow students to do more than just memorize knowledge.

Ask Questions So how do we do this? One recommendation is for educators to work in-depth questioning strategies into a lesson launch.

Ask thoughtful questions to allow for answers with sound reasoning. Then, word conversations and communication to shape students' thinking. Quick answers often result in very few words and no eye contact, which are skills we don't want to promote. When you are asking students questions and they provide a solution, try some of these to promote further thinking:

• **Could you elaborate further on that point?**
• **Will you express that point in another way?**
• **Can you give me an illustration?**
• **Would you give me an example?**
• **Will you provide more details?**
• **Could you be more specific?**
• **Do we need to consider another point of view?**
• **Is there another way to look at this question?**

Utilizing critical thinking skills could be seen as a change in the paradigm of teaching and learning. Engagement in education will enhance the collaboration among teachers and students. It will also provide a way for students to succeed even if the school system had to start over.

Promoting Critical Thinking Into All Aspects of Instruction

Engagement, application, and collaboration are skills that withstand the test of time. I also promote the integration of critical thinking into every aspect of instruction.

In my experience, I've found a few ways to make this happen. Begin lessons/units with a probing question:
It shouldn't be a question you can answer with a 'yes' or a 'no.' These questions should inspire discovery learning and problem-solving.

Encourage Creativity: I have seen teachers prepare projects before they give it to their students many times.
For example, designing snowmen or other "creative" projects. By doing the design work or by cutting all the circles out beforehand, it removes creativity options.

It may help the classroom run more smoothly if

every child's material is already cut out, but then every student's project looks the same.

Students don't have to think on their own or problem solve.

Not having everything "glue ready" in advance is a good thing. Instead, give students all the supplies needed to create a snowman, and let them do it on their own.

Giving independence will allow students to become critical thinkers because they will have to create their own product with the supplies you give them.

This might be an elementary example, but it's one we can relate to any grade level or project. Try not to jump to help too fast – let the students work through a productive struggle.

Build in opportunities for students to find connections in learning. Encouraging students to make connections to a real-life situation and identify patterns is a great way to practice their critical thinking skills. The use of real-world scenarios will increase rigor, relevance, and critical thinking.
A few other techniques to encourage critical thinking are:
• Use analogies
• Promote interaction among students
• Ask open-ended questions
• Allow reflection time
• Use real-life problems
• Allow for thinking practice Critical thinking prepares students to think for themselves for the rest of their lives.

I also believe critical thinkers are less likely to go along with the crowd because they think for themselves.

What Are the Different Types of Problem-Solving Skills?

Before we get to the engaging activities, let's refine our understanding of problem-solving skills, which are any techniques that help you consistently:

• Understand the causes of problems
• Overcome short-term crises
• Create strategies to solve longer-term problems
• Turn problems into opportunities You'll be able to solve problems in your role better as you grow in your industry-specific knowledge.

But there are also a few universal problem solving skills we all need:
• Defining the Problem: Deeply understanding a problem through research, leading to better solutions.

Research can include interviewing, reading books and emails, analyzing financial data, searching your organization's intranet, and organizing your findings.

• Brainstorming: Creating a myriad of new solutions quickly. In group brainstorms, allow everyone to state ideas. Appreciate all input, and avoid criticism. Then, organize solutions into groups around common themes.

• Analyzing: Using disciplined thought processes to evaluate each possible solution. Besides listing their costs and benefits, you might apply deductive reasoning, game theory, and the rules of logic (including fallacies) to them.

• Managing Risk: Anticipating and trying to avoid the downsides of key solutions. Your team can list potential risks, rate how likely each is, predict a date by which each might either happen or no longer be an issue, and devise ways to reduce those risks.

• Deciding: The ability to decide on a solution and move forward with it. After an appropriate amount of time, an analysis of possible solutions, and feedback from team members, a designated decider must choose and implement a solution.

• Managing Emotions: Applying emotional intelligence in order to improve your and your team members' ability to think clearly. This requires you to recognize emotions in yourself and others, manage feelings, and channel emotions into useful work.

27) **Describe some ways you would teach literacy skills in a content area. What strategies might you incorporate to meet the needs of all learners?**

Teachers are often essential in helping students learn effective reading approaches. Literacy strategies can help teachers effectively frame their reading lesson plans, encourage consistent study habits and track the progress of their students.

If you're a teacher looking to improve the reading abilities of your students, it may be important to learn about different literacy strategies so you can learn which option works best for your classroom.

In this article, we discuss what literacy strategies are, why they're important and 17 literacy strategies to consider using in your classroom.

What are literacy strategies?

Literacy strategies are techniques that teachers use to help students improve their reading skills. They target different skill sets and areas of knowledge that involve reading, such as vocabulary, spelling ability, comprehension, critical analysis and language articulation.
Teachers typically incorporate literacy strategies in their daily lesson plans for language arts and other classroom activities to offer students learning support.

Why are literacy strategies important?

Here are some reasons why it's important for teachers to use literacy strategies:

Improves communication skills: Knowing how to approach a text can help students retain more information and learn how to articulate it.

Provides support structures: Using literacy strategies can help you support a student's social and emotional development as they learn new skills.

Develops writing capabilities: Most industries and fields value people who can write effectively, and reading comprehension is an important first step in learning this skill.

Addresses specific needs: As each student processes information in different ways, using varied literary strategies in your teaching can help you evaluate the reading progress of individual students.

17 literacy strategies to use in the classroom

Here are 17 different literacy strategies you can use in your classroom:

1. Annotate the text This strategy includes encouraging students to provide their own commentary on a text by highlighting key sections, writing notes or circling words to research. This practice can help students engage with the nuances of a text and improve their reading comprehension.

It can also allow teachers to understand a student's relationship to reading and their learning process. When assigning a text for homework, it may be helpful to provide some annotation tools, such as a list of shorthand symbols to write next to the text.

2. Work in teams Another helpful literacy strategy is to have students work in groups on class assignments to encourage collaborative discussion when reading and analyzing a text. This strategy can help students develop key communication skills and learn how to ask constructive questions. Students can discuss a reading question in groups and present that information aloud or read a text together and identify important elements. Consider grouping students with different skills and strengths so they can learn from one another.

3. Read aloud Consider dedicating a portion of class time to reading a book aloud.
Listening to a text may help some students improve their active listening skills, which can deepen their ability to concentrate on new information and develop their own reflections. If you read in a conversational tone, students can also learn how to use new vocabulary words and become more engaged in a story. Consider selecting material that discusses a familiar subject to students, such as a topic from a current lesson or a common interest.

4. Host a book recommendation event
To encourage students to read outside of a school environment, try coordinating an event where both students and staff can share their favorite books and discuss them as a group. Seeing mentors enjoy the act of reading and analyzing texts may positively affect how students regard literature assignments in the future.

5. Encourage students to choose their own books
Consider allowing students to pick their own book options for an assignment, including all genres and reading levels. This strategy can motivate students to develop daily reading habits outside of class. You can interview students to learn their preferences and make helpful suggestions about what they may enjoy. Consider assigning a project where students can discuss their favorite aspects of a book and present them to the rest of the class.

6. Make a geographical map When a text describes a particular location, you can have your students design a map of it using information from the text. You can use this activity to teach students how to focus on specific details in a text and incorporate research into a larger project. It can also help students better visualize a book's setting and incorporate outside concepts into their study of literature, such as using mathematics to create an accurate drawing. Merging disciplines can be a useful practice when attempting to accommodate different students' academic strengths.

7. Conduct individual meetings with students Consider also meeting with individual students regularly to discuss their reading development and goals. During these meetings, try to determine their core strengths and some areas of improvement regarding reading so you can determine what literacy strategies might best help them succeed. By focusing on a student's relationship to reading, you can also provide critical context for your data regarding their progress. For instance, you and a student may decide that offering additional reading assignments could improve that relationship and increase their overall confidence.

8. Offer reading rewards To encourage positive associations with reading, you can offer prizes or rewards to an entire class for accomplishing reading goals, such as a completed project or a certain number of books read in a time frame. If you place students in reading teams, you can encourage them to view reading as a community building activity. To include an educational component to the award, consider showing a film adaptation of a book previously read in class and having students discuss the differences between the two versions.

9. Perform the text Another beneficial strategy is having students create music or dramatic reenactments about a text to learn how to express new information in different formats and improve their language fluency. This also encourages creative expression, providing an opportunity for students to develop more personal connections to a text. For instance, students can write songs or poems about characters from a book or pick a scene to develop into a short play. Consider giving students the opportunity to both write and perform so they can benefit from experiencing both mediums.

10. Provide visual organizers Visual organizers are a physical representation of information from a text, such as a chart drawn on a poster or a graph made on a computer. They can help students better understand a text's main idea and retain more details. For example, you can have students divide core themes or significant plot points from the text into distinct categories as they read. Then, they can use those categories to draw a concept flowchart, which is a collection of ideas connected to one larger item by arrows.

11. Play classroom games There are several classroom games that improve literacy. For instance, you can have students play charades using plot points, characters or vocabulary words from a text recently read in class.

To help young students learn how words sound, they can play a clapping game to separate syllables using a physical gesture. You can also use this strategy to learn more about how students remember key information from a text and how they solve problems, which can help you assess their progress in a more informal way.

12. Use a mnemonic device A mnemonic device is a memory tool that associates a concept with a group of letters, including acronyms, expressions or rhymes. When teaching a new form of literary analysis, you can use mnemonic devices to help students frame the process and remember it while reading. You can also use mnemonic devices to guide your lesson plan when discussing literary analysis. For instance, when conducting a spelling lesson, you might teach the word "there" by noting that the word "here" appears in the former. You can then help a student associate both words with the phrase "here and there."

13. "Survey-Question-Read-Recite-Review" Also known as SQ3R, this is a reading comprehension strategy that can help students better understand a text the first time they read it and develop an effective comprehension process. You can have students form questions about a text and try to find the answer as they read, taking notes they can use for future classroom discussions and exams. Consider explaining each step of the process so students can better understand its purpose.

Here are the five steps of SQ3R:

Survey: Students read headings, chapter titles or any charts to preview the topics on which a text focuses. They also consider its overall structure.
Question: Using the information they learned from the previous step, students choose questions to consider while reading.
Read: Students carefully read the entire chapter or section with the purpose of answering the questions they previously wrote. They can use active reading methods, such as underlining key sentences or words and annotating their own reflections.
Recite: After noting their answers to the initial questions, students summarize what they learn in a text and say it aloud to deepen their understanding. They can work in small groups to practice this skill or present their individual summaries to the class.

Review: To clarify information, students review a text again and explain its main ideas. They can also clarify information about the text and further study the effectiveness of their initial questions.

14. Engage with an author Another helpful literacy strategy is having students consider an author's role in a text to deepen their reading comprehension and analytical skills. This strategy also allows students to develop critical thinking capabilities, helping them understand the purpose of a text in a larger context. For instance, you could ask students to reflect on an author's purpose in writing a text or how they phrased a certain sentence.

15. Draw or paint Some students may prefer to engage with a text by drawing instead of writing. To supplement classroom discussions and assess literacy skills in a unique way, consider instructing students to draw a scene from a fictional book or a concept from a nonfiction text. Drawing a visual image can also help students recall more information about a book. It may be helpful to have students select a scene or concept themselves to determine how they identify significant ideas while reading.

16. Use timed reading sessions Consider also assessing the reading skills of individual students by timing them speaking sections aloud. This strategy can help some students become more familiar with a text, including its vocabulary, sentence structure and overall content. It may be helpful to assign students the same passage to read at different times during the school year to gauge how their skills develop. To track this information, you can chart how long each reading session takes using graphing software.

17. Assign journaling projects Teachers can also give students a journaling assignment to record their reading progress in an organized fashion. Having this resource can help students track their thoughts about a text and recall critical information, increasing their overall understanding as they read. For example, students can divide a journal page into two sections, one for an important quote or theme they identify from the book and the other for their reflections. They can write about their personal connections to a text, how one theme connects to another or how the text's main ideas might connect to external topics.

28) Share how you would go about the process of **determining accommodations for a special needs student.**

Who can have accommodations & modifications in school?

Students who are determined to have a disability under the Individuals with Disabilities Education Act (IDEA) (e.g., autism, ADHD, intellectual disability, emotional disability, learning disability) can get accommodations and medications.

Students who have a disabling condition diagnosed by a medical professional (which impacts their ability to perform at their best in school) can also access accommodations/modifications.

Students eligible for accommodations and/or modifications in school have an Individualized Education Program (IEP) or a 504 Plan (described in further detail in the paragraphs below).

These are legal documents that outline the accommodations and modifications, along with other relevant information about the student's needs.

How do we know if a student meets the criteria for a disability under IDEA?

Whether your child meets the criteria for a disability under IDEA is generally determined by an evaluation completed by a school psychologist.

Sometimes other professionals such as a speech-language pathologist, occupational therapist, special education teacher, school counselor, or hearing specialist participate in the evaluation process as well.

These same professionals, along with the child's parents or guardians, can help determine what accommodations or modifications should be included in the student's IEP or 504 plan.

Sometimes the student can give insight into what they need as well.

What is the purpose of giving students accommodations or modifications in school?

The purpose of the accommodations and

modifications is to provide students with disabilities with the tools they need to be as successful.

It is a way to "level the playing field" with peers by removing any barriers to learning that could be related to the disability.

Just like a student who is visually impaired would receive books written in braille or books on tape so they could learn the material, students with other kinds of disabilities or conditions benefit from accommodations and modifications as well.

What is the difference between accommodations and modifications?

An accommodation gives the student an alternative or more effective way of learning the material.

A modification is a reduction in the amount of material or a change to the material itself.

Here are some more examples:

Accommodation:
A student has a learning disability in reading. The teachers read math word problems aloud to the student to ensure understanding. This allows him/her to focus on the math problem without any confusion that could emerge from reading difficulties.

Modification:
A student has a disability in math and has trouble focusing on independent work. They take twice as long as their peers to complete their work.
Therefore, they are given half the amount of homework, so they can get it done in a timely fashion.

What are some common reasons for accommodations or modifications in school?

There are many reasons why a child might benefit from modifications or accommodations such as difficulty focusing, trouble sitting still, seizures, anxiety or depression, learning difficulties, etc. However, in each case, the specific reasons need to be related to the child's disability.

What is a 504 Plan?

Section 504, part of the Rehabilitation Act of 1973, prohibits discrimination based upon disability. According to Section 504 the needs of students with disabilities must be met as adequately as the needs of students without disabilities.

If your child has a medical diagnosis of a physical or mental condition or disability, but does not meet criteria or show a need for special education, they may be eligible for a 504 plan.

The disability must "substantially limit one or more major life activity such as: learning, speaking, listening, reading, writing, concentrating, caring for oneself, etc.," in order to be eligible for a 504 plan.

The 504 plan, created from input from the parents, teacher(s), school records, and sometimes the student, outlines specific accommodations your child is entitled to to meet their needs so she can perform to the best of her ability.

In order to be eligible for a 504 plan, there needs to be evidence at school (e.g., consistent social, academic, or behavioral difficulties) demonstrating that your child is not performing on par with her peers due to their disability.

What is an IEP?

IEP stands for Individualized Education Program
The IEP consists of information such as:
❖ current academic performance
❖ specific academic, behavioral, or social-emotional needs and goals
❖ the level/intensity of services your child will receive
❖ the accommodations/modifications
❖ the level of participation in state and district-wide tests, how progress will be measured
❖ transition services (for students 14 and older) such as what the student's goals/plans are for after high school
❖ To be eligible for an IEP a child needs: an evaluation conducted by a school psychologist a determination from the school psychologist, basd on the evaluation, that the student has a disability under the Individuals with Disabilities Education Act (IDEA).

Examples include, ADHD, autism, intellectual disability, learning disability, emotional disturbance, speech language impairment, visual impairment, hearing impairment, traumatic brain injury). the school team decision that the child needs special education services to meet their academic, behavioral, and/or social-emotional needs. You may not know if your child or student needs an IEP or 504 plan. If you are wondering if a child has a disability or needs an IEP or 504 plan, arrange a meeting with the school team (teacher, administrator, counselor, etc.) to determine the next steps to ensure the child's educational needs are met. You can request an evaluation from the school to determine what your child needs.

KNOWLEDGE OF CONTENTS/ MATERIALS

1) What special course work have you taken that you feel has made you especially suited for the position you are applying?

B.Ed., Google Certified Educator & Ph.d

2) What kinds of materials and supplies would you need to do your best job?

Things that no teacher should go without in their classroom with the equipment below, teachers can give children the very best education every day.

1. A classroom set of tablets The tablet in the classroom brings education to life. Students have endless access to valuable information such as a dictionary and thesaurus, which previously were only available in printed format.
Interactive technology makes learning more engaging and memorable and tools such as audio and video recorders can change the way that learning takes place and homework is completed.

Technology plays a huge role in the lives of younger generations growing up today. Embrace their skills with technology and adapt the classroom to suit by investing in tech like tablets, robots and other computers and gadgets.

2. A teaching assistant Evidence shows that TAs have a positive effect – around two- or four-months' worth of extra academic progress across the year – if their interventions are formal and in small groups. A report says: "Crucially, these positive effects are only observed when TAs work in structured settings with high-quality support and training." Some label TAs as the unsung heroes of education. Ultimately, they deliver better learning outcomes for students – making them an indispensable part of a teacher's classroom.

3. Interactive whiteboard This is somewhat similar to the idea of bringing in more technology, but interactive whiteboards are so important they deserve a special mention. Interactive whiteboards not only bring an element of fun and modernisation to the classroom, teachers are also able to expand the delivery of education if they one at hand.

More learning styles are possible, with students seeing, hearing and interacting with the lesson, with a wider range of mediums available – such as image, video or interactive games. And if nothing else, it injects some life into a lesson, leaving outdated whiteboards, markers and paper printouts in the dust.

4. Sturdy & solid school furniture Without solid, specially designed school chairs and desks, students can end up distracted, uncomfortable and unable to focus on their studies. Good furniture not only encourages students to have better posture, it looks after their long term health and leaves teachers with one less thing to worry.

5. Cleaning and hygiene supplies Maintaining the highest standards in any setting is important – especially under the circumstances of today. From disinfectant, and air-fresheners, to washing-up liquid, first aid and hand sanitisers, they all have important roles to play. These supplies never get old, and their importance is only growing. Keep a well stock cupboard full of cleaning and hygiene supplies and help teachers to maintain a clean educational environment.

6. Tissues From accidental spills to unfortunate tears, tissues are an undervalued part of every classroom. Keep them well stocked so, just when emergencies occur, your teacher can reach for a tissue and quickly make everything better.

7. Classroom decorations the environment a teacher works in is just as important as the tools they have for the job. It's the job of the school to develop a stimulating environment that helps students concentrate on their studies and encourage creativity.

Make use of the walls of each classroom, decorating with colourful posters, pictures and progress charts to create a culture of learning that helps keep students engaged in their work.

8. A diary and wall planner Teachers are incredibly busy people, so any help they can get to remain organized will be welcomed with open arms. Work-based diaries can help teachers stay on top of deadlines, meetings and other major events that go on throughout the school calendar. You could a spread a little organization around too with a wall planner.

Marked up with important events and special days, it's not teachers who will be aware of the daily on goings of their class – but students too.

9. Students willing to learn Even with all the right supplies, teachers need students who are alert and willing to learn, a good attitude and work ethic can make a classroom with no supplies an absolute learning zone.

Thankfully, all the things listed in this article will contribute to that. A well-stocked classroom gives teachers the confidence to teach and students the ability to be the best they can be!

10. Essential supplies every teacher needs All of the things above are incredibly important to getting the best out of every teacher – but what about the everyday essentials?

Keep the classroom functioning at it's best my keeping these 23 essentials in constant supply.

√ Pencils √ Pens √ Ruler √ Plastic wallets √ Dividers √ Ring binders √ Pencil sharpener √ Exercise books √ Scissors √ Glue √ Paint √ Coloured pencils √ Erasers √ Sticky notes √ Notepads √ Tape √ Storage √ Desk organizer √ Stapler √ Magnetic clips √ Paper clips √ Hole punch √ Highlighters.

3) What kinds of materials have you used to assess pupil strengths and/or weaknesses?

If you're a teacher, it's important to be aware of your students' strengths and weaknesses. Strengths and weaknesses can help you determine how best to support your students and help them grow in their education. One way to determine the strengths and weaknesses of your students is to give them a standardized test. This will give you an idea of their academic abilities. You can also ask your students to complete a questionnaire or assessment that will help you understand their individual strengths and weaknesses.

Once you have an understanding of your students' strengths and weaknesses, you can target instruction to meet their needs. In this article, I will explore in detail the various ways to help you identify your students' strengths and weaknesses. Step-by-Step Guide on How to Determine Students' Strengths and Weaknesses

The following are the key steps to follow when trying to determine the strengths and weaknesses of your students:

Step 1: How to Collect Data About the Strengths and Weaknesses of Your Students. When collecting data about students' strengths and weaknesses, consider the following:

1. Survey all students in the classroom to get a general idea of their strengths and weaknesses. When surveying all students in a classroom, it is important to assess their general strengths and weaknesses. It is also important to identify any specific areas where they may need more help or support. By understanding the areas in which students struggle, you can better tailor your instruction to meet the needs of each individual student. Some general strengths that students often exhibit are creativity, determination, and resilience. On the other hand, some weaknesses may include difficulty paying attention in class, not being able to stay on task for extended periods of time, and having difficulty studying for exams. By surveying all of your students and taking into account their individual strengths and weaknesses, you can create a personalized learning environment that will help them succeed in school.

2. Observe students in class, individually and in groups, to gather more specific data.

Observe students in class, individually and in groups, to gather more specific data. This data can be used to determine which students are struggling and need more support.
It can also be used to identify which students are excelling and demonstrating strengths in specific areas.

By observing students in class, you can quickly identify which students are struggling and need more support. This information will help you tailor your instruction to meet the needs of each student.

3. Have students write essays or articles about their strengths and weaknesses.
In order to help a student grow in their academic endeavors, it is important to have an understanding of their strengths and weaknesses. This can be done by having the student write essays or articles about these topics.

In this way, you can better understand the areas in which the student needs improvement as well as their strengths from their own perspectives. Combining the results from this exercise with the survey results can help you to fully understand your students.

Also, involving your students in the process of determining their weaknesses and strengths helps them feel more confident in their abilities and builds trust between you and them.

4. Take into account parents' input when collecting data about students' strengths and weaknesses.

Parents are an invaluable resource when it comes to assessing their children's strengths and weaknesses. Collecting data from parents can help you identify areas in which students need assistance and can provide valuable feedback that can be used to improve student learning.
It is important to take into account parents' input when collecting data about students' strengths and weaknesses. Parents often know more about their children than anyone else, and they have a unique perspective on what makes them unique as individuals.
By working with parents, you can create a more accurate picture of your students and make the most effective use of resources available to them.

5. Use all available data to help you determine the strengths and weaknesses of your students
When it comes to assessing the strengths and weaknesses of your students, you cannot rely solely on what they tell us. You must use all available data, including their test scores, class grades, previous and continuous assessments, observations, conversations with students, and attendance records. By doing so, you can better understand where your students need more help and which areas they excel in. This information can then be used to plan interventions and provide support that will help them reach their full potential. By using data wisely, you can provide individualized support for your students while still ensuring that they are learning the essential material.

Step 2: How to Analyze the Data gathered about the strengths and weaknesses of your students

There are a few ways to analyze the data gathered about your students' strengths and weaknesses. One way is to use a rubric to determine how well each student meets the specific goals of the assessment. Another way is to use a rating scale, where students receive either a high, medium, or low rating for each area. A final way is to simply list out the areas in which your students excel and those in which they need improvement. This information can help you target interventions and support your students as they progress towards their academic goals.

It is important to be aware of the different ways in which data can be analyzed in order to best support your students. However, it is also important to remember that each student is unique and will respond differently to different types of interventions and support. Thus, it is important to monitor and adjust interventions as needed.

Step 3: Make a Diagnosis

In Step 3, you need to determine the strengths and weaknesses of your students. This step is essential in order to help your students reach their potential. By understanding their strengths and weaknesses, you can help them learn and grow in the right areas. Some of the most important things to look for when making a diagnosis are:
-What skills or abilities do your students have that are strong?
-What areas do they need to work on?
-How can you help them develop these skills or abilities? It is also important to consider:
-What obstacles are stopping your students from achieving their goals?
-What helps them overcome these obstacles?
-How can we help them use these resources to their advantage?

Once you have made a diagnosis, you can start to develop a plan of action. This plan will help your students reach their academic and personal goals. Other Strategies to Improve Your Ability to Determine the Weaknesses and Strengths of Your Students. The following are other variables that can facilitate the process of determining the strengths and weaknesses of your students:

1. Build a Strong and positive relationship with students to help you determine their weaknesses and strengths Building a strong and positive relationship with students can help you in understanding their weaknesses and strengths. It is important to identify these so that you can build a positive bond with them.

This will make them trust and open up to you thereby helping you understand them. By understanding your students, you can be able to determine their strengths and weaknesses quite accurately. One of the most important ways to build a strong relationship with students is to LISTEN. Give them the opportunity to talk about what they are working on, what they are enjoying in class, and any problems they are experiencing. This allows you to understand their needs and help them overcome any obstacles they may be facing. Check here for our guide on how to build positive relationships with your students.

2. Use assessment tools to help you determine students' weaknesses and strengths There are a variety of assessment tools available to help you better understand your students. Some of the most common include quizzes, tests, and surveys.

3. Be approachable and open to help you determine your students' weaknesses and strengths One of the most important responsibilities of a teacher is to help students grow and learn. To do this, teachers must be able to assess their students' strengths and weaknesses.

One way to do this is by being approachable and open to helping the student improve. If a student is shy or quiet, for example, it can be difficult for you to get them to talk.

However, if you make an effort to be friendly and open, the student may feel more comfortable opening up and talking about what they are struggling with. This can help you better understand where the student needs more assistance and how to best provide it.

The same principle applies to students who are naturally very strong in one area but may need some extra encouragement or support in others. By being open and approachable, you can help the student build on their strengths while also addressing any areas where they may need more assistance

By using these tools, you can get a snapshot of your students' strengths and weaknesses as well as their progress over time. This information can help you provide the best possible instruction and support. Click here for some assessment strategies to help you in your diverse classroom.

4. Establish effective communication channels to help you determine your students' strengths and weaknesses Effective communication is key to successful teaching and learning.

In order to effectively communicate with your students, you must establish effective channels of communication. These channels can be verbal, written, or electronic. To determine your students' strengths and weaknesses, you must use these channels of communication in combination with each student's individual characteristics. For example, if you are teaching a math class, you might use verbal communication (such as conversation or discussion) to help your students learn the concepts. You could also use written notes and homework assignments to help reinforce the material. Additionally, you could use electronic tools (such as online videos or calculators) to help the students practice the concepts.

By using these various methods of communication and applying them to each student individually, you can effectively assess their strengths and weaknesses and provide the appropriate assistance.

5. Develop your icebreaking skills to help you determine your students' strengths and weaknesses.
Icebreaking is an important tool to use when trying to better understand your students. By getting to know them better, you can identify their strengths and weaknesses.
This information will help you develop more effective teaching methods and strategies that will help your students succeed.

There are a few things that you should keep in mind when icebreaking with your students. First, it is important to be aware of their personality types so that you can cater the icebreaking activity to them. Next, be sure to vary the icebreaker activities so that everyone has a chance to participate.

Finally, make sure that the icebreaker is actually fun for the students! By using these tips, you can develop a successful icebreaking strategy for your classroom!

6. Collaborate with parents to help you determine your students' weaknesses and strengths

Collaborating with parents is an important part of helping determine a student's weaknesses and strengths. By discussing what the student is good at and what they need help with, both the teacher and the parents can work together to provide the best possible education for their child.

This process can be aided by using assessments to help identify areas of strength and weakness, as well as by speaking with family members about their experiences teaching their own children. Ultimately, the collaboration between you and the students' parents is essential to helping students achieve their goals.

7. Collaborate with other teachers to help you determine your students' weaknesses and strengths Collaborate with other teachers to help you determine your students' weaknesses and strengths. Other teachers teaching your students can have different perspectives regarding their strengths and weaknesses. Understanding what your colleagues think about your students and their strengths and weaknesses can contribute a lot to the process.

This will allow you to provide the most effective instruction possible.

Other teachers can offer you more useful information regarding your students. Therefore, make sure to collaborate with them. By working together, you will be able to help your students reach their full potential. Be sure to check out our tips on how to collaborate with other teachers for effective teaching and learning in your classroom.

Conclusion The strengths and weaknesses of your students can be determined by analyzing their data. This will help you diagnose their areas of weakness and target the appropriate instruction for them. By doing this, you will help your students to achieve their academic goals.

Second Idea An important activity is for students to understand that each and every one of them has strengths. These can come in the form of activities (ex. dance, hockey, math, etc) and in the form of character strengths.

It is also important to share what these strengths could look like in each student; strengths are not something that a student needs to be the best at but more about personal skills, qualities, traits and virtues that students have developed. For a poster of 24-character strengths (developed by Dr. Martin Seligman) click here.

This poster can be used as a way for students to choose character strengths that may represent them. For middle and high school students, I recommend watching the short film "The Butterfly Circus" as a way to lead to deeper dialogue on the view that every person has strengths and it depends on the perspective we choose. Through the work of many passionate educators whom I have had the chance to work and/or learn with (in schools as well as online and in workshops), I have come across the following ideas:

"All About Me" Activities – These are common in many classes and provide students with the opportunity to share a bit about who they are through a visual art or writing process.

The Identity Tree – family and friends make up the roots, interests and strengths make up the trunk and character strengths/virtues make up the leaves Identity Trees Identity Trees at James Hill Elementary

Student Identity Crest – include family, culture, strengths and interests
Presentation – each student creates a slide/poster that includes important images and words of strengths and interests.
All About Me Book – often used for students with special needs but is something that can be used for all students. Some of the students at our school have been doing this with the "Book Creator" app on the iPad.
Movies – some of our students have used iMovie to share a bit about themselves to share with peers and educators in the school.
Class Survey – use a paper survey, a google form, or other online surveys (with permission) to ask questions about strengths and interests in and out of school.

You can also survey family members to provide thoughts about the student. This would be great to be included in a student's file.

Shared Stories – through prompts, students can share stories of themselves that reveal strengths.

"What makes your heart sing?"

If I had a day to help someone/something I would…

I was most proud of myself when I…

Spend Time With A Student – A 2×10 strategy can be done for students who are struggling but can also be used as a way to get to know any student. Spend 2 minutes a day for 10 days straight having a natural conversation with a student. Find out what brings out the smile and move deeper in the following days. Other teachers I know have lunch (or "tea") with one or two students each week engaging in natural dialogue. Something as simple as spending quality time can have a lasting impact on a child and open up our eyes to their lives beyond school.

Identity Day – Although this is generally done as a school-wide event, it can also be done within a class. During Identity Day, students plan, prepare and share a presentation about themselves.

They can present on a strength, an interest, their family, culture… anything that represents who they are. I have been involved in two school-wide Identity Days and it is a great way for students and staff to better connect with each other on strengths and interests.

For a description of Identity Day, click here. For resources that can help you run an Identity Day click here.

Create Space for Strengths to be Revealed – More and more teachers are providing time each week for students to explore and create in areas of strength and interest. Ideas like 20% Time, Genius Hour, and Innovation Days provide opportunities for students to showcase and bring out their strengths.

Strengths Chats – For educators struggling to find the strengths in one or two students, Kathy Cox has developed a strengths grid that can be used to frame individual conversations with students (called "strengths chats"). She has divided strengths into social, academic, athletic, artistic, cultural/spiritual, and mechanical. You can view the strengths grid in her article here.

Observe – Take the time to watch and listen to your students. Ask the right questions. Instead of asking "how was your weekend?", ask "what was good about this weekend?" or be like Dora and ask "what was your favorite part?" . Create space in the lessons for students to share stories that reveal skills, traits, and virtues. You can also ask family members and friends to share what they feel a student's strengths are. In elementary, watch a child during choice times and recess.

Ask Adults – If you are struggling to see the strengths within a student, check with a former teacher, coach, family member who has observed the student in his/her element doing something that helped them to flourish in that moment. If a student had success with a former teacher, tap into this!

BONUS: For older students, you can use the VIA Character Strengths survey to get a ranked list of 24 character strengths. For intermediate students and older (including adults), Karen Copeland and I created an "Identity Tree" which is a fantastic way for people to acknowledge their strengths and realize the impact these strengths have on ourselves and those around us.

You can download the PDF with instructions here. For the vast majority of our students, it is not difficult to create the conditions for strengths to be revealed. The challenge is often to create ways for these student strengths to be used more often within the school.

For some ideas to get you started on including the strengths of students, click here.
For some of our students, though, life has been a series of challenges and they often hesitate to open up to let us in.
For students with years of struggle, the fact that they come to school most days can show a real strength in resiliency, determination, or courage so this can be a starting point to embracing character strengths.

4) Are there any materials you have used that you find are especially effective for slow learners or bright students?

A slow learner is a child who learns at a pace a little behind others of their age and grade level. Slow learners are not always learning disabled, and may have ordinary lives outside of the classroom. However, academic subjects are a challenge for them. To help slow learners, take a variety of approaches to teaching important subject matter. Get support for the students inside and outside the classroom. Most importantly, encourage slow learners by working with them patiently and by celebrating their successes.
Children who are labeled 'slow learners' are those that:

• Reach normal infant and toddler milestones later than the average child on a consistent basis. These milestones include crawling, walking, speech and vocabulary and motor skills such as clapping, hopping, skipping, recognizing eyes, ears, etc.

• Have trouble concentrating–all children have limited attention spans. but those who have trouble concentrating for more than two or three minutes at a time and are unable to recall what they did in that time and/or repeat what they did without instruction or prompting later on, will likely be in need of specialized attention and be labeled 'slow learners'.

- Struggles with the simplest of concepts and has difficulty retaining what they learn. This is a true indicator of a child with a learning disability. But rather than focusing on the disability, focus on finding how to work with the disability to make it less of an issue.

- Is socially immature or reclusive. Children who are labeled 'slow learners' will a) notice the fact that they are 'slow' or learning at a different pace or b) be singled out by the teacher and/or their peers as being 'slow'. This is embarrassing, humiliating and demeaning to a child.

Method :1 Teaching to the Slow Learners in Your Class

1.Repeat each learning point more than you normally would

Slow learners need to hear information a few times more than other students in order to understand it.
- Keep the other students interested by asking them questions and having them answer. Echo back their answers and explain how they relate to the point you are trying to teach.
- For instance, in a lower elementary class, you might say, "Saranda says 2x2 is 4, and she's right. We know this because 2 and 2 is 2 + 2, and that's 4."
- With older classes, you can reinforce learning points by leading discussions that encourage students to repeat the learning points. Ask questions about the subject matter, and ask students to explain their reasoning when they answer you.

2)Use audio and visual aids

Slow learners may struggle with basic skills such as reading, so movies, pictures, and audio can help them learn things that they would not pick up from reading alone. Use various media to repeat the information you want them to learn.
- For instance, if you are teaching conjunctions to elementary students, you can supplement your explanations and worksheets with the classic "Conjunction Junction" cartoon from Schoolhouse Rock!

- When teaching a novel to high school students, help slow learners by passing out worksheets and supplementary materials with visuals, such as family trees of the characters involved, timelines of the plot, and images of historical maps, costumes, and houses from the period of the novel.
- You may even have all your students take a learning style quiz to find out what types of learners you have and what approaches would be the most effective.

3)Guide students to the main points of lessons and tests

Slow learners may struggle to identify the main points of a lesson or a test, and may be overwhelmed by supplementary information. When teaching, make sure to identify and emphasize the learning points. Don't overwhelm your slow learners by moving on too quickly or asking them to learn many details beyond the main points.
- Before you start a lesson, summarize the main points so all your students know what they should be paying attention to.
- Provide study guides for tests so that slow learners know what information they need to concentrate on.
- Assign quicker learners supplementary reading and worksheets that fill them in on supplementary details about the topic.

Their self-esteem and confidence levels suffer tremendously and they withdraw in an effort to shield themselves from the pain–holding it inside themselves.

4)Use real-life examples when teaching math Introduce new math concepts by applying them to situations that your students can relate to. Use drawings and props, like pennies, beans, or marbles, to help students visualize the numbers.
- For instance, to introduce division to elementary students, draw a circle on the board and tell students it is a cake that has to feed 6 people equally. Then draw lines to divide it into 6 slices.
- For older students, some concepts may be more confusing using real-life scenarios. For concepts such as solving for an unknown variable, teach the form directly.
- Slow learners may be missing math information from previous years. If a slow learner is struggling with a new concept, check to make sure they know how to do more basic skills.

5)Teach reading skills Slow learners may struggle to read "automatically," the way their peers do. To help them catch up, teach reading skills to your whole class, or to a small group of slow-readers while other students work on supplementary projects.

- Encourage struggling readers to follow the words with their finger across the page as they read.
- Teach students to recognize phonemes and to sound-out unfamiliar words.
- Help your students with reading comprehension by training them to ask questions, such as "How does this character feel?" "Why did the characters make this decision?" "What could happen next?"
- Older students who are slow learners may also be helped by learning how to summarize chapters and otherwise annotate their reading.

6) Give your class lessons on study skills Slow learners need to go over material more than other students.
Help them speed up their study time by teaching them efficient methods of outlining, notetaking, and memorizing.
- Give your class demonstrations of note taking and outlining.
- Teach students to break down big tasks into small pieces so they aren't overwhelming.
- Teach them how to memorize using mnemonic devices. For instance, "Never Eat Shredded Wheat" is a way to remember the directions "North, East, South, and West.

METHOD:2 Facilitating Success in the Classroom

1) Schedule daily reading Slow learners need a lot of reading practice. Schedule sustained, silent reading time for your students every day. Provide a variety of reading materials, including books a little below grade level. Graphic novels may also be engaging for slow readers.

2) Assign peer tutors and homework buddies Rather than encouraging competition among your students, facilitate a culture of mutual helpfulness. Put your students in pairs so they can help one another learn new materials. Alternatively, you can train some of your quicker and more patient students to be "peer tutors," students who help other students understand their assignments. Assign jobs to all your students if you do this: put some in charge of passing out papers or feeding a class pet, for instance.

3) Give slow learners work that plays to their strengths Slow learners may become discouraged at having to work longer at things than other students. Provide them with daily breaks, and chances to excel. Identify areas where these students shine, and offer them the opportunity to pursue these activities in between more difficult tasks. For instance, a slow learner may be skilled at drawing, at sports, or at organizing. They may enjoy helping in the classroom, tutoring younger kids, or leading a team. Figure out the skills they take pride in, and give them opportunities to employ them.

4) Praise their successes When a slow learner completes a task, masters a concept, or otherwise triumphs, praise them wholeheartedly. You can praise them for trying, but don't focus on it: instead, praise them for finishing projects and figuring things out. They'll be less discouraged at how long things take if they know they receive congratulations at the end.

5) Check for understanding during lessons Develop a discrete way for your students to let you know how well they are understanding the material you are teaching. Avoid asking students to raise their hand if they do or do not understand.

Instead, try giving students numbered or color-coded cards to raise to indicate their level of understanding. For example, you could provide each student with a red, yellow, and green card. Then, ask students to raise up the card that indicates how well they understand.

Red could mean they are confused, yellow could mean they need you to go slower or repeat something, and green could mean that the lesson makes sense so far.

STRATEGIES FOR "SLOW LEARNERS"

To keep these students actively engaged in the learning process requires more than the usual variation in presentation methods (direct, indirect), classroom climate (co-operative, competitive), and instructional materials (films, workbooks, co-operative games, simulations). If this variation is not part of your lesson, these students may well create their own variety in ways that disrupt your teaching. Other immediately noticeable characteristics of slow learners are their deficiencies in basic skills (reading, writing, and mathematics), their difficulty in comprehending abstract ideas, and most disconcerting, their sometimes unsystematic and careless work habits.

1. Compensatory Teaching Compensatory teaching is an instructional approach that alters the presentation of content to circumvent a student's fundamental weakness or deficiency.

Compensatory teaching recognizes content, transmits through alternate modalities (pictures versus words), and supplements it with additional learning resources and activities (learning centers and simulations, group discussions and co-operative learning). This may involve modifying an instructional technique by including a visual representation of content, by using more flexible instructional presentations (films, pictures, illustrations), or by Shifting to alternate instructional formats (self-paced texts, simulations, experience-oriented workbooks).

2. Remedial Teaching This is an alternate approach for the regular class room teacher in instructing the slow learner. Remedial teaching is the use of activities, techniques and practices to eliminate weaknesses or deficiencies that the slow learner is known to have.

For example, deficiencies in basic math skills are reduced or eliminated by re-teaching the content that was not learned earlier. The instructional environment does not change, as in the compensatory approach. Conventional instructional techniques such as drill and practice might be employed.

3. Instructional Strategies for Slow Learners While no single technique or set of techniques is sufficient teaching the slow learner, the suggestions that follow are a starting point for developing instructional strategies that specifically address the learning needs of the slow learner.

Develop Lessons that Incorporate Students' Interest s, Needs, and Experiences.

This helps address the short attention spans of slow learners. Also, these students should be made to feel that some of the instruction has been designed with their specific interests or experiences in mind. Oral or written autobiographies at the beginning of the year, or simple inventories in which students indicate their hobbies, jobs, and unusual trips or experiences can provide the structure for the lesson plans, special projects, or extra-credit assignments in the year.

Frequently Vary Your Instructional Technique Switching from lecture to discussion and then to seat work provides the variety that slow learners need to stay engaged in the learning process. In addition to keeping their attention, variety in instructional technique offers them the opportunity to see the same content presented indifferent ways. This increases opportunities to accommodate the different learning styles that may exist among slow learners and provides some of the remediation that may be necessary.

4. Incorporate Individualized Learning Materials Slow learners respond favorably to frequent reinforcement of small segments of learning. Therefore, programmed texts and interactive compute r instruction often are effective in remediation of basic skills of slow learners. In addition, an emphasis on frequent diagnostic assessment of the student progress, paired with immediate corrective instruction, often is particularly effective.

5. Incorporate Audio and Visual Materials One common characteristic among slow learners is that they often learn better by seeing and hearing than by reading. This should be no surprise, because performance in basic skill areas, including reading usually is below grade level among slow learners. Incorporating films, videotapes, and audio into lessons helps accommodate the instruction to the strategies learning modalities among slow learners. Emphasizing concrete and visual forms of content also helps compensate for the general difficulty slow learners have in grasping abstract ideas and concepts.

6. Develop Your Own Worksheets and Exercises Textbooks and workbooks, when written for the average student often exceed the functioning level of the slow learner and sometimes become more of a hindrance than an aid. When textbook materials are too difficult, or are too different from topics that capture your students' interests, develop your own. Sometimes only some changes in worksheets and exercises are needed to adapt the vocabulary or difficulty level to the ability of your slow learners. Also, using textbooks and exercises intended for a lower grade could ease the burden of creating materials that are unavailable at your grade level.

7. Provide Peer Tutors for Students needing Remediation Peer tutoring can be an effective ally to your teaching objectives, especially when tutors are assigned so that everyone being tutored also has responsibility for being a tutor. The learner needing help is not singled out and has a stake in making the idea work, because his or her pride is on the line, both as a learner and as a tutor.

8. Encourage Oral Expression Instead of Written Reports For slow learners, many writing assignments go un - attempted or are begun only halfheartedly because these learners recognize that their written product will not meet even minimal writing standards. A carefully organized taped response to an assignment might be considered. This has the advantage of avoiding spelling, syntax, and writing errors.

9. When Testing Provide Study Aids Study aids are advances organizers that alert students to the most important problems, content or issues. They also eliminate irrelevant details that slow learners often laboriously study in the belief that they are important. The slow learner usually is unable to weigh the relative importance of competing instructional stimuli unless explicitly told or shown what is important and what is not.

Example: test questions or a list of topics from which questions may be chosen help focus student effort.

10. Teach Learning Skills You can increase learning skills by teaching note-taking, outlining, and listening. These skills are acquired through observation by higher ability students, but they must be specifically taught to slow learners. Unless your slow learners are actively engaged in the learning process through interesting concrete visual stimuli, there will be little contact emotionally and intellectually with the content you are presenting. This contact can be attained most easily when you vary your instructional material often and organize it into bits small enough to ensure moderate-to-high rates of success

11. Be patient with slow learners. The foremost aspect of teaching a slow learner is that the educator should be patient and consistent throughout the entire process. The core problem of slow learners' education is their weak cognitive skills coupled with the slow speed learning. A teacher has to be understanding and patient toward their ability to get distracted easily and having a low attention span. Moreover, teachers must find creative ways to cope with this situation so that the entire class is not affected. One of them is patient repetition. Try repeating every basic instruction, keyword and concept time and again without being boring. Do not over speak, but over teach.

12. Seek school management's help Request the school to arrange special classes for slow learners after/before school. Also, check whether you can get a co-teacher or an assistant teacher for your class. This will help you concentrate better on them.

13. Engage fellow classmates in your efforts Teach the other students to empathize with the special students. Specially ask them not to bully or tease slow learners. Inform them about their condition and how they could make a difference. Ensure you have these timely sessions in the slow learner's absence.

14. Provide minimum homework We all agree that homework although with its benefits is more of a burden for a child and her parent. Slow learners, in particular, find it difficult to be attentive throughout the school day, let alone coming home and completing homework assignments. For such children, quality matters over quantity.

Having minimum homework would help them understand learning and reduce their anxiety. This, in turn, would maintain their enthusiasm toward school. An educator can assign and alter homework personally and leave out small details that may be of little importance. For example, a homework of writing an essay on an English chapter could be modified to reading the chapter twice, and telling the summary to the teacher would be a better idea.

15. Let a buddy teach Peer tutoring works better for slow learners. When their teachers are of the same age, they get encouraged. Let them select 1 or 2 of his friends to form a study group. Assign the study group the task of reiterating the new teachings of the day and assisting with homework.

16. Encourage and Teach the right things Invite them to come forward during art classes, school activities, or volunteering.

Recognize and reward their participation. This would do wonders to their self-confidence. Teach special skills rather than unnecessary skills. This may include following the correct instruction words (count, color, circle, etc.) or listening and focusing on keywords. Remember the main goal is to make them self-sufficient.

17. Give them special takeaways Hand out special cheat sheets, mini dictionaries, or visually graphic information sheets. One good idea is to give lesson pamphlets for pinning them to their soft boards so that they are surrounded by constant reminders of lessons and activities. Do check out our stash of Math tips and tricks to help motivate them.

18. Praise and raise them Always praise every tiny effort of a slow learner in front of the class or in public. This would raise their self-esteem and confidence.

19. Encourage constant Parent–Teacher Association Work very closely with their parents.

Ensure the homework and tasks assigned are successfully completed on a daily basis. Be accessible and open to communication. Make sure to listen out to parents' problems and help to solve them. Conduct special meetings for their parents of apart from the general PTA meets.

20. Most Importantly Demonstrate effective teaching, classroom organization and management skills in order to ensure that students' learning needs are appropriately addressed Monitor the effectiveness of their instructional methods as well as the learning profiles (preferences, characteristics, strengths, interests, talents, tyles, etc.) of the students they teach• .Adjust or change their teaching methods as required to meet the learning needs of each of their students •As part of their responsibilities as professional educators, engage in appropriate professional development and in-service activities, particularly in the areas of literacy and mathematics, in order to gain new knowledge, skills and attitudes that relate to teaching students who experience difficulties •Maintain an awareness of the performance level of all students in their classes so that the school-based student services team can discuss those students experiencing difficulties.

Lastly, a few don'ts: Do not reprimand in front of the class. You may do that in private.

Do not emphasize on writing, concentrate on reading. Oral education is more beneficial for them.

Do not let them quit trying. Encourage them to continue their hard work to complete their tasks even if it means postponing it.

Do not be overprotective. Let their slow learning not become their introduction.

5) What kinds of tests do you like to give?

Different Types of Testing There are four types of testing in schools today — diagnostic, formative, benchmark, and summative. What purpose does each serve? How should parents use them and interpret the feedback from them?

1. Diagnostic Testing This testing is used to "diagnose" what a student knows and does not know. Diagnostic testing typically happens at the start of a new phase of education,

like when students will start learning a new unit. The test covers topics students will be taught in the upcoming lessons. Teachers use diagnostic testing information to guide what and how they teach. For example, they will plan to spend more time on the skills that students struggled with most on the diagnostic test. If students did particularly well on a given section, on the other hand, they may cover that content more quickly in class. Students are not expected to have mastered all the information in a diagnostic test. Diagnostic testing can be a helpful tool for parents. The feedback my kids receive on these tests lets me know what kind of content they will be focusing on in class and lets me anticipate which skills or areas they may have trouble with.

2. Formative Testing This type of testing is used to gauge student learning during the lesson. It is used throughout a lecture and designed to give students the opportunity to demonstrate that they have understood the material, like in the example of the clock activity mentioned above. This informal, low-stakes testing happens in an ongoing manner, and student performance on formative testing tends to get better as a lesson progresses. Schools normally do not send home reports on formative testing, but it is an important part of teaching and learning. If you help your children with their homework, you are likely using a version of formative testing as you work together. For example, while watching my son, Luke, measure objects using inches and centimeters this week, I was able to see when he chose the wrong unit or when he did not start the measurement at the zero point on the tape measure. That was a form of formative testing.

I find it helpful as a parent because it lets me correct any mistakes before they become habits for my sons.

3. Benchmark Testing This testing is used to check whether students have mastered a unit of content. Benchmark testing is given during or after a classroom focuses on a section of material, and covers either a part or all of the content has been taught up to that time.

The assessments are designed to let teachers know whether students have understood the material that's been covered. Unlike diagnostic testing, students are expected to have mastered material on benchmark tests, since they covers what the children have been focusing on in the classroom. Parents will often receive feedback about how their children have grasped each skill assessed on a benchmark test. This feedback is very important to me as a parent, since it gives me insight into exactly which concepts my boys did not master. Results are broken down by skills, so if I want to further review a topic with my boys, I can find corresponding lessons, videos, or games online, or ask their teachers for resources.

4. Summative Testing This testing is used as a checkpoint at the end of the year or course to assess how much content students learned overall. This type of testing is similar to benchmark testing, but instead of only covering one unit, it cumulatively covers everything students have been spending time on throughout the year. These tests are given — using the same process — to all students in a classroom, school, or state, so that everyone has an equal opportunity to demonstrate what they know and what they can do. Students are expected to demonstrate their ability to perform at a level prescribed as the proficiency standard for the test. Since summative tests cover the full range of concepts for a given grade level, they are not able to assess any one concept deeply. So, the feedback is not nearly as rich or constructive as feedback from a diagnostic or formative test. Instead, these tests serve as a final check that students learned what was expected of them in a given unit.

As a parent, I consider summative testing a confirmation about what I should already know about my sons' performance. I don't expect to be surprised by the results, given the regular feedback I have been given in the form of diagnostic, formative, and benchmark testing throughout the year. Combining Test Results We need a balance of the four different types of testing in order to get a holistic view of our children's academic performance.

Each type of test differs according to its purpose, timing, skill coverage, and expectations of students. Though each type offers important feedback, the real value is in putting all that data together:

• Using a diagnostic test, you can gauge what a student already knows and what she will need to learn in the upcoming unit.

• Formative tests help teachers and parents monitor the progress a student is making on a daily basis.

• A benchmark test can be used as an early indicator of whether students have met the lesson's goals, allowing parents and teachers to reteach concepts that the student may be struggling with.

Ideally, when heading into the summative testing, teachers and parents should already know the extent to which a student has learned the material. The summative testing provides that final confirmation. Hopefully, the next time parents hear the word testing, they don't just think of summative testing. Instead, they think of all four types and the value of putting the feedback from them together to get a richer, more thorough understanding of their child's progress.

6) How do you organize you teaching supplies and/or materials?

1. Create a separate space for resources you don't use but must keep You may have a reading curriculum that comes with ESL components and you have no ESL students. Perhaps your math guides don't all align with the Common Core and you are using supplemental materials, but the school has not said to recycle the old ones. We all have stuff that we are housing simply because we need to. Don't let it be clutter, but instead package it up neatly and out of sight.

That way, if you leave your position and need to leave the resources behind they will be gathered already. I find a great way to do this is to place them in a copy paper box and attach an inventory of what is inside onto the box. That way you can leave the entire box behind or turn it in if that is what you need to do. In my situation, I have a deep shelf and simply store them in the back with items I use regularly placed in front of the box.

2. Store teacher materials out of sight
I prefer to house my teacher guides, manuals, resource books, etc. out of student view. This helps reduce visual clutter.

Since the books are not something the students need to access, I keep them out of sight. I use the small group table as my teacher workspace. There is open shelving behind it so I keep my books in decorative boxes without tops grouped by subject area. These function almost as drawers. The students can't see what is inside and I can access them easily when I am sitting there planning.

3. Keep subject areas together If you use a teacher desk, you may want to store them in the drawers. You could also use the drawers of a filing cabinet. Regardless of if you use a drawer of a shelf, it is important to keep subject areas together. Dishpans can be purchased at the Dollar Store and work great on shelves to cluster books together. If you use a drawer, create tabbed sections using file folders. Add in related items like pacing guides, curriculum maps, a binder or CD of printables to the related section or bin.

4. Go digital when possible Many teacher guides are available online. Ask your curriculum coordinator if this is an option. Even if you've had the books for several years you may be able to use their online manuals by obtaining the code.

5. Collaborate with colleagues Take a tour of your building. Most schools have classrooms with similar furniture, built-ins, closets and shelving. See how other teachers are housing their books. Ask if they are happy with their systems. Use their methods as inspiration.

Teacher Resources You Purchase Below are 3 tips for organizing your teaching materials that you have purchased.

1. Declutter your collection of resources Go through your personal resource collection with a critical eye. Tear out pages you want to keep and put them in a binder.

2. Go digital Scan resources and go paperless. Then pass the book onto a colleague or recycle it.

3. Use dividers If you use a traditional bookshelf, be sure to add dividers that make it easy to see where things are. You might also want to label the front of the shelf as well.

How to Keep Track of Borrowed and Lent Items When creating a clutter-free learning environment, we need to purge, sell and donate anything and everything that is not essential to teaching our students.

Borrowing from others is a great way to minimize clutter, to save money, and to provide students with a variety of resources.

However, in order to establish a good reputation as a borrower and to be sure that you don't lose track of your own valuable items that you lend to others, it's important to develop an organized system for managing borrowed/lent materials. Read below to get tips for managing and organizing the teaching materials you borrow and lend out!

5 Tips for Managing Lent and Borrowed Teacher Resources Below are 5 simple tips for managing and organizing the teaching materials that you lend out and borrow.

1. Create one specific place to list and track borrowed items. I recommend designated pages in an all-purpose teacher binder. This helps keep everything you reference and need in one place.

2. Whenever you borrow or lend something, be sure to immediately record it. Don't let it take up any space in your brain. As soon as you borrow or lend something right it down in a designated space so you don't forget.

3. Log in items when they are returned. Similar to writing it down when you borrow or lend something, you'll want to note when it is returned. This will help you stay on top of things without a lot of mental effort.

4. Keep a running list of book titles that you borrow from the library. I like to keep two different lists. One of my school library and one for the public library. As an alternative, you could put a sheet protector into your binder and use it to slide in printed out lists from the library's system.

5. Return items promptly. As soon as you are done using a resource, return it to the owner of it. This will make it so you have less items to manage and your lender will greatly appreciate it.

How to Use Binders to Organize Teaching Resources

There are So many teaching resources we need at our fingertips as classroom teachers. Do you have one place where all of your teaching resources and worksheets are organized? Can you easily bring it home and to planning meetings when you need to? If not, you must consider using binders to organizing your teaching materials!

It's true: a great, but simple tool for classroom organization and management is a 3-ring binder. They are perfect for organizing your teaching units and lesson plans as well as for creating student portfolios, collecting documents for your Teacher Evidence Binder, housing meeting notes, and about a million other things.

Must-Haves for Your Teaching Binders Teachers have so many things to manage. One way to be successful at being organized in the classroom is to be proactive in setting up a system for managing paperwork.

A simple way to manage all important documents and paperwork that need to be easily accessible is a binder or folder system. Binders are ideal because they offer the flexibility to move papers around as well as adding and removing them as needed. They are durable. You can add addition pockets for sorting, holding pens and other tools and best of all you can customize them by inserting your own cover and spine.

1. Binder Covers Binder covers allow you to quickly identify which binder you are looking for by flipping through them in your basket.
• Bright Polka-Dotted Binder Covers
• Primary Polka-Dotted Binder Covers
• Bright Chevron Binder Covers
• Primary Chevron Binder Covers
• Bright Quatrefoil Binder Covers
• Primary Quatrefoil Binder Covers

2. Binder Spine Labels Another binder must-have is a spine label. Binder spine labels are a great way to quickly find which binder you need on your bookshelf. My teacher binder resources include tons of spine labels to choose from. Plus, they are editable. This makes it so you can customize them to fit your needs. Check out the different options below:
- Bright Polka-Dotted Binder Spine Labels
- Primary Polka-Dotted Binder Spine Labels
- Bright Chevron Binder Spine Labels
- Primary Chevron Binder Spine Labels
- Bright Quatrefoil Binder Spine Labels
- Primary Quatrefoil Binder Spine Labels

3. Dividers

Binder dividers are a great organization tool for maintaining an organized binder that you can easily navigate. You'll be able to flip through your binder quickly to find exactly what you need. They are a big time saver! In closing, we hope these tips for organizing teaching materials in your classroom was helpful! If you did, then you may also be interested in these posts:

• Classroom Paper Organization Ideas for Elementary Teachers
• Why It's Important for You to Have an Organized Classroom
• 20 Back to School Read A louds for Elementary Teachers.

7) Describe your educational background and teaching experience related to your subject area?

Example:
10 +2- Physics, Chemistry, Math's, Biology
B.Sc., Physics M.Sc., Physics B.Ed., Physical science GCE.

8) How do you stay current in your teaching field.

Teaching is not the same today as it was even 10 years ago, much less four decades ago, which is when many of today's retiring teachers first entered the classroom as an instructor.

How To Stay Fresh As a Teacher

1) Take Continuing Education
Classes Teachers can be students, too, and one of the best ways to stay fresh is to continue your education.
Many teachers are required to earn a specific number of continuing education credits each year, but it's important to pick the right classes to take. Classes should expand the teacher's tool set rather than reviewing existing skills. Both online and traditional colleges offer continuing education diplomas and certificates.
These programs take around one year complete, depending on the number of credit hours. A great way to find the best programs is asking colleagues what they have taken.

2) Revamp Lesson Plans

Teaching the exact same lessons every year can get stale, so take the time to revamp lesson plans on a regular basis. This is especially important for teachers who only teach one or two courses with multiple sections each day. After knowing the material so well and teaching it so many times, it's easy to get stuck in a rut.

One useful exercise is to start from scratch on a lesson that has seemed to flop lately and rethink the best way to teach the material. Or, connect with a fellow teacher who may teach at a different school, and compare and improve on your current lesson plans!

3) Add Technology to Courses Stanford professor noted recently is that technology is one of the best ways to connect with students these days. Many teachers have already made the switch from overhead projectors and blackboards to slideshow presentations, and laser pointers, but there's always more to add. Smart Boards help teachers create interactive lectures that students can access from their own computers later, and many teachers are finding ways to let students use their smartphones to vote on polls or collaborate on projects. Gamifying your lesson plan can also engage tech-driven students of modern-day as well.

4) Work Toward an Advanced Degree Although most elementary, middle, and high school teachers don't need to hold a master's degree, many teachers still choose to work toward a higher degree, often a Master or Doctorate of Education. Doing so gives the teacher a chance to learn more about educational methods and specific subjects stay on top of things in the classroom. As The Weekly Herald points out, advanced degrees in education are particularly helpful to stay up-to-date with the latest teaching methods for kids growing up today. Plus, many school districts give a raise to teachers who hold an advanced degree. Work Toward an Advanced Degree.

5) Read Industry Books There are thousands of books about education, and picking and choosing some of the best new books can provide a lot of food for thought. It's important to choose wisely, focusing on books that others are buzzing about or books about specific aspects of being a teacher that can motivate improvement in weak areas. Even memoirs from other teachers can give the sense of being part of a bigger movement and inspire excellence! Our picks are:
The First Days of School: How to Be an Effective Teacher, The Creative Teacher: An Encyclopedia of Ideas to Energize Your Curriculum, Teaching with Love & Logic, and How to Differentiate Instruction in Mixed-Ability Classrooms.

6) Brainstorm with Other Educators Colleagues are sometimes the best places to get ideas, particularly if they work at the same school or type of school.

Picking someone else's brain can provide tons of ideas on how to incorporate new techniques to connect with the students and help them learn more effectively. It can also help refresh educators who are feeling burned out or discouraged, as teacher Jim Burke explained in his ASCD article.

7. Establishing Goals Educational technology is often developed to suit a specific problem that makes selecting the right solution for the school's specific strengths and weaknesses an essential part of modernizing the classroom. Teachers thus have to undertake a thorough research on different solutions to know their distinct characteristics and avoid random selection of tools that are hardly of much use to them. Establishing goals is important for the teachers as in the present age; innovation without direction is the path to a woefully misplaced investment. Also, with so much technology now available to educators, it makes all the sense to actually gather a few resources on how to use current technologies in the classroom. As teachers create a guideline for them, it will help lay the foundation for understanding popular platform and concepts being applied to the classroom. To enhance understanding of how to use technology in the classroom is to subscribe to or follow some of the latest tech blogs related to classroom instruction.

8. Discuss with Peers and Experts from Across the World With social media going conventional, communication with natives and people situated in different corners of the world from the community has become way too easy. Discuss on how other teachers apply new style of pedagogy and ways of relating to students, share with each other and this way teachers will not only learn new things but improve and grow together in the community. The other side of the thing is that, it is true that, teachers cannot alwaysstay up-to-date in the loop on all the latest trends. However, it's important to be aware of the trends that are far reaching so that school staff members are all on the same page when it comes to addressing issues like cyberbullying and topics like digital literacy and digital citizenship. The more teachers share about what the students are interested in, the more does it open up avenues for the teachers to connect with the students.

9. Don't Panic and Keep Things in High Spirits

While trying out any new technology enabled pedagogical practice or for that matter incorporating a new tool into learning, it is pertinent to step into it thinking it is to one's advantage.

This gives the much-required initial push to start things new and afresh. Trying out new technology trends can actually be fun for not just the teachers but the students too. As teachers adopt new approaches, they will find it gives new life into material and creates excitement among their learners. Further, the significant benefits of integrating technology into the classroom are that it offers a certain degree of flexibility that was unimaginable in the traditional model of education. For instance, in the flipped classroom setup, teachers can use class time for homework and deliver lectures after school through digital media, has been causing significant waves in the world of education. It may not suit every topic, but despite some detractors the method has shown to be remarkably useful in certain environments. As one is developing their plan, its crucial to consider what new things these technologies can do.

10. Utilizing Social Media
Social media is an easy and effective way to learn about new technologies. Teachers should take optimum advantage of social media platforms like Twitter and Facebook, where they make it easy for the teachers to track what's trending in the world of educational technology. All that's required for a teacher is search hashtags on both platforms like 'edtech' or 'edchat 'to read all about the latest educational innovations. One can also chat with the experienced techies and get all of their questions answered related to technical confusions. At any rate, using social media in the classroom is certainly a tricky exercise, but can be very rewarding to both the student and the teacher. Directing activities with complete, well-planned guidelines can lead to an incredibly active, organic student community, encouraging students to learn for themselves not just for grades.

11. Proceed to Continued Education Bracing up skills and reskilling is what every profession demands in the fast-paced evolving economy and teaching being no different.
Effective teachers' professional development course programs enable educators to develop their knowledge and improve their instruction.
It is about acquiring new skills and becoming a better teacher and gaining the confidence by learning new methods and information regarding the technology enabled pedagogical approaches- benefits as well as its implementation process. In the course of completing the program, teachers can learn on online teaching and learning, the fundamentals of using digital tools to streamline assignments, organize the assessment process and how teachers can provide students with constant access to learning materials.

PLANNING SKILLS

1) How well organized are you? Why is organization important for a teacher?

Teachers in the 21st century need to be good at many different things. They are, of course, expected to know their subject well or to have a wide range of knowledge if they are teaching one grade many different subjects, but as well as this, teachers need to be technologically savvy, they need to be caring and patient, and, perhaps above all, they need to be organized. Just what is it that is so important about organization for teachers that makes it something they all need to be able to do? Read on to find out.

Beginning Of the School Year There are basic principles and ways of operating to get yourself off to the best start at the beginning of the school year. Revisiting at any time during the year is a great idea also. Take a look at our series where Marie Amaro walks through these principles in a fantastic step-by-step practical guide.

No Wasted Time The school day is full – very full – of lessons, breaks, sports, and lunch, as well as additional activities depending on the student's own choices. This means that, in order to offer the best education to each child, a teacher will need to be highly organized because, in this way, there will be no wasted time. A disorganized teacher, one who doesn't know where their class notes are or who hasn't checked they know how to use the equipment they need for the lesson, will waste a lot of time getting ready. Even a few minutes can mean that an entire topic can be lost.

If you organize your files online, if you have your handouts pre-printed, if you have checked that you have everything ready before the lesson begins, you can make the most out of the time you have with your class, even if it's a single period.

If you are organized as a teacher, you can make great use of your time. You don't want to waste any of your precious class time by being unprepared or not knowing where things are located in your classroom.

If you know exactly where everything is located within your room, then you won't waste valuable minutes looking around for something.

This will allow you to get right into the lesson without wasting time searching for items. It's much better to have all materials ready before starting than to find yourself running late because you couldn't locate an item quickly enough.

Important Life Habits As well as ensuring that students get their full lesson quota by being organized, an organized teacher will also be able to help students develop good life habits now and in the future.
They will learn the difference between having everything they need with them and being able to enjoy a smooth and interesting lesson, and not having what they need, in which case they will be

stressed and tense and won't learn so well. The earlier this can start, the better.

A child who can emulate an organized, punctual teacher from when they are very young will keep these lessons with them well into the future, including when they start work.

Fewer Discipline Problems It might be surprising to learn that a more organized teacher is a teacher who has fewer discipline issues in their classrooms, but it's true. Students will know that this teacher is ready to start teaching, and they need to be prepared to start learning; there is no time for messing around and playing games because work begins right away.

When the work begins immediately – thanks to the teacher's organizational skills – the children in the class will have much less opportunity to talk among themselves and disrupt the rest of the class. Even those who might want to act up won't have the chance to, and soon enough, they will learn that it's not worth even thinking about.

Plus, an organized teacher will gain a reputation for being aware of everything that is happening around them as they won't be distracted by their lack of organization. Again, this means that anyone attempting to be disruptive will be stopped much sooner.

Improves Personal Relationships Teachers work hard, and they don't just work in the classroom – there are lessons to plan and papers to grade, and this all has to happen after or before school hours. This can have an impact on personal relationships, as there isn't much time for anything other than work. However, the more organized the teacher is, the more time they can save overall, and the better their relationships with friends and family will be. Students and their parents will expect teachers to meet their deadlines and keep their promises. Being organized and therefore saving time by not searching for books and papers and other important items means this can happen and you can still find time to relax and enjoy your time with others or by yourself, depending on your preference.

Better Health We've mentioned that teaching is hard work, and that can also sometimes be stressful work as there is a lot to do and a lot of responsibility. Being disorganized on top of all this can certainly have a negative effect on the body and mind and potentially make your stress levels even higher. If you are organized, no matter what the job might throw at you, you will always be able to stay calm and focused, and you should be less stressed,

improving your health and helping you become a calmer, more focused teacher overall.

It Reduces Stress How much stress is usually thrust onto the shoulders of a teacher? It often feels like we're juggling balls in the air, just waiting for one to fall and break. When teachers get stressed out, they tend to become less effective at their jobs.

Being organized helps reduce this stress by making sure everything has its place. This means fewer things on our desks or shelves, which makes us feel better about ourselves and our work. We also have time to focus on what's important instead of worrying about where something went when it was supposed to be somewhere else.

It Improves Students' Learning Getting organized as a teacher can be difficult. There are many tasks that need to be done, and you might not have the time to think about organization. However, being organized as a teacher can help students learn better because they will have a sense of order.

Getting organized, as a teacher, can help you improve learners' learning. It is important for teachers to keep track of what needs to be done in class. If there is too much work to do, then it could cause stress among students.

Students should know where things stand at all times. They should understand what has already been completed and what still needs to be finished. You must also make sure that your lesson plans are well-organized.

The best way to organize your lessons is by using an outline or schedule. You may want to use different colors depending on whether something is due today, tomorrow, next week, etc.

It Improves Your Teaching Being organized helps improve your teaching efforts. It makes you more efficient because you can easily find the information you need when needed. When teachers have a clear understanding of how they will teach each day's material, they can better prepare for classes.

This means less time spent preparing materials and more time spent actually teaching. In addition, it also allows students to focus their attention on learning instead of having to spend extra time trying to figure out what lesson activities they should be doing that day.

It Makes You Confidence Organized teachers

always have confidence in themselves. This is because they are able to achieve much within the limited time in school.

They can easily organize their lessons and make sure that students understand what they need to learn. When a teacher has organized his/her class, he/she knows how long it takes him/her to teach each subject or topic.

His/her also knows which subjects or topics require more attention from other classes. Therefore, when teaching any given lesson, he/she will be confident of its success.

It Teaches Life Lessons to Students learn to be organized, responsible, and accountable from organized teachers. When a teacher teaches his/her class in an orderly manner, he/she will also teach life lessons such as being organized, responsible, and accountable. These three things are very important for people who want to succeed in life because these traits make it easier for someone to achieve success. For example, if you have good organizational skills, then you won't forget anything when preparing to teach a lesson. If you're responsible, then your schoolwork is always done on time or before the deadline. And lastly, if you're accountable, then you'll know that you must do something about any mistakes that you made during teaching.

Have a Purpose Both in and out of the classroom, the very best teachers and the happiest people have a clear sense of purpose. On a grander scale, they have a dream, a vision, and a view of their world as they would like to see it become.
Thus, have a goal of how you want to be organized, both in and out of your classroom. It will help keep you focused on what is important for yourself and your students. You can also use this list as an outline or guide when planning lessons, projects, etc.
This way, you won't get lost in all the details that go into teaching. Instead, you'll focus on the big picture.

Plan for Success Whether teaching a lesson or building a house, a good plan helps us get things done efficiently, effectively, and correctly. A good plan stimulates creativity.

Plan the process of making decisions about what to do, when to do it, and how to do it. Make sure your plans include all aspects of the lessons, so nothing is left out.
When planning your lessons, think through every step-in detail before starting. It will save time later if something goes wrong.

Also, make sure you have enough supplies available to deliver the lesson. If not, don't start a topic or lesson until you can deliver it with everything on hand.

Discover Your Prime Time Don't waste your most creative time doing menial tasks like photocopying, stapling, cleaning, filing, or grading objective tests. Safeguard those precious hours when you are at your intellectual peak to do the most cognitively challenging tasks: writing, planning, and creating. You may be surprised at how much more productive you become during this prime time than at any other period of the day.

Set Up a Schedule for Yourself It takes discipline to stick to a schedule, but it pays off big-time. The key is to set up an efficient system that works best for you. For example, if you have trouble getting started in the morning, try waking up early so you can get some work done before others wake up. If you're not sure what's going on with your life right now, use a calendar app such as Google Calendar to keep track of important events. It will help you stay organized and avoid missing out on anything significant.

Get Rid of Distractions If you find yourself constantly distracted by social media or email notifications, turn them off completely until after you've finished working. This way, you won't be tempted to check those apps while trying to focus on something else. You'll also save time because it takes less effort to ignore distractions than it does to actually complete tasks.

Use the Pomodoro Technique The Pomodoro technique is an effective method for getting things done in short bursts. The idea behind this approach is that if you break down large projects into smaller chunks, then you can work more efficiently without feeling overwhelmed.
It's a simple concept: set aside 25 minutes of uninterrupted, focused work and take breaks every four hours. If you're not sure how long your task will take, estimate about 20% longer than you think it should take.
This way, when you get stuck on something or feel like giving up, you'll have some buffer room before you start working again. You might even find yourself finishing early!

Keep a Personal Calendar A daily calendar is the single most valuable time management tool. It doesn't matter which kind you use, as long as it meets your needs. If you don't have one already, try using Google Keep or Evernote instead of pen and paper.

They're free, easy-to-use tools with built-in reminders. And they sync across all devices, so you won't lose any information when switching between them.

You'll also be able to see what's coming up next on your schedule at a glance. This will help keep you organized and avoid getting distracted by unplanned events that pop up during the day.

Lead a Balanced Life First, lighten up a little! Grab a little gusto. Live each day as though it might be the last. The second part of my guiding philosophy is a commitment to do at least one thing each day that will make for a better tomorrow—for my family, my community, and myself.

I believe in balance because life isn't fair; we can only control what happens today. But if we are going to live our best lives, we must commit ourselves to live well every single day.

We need to take care of ourselves physically, emotionally, spiritually, mentally, financially, socially, and environmentally. It's not always easy, but it's worth it. I am committed to being an advocate for those who have been left behind by society.

My goal is to help others understand how they too can find their way back home. I want to be the kind of person who makes people feel good about themselves when they look at me.

I don't want to just talk about things or give advice. I want to inspire people with my actions. I want to show them that there is hope after all.

Find Time for Really Important Things No matter how well organized we may be, unanticipated tasks occasionally demand our attention.

It may be a report requested by an administrator, a favor for a friend, a school or personal crisis, or simply something important we just didn't have time to get done earlier. When these interruptions occur, it's easy to let other priorities slide and put off what really matters until later.

But if you're like most busy professionals, your schedule will never allow you to do everything on your list in one day. So, when the unexpected happens, don't panic! Instead of letting yourself become overwhelmed with too many things at once, take some time out from your daily routine to focus on those truly important items. You'll find they are easier to accomplish than you thought possible.

2.What do you include in your daily lesson plans?

For students, it's important to include clear and concise information that helps them understand what they will be learning, why it's important, and how they can succeed.

Some key components to include in daily lesson plans for students:

1. Learning Objective: A statement that describes what students will be able to do by the end of the lesson.

2. Agenda: A list of activities and the approximate time for each, so students know what to expect and can manage their time effectively.

3. Materials: A list of any materials or resources students will need for the lesson, such as textbooks, worksheets, or online resources.

4. Instructions: Clear, step-by-step instructions for activities or assignments, including any expectations or guidelines for completion.

5. Learning Tasks: Specific tasks or activities that students will engage in to achieve the learning objective, such as reading, writing, discussing, or problem-solving.

6. Assessment: Information about how student learning will be assessed, including any quizzes, tests, or projects that will be completed.

7. Support: Information about where students can go for help or additional support, such as office hours, tutoring resources, or online forums.

8. Reflection: Opportunities for students to reflect on their learning, such as discussion questions or journal prompts.

9. Extensions: Optional activities or resources for students who finish early or want to explore the topic further.

10. Homework: Any assignments or tasks that students are expected to complete outside of class.

Including these components in your lesson plans can help students stay organized, engaged, and motivated to learn.

Write a standards-based lesson plan that includes the elements described in this module. You should include at least the following:

I. Lesson information: content area, grade level of target group of students, and timeframe of the lesson.
II. Lesson topic

III. Standards, benchmarks, or performance standards addressed in the lesson
IV. Intended learning outcomes for students
V. Instructional resources
VI. Arrangement of environment (e.g., independent seat work, cooperative groups, work on projects or presentations, specific modifications)
VII. Instructional activities:
VIII. Introduction to lesson
IX. Lesson development (be sure to include lesson adaptations for students with special needs)
X. Assessment activities (be sure to include adaptations for students with special needs)
XI. Wrap up
XII. Teacher reflection

3) Do you prefer to do long term or short-term plans? How do you plan for instruction?

I think both short term and long term plans are equally important and necessary.
I start long-term planning over the summer months to really think through what I want my students to have learned after the course of a year. For long-term planning, I think broadly about concepts and ideas I want students to gain.
I formulate units in various subjects around those big ideas.
I get much more specific for short-term planning and consider which skills I want students to master within a unit or even within one lesson. I backwards plan my short-term plans to ensure that my assessment at the end of a week or a unit aligns with my daily lessons and objectives.
I enjoy planning with a team because of the value of added contributions."

The long-term plan will:
• provide a forward vision of the range, content and curriculum coverage, and focus over a longer period of time
• provide a shared, agreed pathway through the years of the key stage for the cohort, group, year, etc.
• link to the medium-term plans and, by implication, the short-term plans
• provide a form of curriculum 'road-map' that may draw on wider departmental, school and local events, processes, timetabling and links
• be adaptable and evolve according to changing circumstances and needs
• draw on broader strands of progression that can be traced and linked across the timescale of the plan

• be evaluated through feedback to see that it matches the needs of the learners.

The short-term plan:
A successful medium-term plan will result in a range of possible formats and ideas for what a short-term plan or resource might be.

For example, while the short-term plan may still in many cases provide a clear, structured lesson plan with starter, introduction, development and plenary session, this will be one of a range of pedagogies and learning designs chosen because of the stage pupils have reached in their learning.

Other plans may more appropriately begin, for example, with investigation and group discussion, leading to presentation and peer review.

Alternatively, they may start with experiences outside the classroom and lead to independent research followed up by direct teacher-led instruction on how to interpret or process findings or responses for specific purposes and audiences.

Whatever the format, style or content of the resource that will guide short-term work, it will need to have personalization at its heart and, alongside it, an understanding of how the short-term plan will aid progression.

Above all, the detail of the plan will ensure a rich and engaging learning experience that will build upon what has happened previously in a teaching sequence, and link into what is to happen thereafter – guided by the medium and long-term planning.

The following set of principles may assist you in the short-term planning process.

There are three areas against which to reflect on your plans and processes:
• building, practicing and applying skills
• the learning processes
• progression through levels and leading to independence.

BELOW ARE 8 WAYS TO INCREASE STUDENT MOTIVATION THROUGH GOAL SETTING

a) Identify a Goal b) Visualize the Results c) Plan Backward with a SMART Goal-Setting Plan d) Identify Motivation e) Overcome Obstacles f) Find a Support System g) Avoid Procrastination by Increasing Accountability h) Plan for the Future.

4) How closely do you follow your plans?

Sticking to the plan is good when it's reviewed, and thought through. Consistency is good most of the time. There are two dangers, however:

I. It's bad to stick to a plan that was based on assumptions that have since changed. It happens far too often.

II. The idea that having a plan means being locked in, forced to stick to it, confuses the daylights out of people. They start to argue against having a plan because of it. As if having a plan doesn't help you navigate better when there are changes. As if having a plan reduces your freedom to change course, which is simply not true.

Follow these tips to increase your chances of successfully following your plans.

Write it down Write down your career plan so that you will remember it and can track your progress. You are more likely to commit to your plan that is specific, measurable, achievable, realistic, and timely (SMART).

Put a copy of your plan some place where you can see it often such as on your bedroom mirror or the refrigerator door.

Set deadlines Make one of two goals that you can achieve within a few days or a week.

Then make other short-term goals that only take a few months to complete. Over time you will see how many tasks you have completed and how much closer you are to accomplishing your long-term goals.

Reward yourself Working toward your goals is hard work. Think of small rewards to give yourself when you accomplish something big or small.

These bonuses will help you stay motivated.

Have an accountability partner It's important to not try to complete your goals alone.

Find one or two people who will help you stick to your plan. This can be a friend, a job coach, or your supervising agent (or corrections agent). Your partner will remind you of deadlines and give you encouragement when you face setbacks.

5) How do you feel when you don't meet a deadline as a teacher?

While missing a deadline can feel overwhelming, it happens even to the most experienced professionals. Whether you missed a deadline due to an emergency or other obligations, there are some steps you can take to explain yourself and ask for an extension. If you recently missed a deadline, then you might be wondering what you can do to remedy the situation. In this article, we discuss the benefits of addressing a missed deadline, provide instructions to help you explain the situation to your supervisor and provide tips to help you get your work back on track.

Benefits of addressing a missed deadline
Addressing a missed deadline can make you seem more professional, especially if you're proactive. Taking the initiative to start a conversation with your supervisor or client to explain the situation can also show you respect them and care about making things right.

Some other ways addressing a missed deadline can benefit you include by helping you:

➢ Regain trust ➢ Formulate a solution ➢ Take responsibility for your actions ➢ Protect your reputation in the workplace ➢ Decrease stress ➢ Improve communication.

How to tell a supervisor you missed a deadline If you recently missed a deadline, it's important to let your supervisor know.

By handling this situation professionally, you can likely develop a solution to help both of you move forward. Here are some steps you can take to tell your supervisor you missed a deadline:

1. Address the situation as soon as possible While the deadline may have already passed, addressing the situation as soon as possible is still important. This can give your supervisor the time they need to make necessary adjustments to keep the rest of your department or your project on track.
If possible, notify your supervisor in person. However, if a phone call is the quickest way to contact them, this may be your best option.
If you're unable to contact your supervisor via phone, leave a brief message and follow up with an email to show you're doing your best to notify them.

2. Provide a brief explanation Offer a brief explanation of why you were unable to meet the deadline. While you don't have to share personal details, letting your supervisor know if there was an emergency you needed to take care of or there was another reason for the delay can help them understand the situation.
Instead of making excuses, be honest and admit if there's something you could have done to prevent the situation.

Explaining that you understand why you were unable to meet the deadline can show your supervisor you know what steps to take to make sure you complete future tasks on time.

For example, if you missed a deadline because you were waiting on a key piece of information from another team member, you might share that you understand you could have followed up with that team member earlier in the week to ensure they were on track and prepared to deliver their portion of the project on time.

3. Apologize for the delay While it may seem like a small act, simply apologizing for the delay can improve how your supervisor reacts to the news. Try to understand how missing this deadline may impact their job, your team's workflow or the organization.

For example, if your supervisor was waiting on you to share a data analysis report so they can finish a slide show presentation to share with the rest of your team, let them know you understand how important the project is and apologize for delaying their portion of the project.

Showing you understand the impact of your actions can make your apology seem more sincere.

4. Propose a new timeframe Consider what other priorities you have on your list and whether you can move some of them around to make sure you can finish the project you need to complete.

Then propose a new timeframe that works for both you and your supervisor. Make sure you agree to a deadline you can meet this time to help you rebuild trust.

If you're overwhelmed with the amount of work you currently have, you might suggest moving another task to a different team member or delaying a less important project so you can focus. This can show your supervisor you're dedicated to finding a solution to remedy the situation.

5. Show your appreciation Finally, make sure to thank your supervisor for understanding your situation and working with you to find a solution. Let your supervisor know you're grateful for the extension and reassure them that you can meet the new deadline. While you can keep your statement of appreciation brief, try to be specific about what you're thanking your supervisor for and why it means a lot to you. Taking the time to show your appreciation can help you end your conversation on a positive note.

Tips for handling a missed deadline Here are some additional tips to help you handle missing a deadline and prevent it from happening again in the future: Be proactive If you notice that a project is taking you longer to complete than expected, let your supervisor know ahead of time.

Requesting an extension before the due date can reduce stress and give other members of your team time to adjust their schedules or priorities.
If you miss a deadline due to unforeseen circumstances, you can still be proactive by reaching out to your supervisor before they notice the delay.

This may involve sending an email during hours outside of work, especially if there's an emergency situation. Being proactive can show your supervisor and your team members that you care about your work.

Take responsibility for your actions Instead of placing the blame on another coworker, your current workload or a faulty computer program, take responsibility for the missed deadline.

While there may have been other extenuating circumstances at play, it's important to show your supervisor that you understand where you may have been able to mitigate these challenges.

For example, if you were unable to meet a deadline because you took on too many responsibilities, you could share that you understand you need to prioritize your work more effectively in the future.

This can show your supervisor that you're responsible and capable of improving your workflow in the future.

Provide frequent updates as you work toward your new deadline, provide frequent updates to let your supervisor know you're on track.

This can alleviate some of the stress they may be feeling and help you ensure you complete the project by the upcoming due date. For example, if you're working on a large report, you might let your supervisor know when you're halfway finished and ask if they would like you to send them the information you have completed so far.

If they need this information to complete another task, it may be helpful and allow them to continue working while you finish the rest of your report. Improving your communication can also help you rebuild trust with your supervisor.

Take steps to prevent missing future deadlines
Identify what steps you can take to prevent missing future deadlines.
This might involve working ahead during slower periods, being more selective about the projects you take on or maintaining a more organized to-do list.
Another great option is to give yourself a soft due date for future projects. For example, if you have a report due on March 14, you might make it a goal to have a rough draft finished by March 7.
This can help you break large projects into smaller, more manageable pieces that you can make regular progress on to ensure you meet your deadline. Once you've identified a few steps you can take to improve your performance, share them with your supervisor.
This can show them that you're committed to taking actionable steps to prevent missing future deadlines.

6) What do you do when students do not meet their deadlines?

Any reluctance shown by a student in meeting a deadline has two aspects. One is the laziness of the student and the other some short comings of the teacher.

The first one is very clear but the second aspect needs clarification. When we say short comings of the teacher it includes failing to make your student understand enough the given task., loose command and indiscipline.

Certainly, it is a matter of disappointment for a good teacher but we have to remove the hurdle after proper analysis and encourage the student to proceed with confidence.

Time Management and accountability should be taught at a young age. Working for a specific target teaches this to a child. Not meeting a deadline should not be left unchecked even at elementary level because it conveys a wrong message that it is alright not to be punctual. That is why an adult or a teacher should be strict in this issue. It is best to reduce points for late assignments proportionately. If you do not want to be strict with marks you can ask the child to do some extra work because he was late with the assignment. Or you can give pair work and ask them both to motivate each other and see that they stick to the time. This enhances team work and punctuality.
Always compliment punctuality and encourage it openly in the class. This helps as reinforcement. It also increases peer estimation which again helps in motivation to the student.

7.How can teachers ensure students never miss a deadline?

A student's life is largely the summation of classes, assignments, tasks, co-curricular activities. It's all about widening knowledge base, developing skills and pushing forward. Often, however, teachers find their students tumbling from one task to another and missing deadlines. Somewhere in the middle, many lose track of what they were supposed to do and when, consequently missing out on the excitement of discovering new things. But with technology, life really can be much more sorted out. So here we have a list of apps and online tools that teachers can share with their students to help them manage tasks and assignments better.

Any.DO: When you are collaborating with peers on projects or assignments and have separate tasks for individuals to do, do not get too stressed about organizing it because that job can be handled by Any.DO.

This app, which was originally launched for Android devices and is now available for iOS and Chrome apps too, lets you create to-do lists and share them with your friends and colleagues.

On Any.DO you can type out a list of tasks or enter tasks by speaking into your phone. Once you've entered your task you can assign it to a day and time for completion, and also set a reminder if you like. Then you share it with anyone in your contacts list, regardless of whether the person has the Any. DO app installed on his or her device.

Fetchnotes: This is a neat service for creating and keeping notes online. It feels a little like using Twitter — you write a note and use a hashtag to label it. Then whenever you want to search for a note just enter a hashtag. For example, if you are taking notes in a literature course you might use the hashtag "#renaissance" for all notes related to the period. Then you can go back and read all of your notes about the writings of the period by just searching for that hashtag. If you want to share a note with someone in your contacts you can do that too by just putting "@" before the person's name. Fetch notes works on the web and offers Android and iOS apps.

Google Apps: Those using Gmail accounts can use it to keep a tab on their tasks. You have to select "tasks" under the "GMail" drop-down menu. That will open a small pop-up window in which you can enter the lists.

Google Calendar can be used for keeping track of long term projects. After entering a project due date, you can set reminder alerts to be emailed to me at various intervals. This is helpful because it keeps refreshing your memory.

Todoist: Move over sheets of paper with cryptic notes scribbled on them. Todoist on the web makes your job easy by letting you create to-do lists in chronological order or in order of priority.

The design is uncluttered and the user interface intuitive. The Android and iOS apps provide a variety of ways to manage your to-do lists on the go. Here's how you can use it: You can synchronize it with Outlook and Gmail and set reminders to follow-up on emails.
You can also share your lists with others, by which it becomes easy to divide the work load particularly in group projects.

Flask: When you want to keep things really simple and minus any process of creating accounts, etc., Flask could be a good option for you. It is a simple way of making to-do lists and sharing them with others.
You just go to the site and start writing your list. It assigns unique URLs to each list you create. To share your lists, click the share button to send the link to your list to others.

Workflow: Use this intuitive outline format for the e-version of a regular to do list you would write in a little diary. You can click "+" to add an item and use the tab key to indent an item so that there is some segregation when you're looking at the list. You can prioritize tasks by typing a hashtag like #today or #tomorrow. When you have completed a task just click on it and strike it out.

Thought Boxes: This works a little like a mind mapping tool, where you connect your thoughts. The idea is that you create a category – 'train' (as in train of thought) — and create several to-do lists under it that are connected to the category. Your lists can include basic text notes as well as links to other sites.
For example, if you are organizing a play, your "train" could be "School Play" and under it you could have one list about budget, another about props, another one about physical arrangements or invitations, actors etc. All these "thought boxes" will show on a single page which is your "train".

You can rearrange the boxes in each of your trains in your Thought Boxes account by just dragging and dropping them into place. The free version does not allow you to share your trains with others

Meeting Deadlines and Keeping Schedules:

Impact of Temporal-Sequential Thinking For many students, time is their most precious resource. Making the most of the time they have enables students to be as efficient and successful as possible, leading a balanced life of work and play.
A clear understanding of time is required for students to manage their own time effectively, e.g., plan long term projects, organize schedules, etc.
As such, time management skills are an important component of a student's success – in school and beyond. In order to meet assignment deadlines and to keep up with schedules related to school and schoolwork, students must engage their temporal-sequential thinking abilities.
These skills help us interpret, retain, or create information that is in a serial order. Students with strong temporal-sequential thinking skills are able to manage their schedules, organize their work, and make efficient use of their time.
Such students are also able to avoid procrastination (putting off a task that must be done).
For students with weak time management skills, procrastination can have painful consequences, affecting both academic and personal success.

Here are some strategies to help students meet deadlines and adhere to school schedules. Managing Time Examine students' management skills to identify poor management techniques. For example, help students see the ineffectiveness of "to do" lists which do not include objectives, are not prioritized, or whose schedules are not met. In addition, help students understand how compulsive over-planning, e.g., including too much detail or requiring too much time, may also be an ineffective time management technique. Talk with students about procrastination. Encourage them to think about why they or others may procrastinate. Do they fail to manage time wisely, are they uncertain of priorities, goals and objectives, or perhaps, are they overwhelmed by the size or complexity of tasks? Have students practice estimating and managing their time. For example, have students keep track of activities in a log, first recording the estimated time they think the activity will take, and then documenting the actual time it took to complete the activity. Help students come up with strategies for adjusting their work schedule, if time estimations were off target, or if work is ahead of – or behind schedule. Teach students how to budget time to create long term schedules, such as when managing a schedule of work and recreation, or planning the timeline of a school project. Allow students to practice being "time managers," having the responsibility for working out and monitoring schedules for activities.

In essence, this requires students to become project managers, making sure activities lead to products on schedule. Incorporate time management practice into cooperative learning activities in which one student sets and manages the schedule for the group.

Keeping Assignment Books To improve students' abilities to "follow through" on directions, have them keep assignment books that help them stay organized and keep up with work demands.

(Many schools or PTA's will provide these books.) Many students, even early adolescents, will need direct instruction in effectively maintaining assignment books based on the expectations of the school and individual teachers.

Create a simple system for keeping track of short- and long-term assignments, tests, and quizzes where students record, check off, etc.

Discuss different ways to organize assignment books. Suggest that these books may be most effective if students break each day or even individual assignments into a series of "to do" lists. Incorporate time management skills into assignment books. For example, have students include areas for notes specifying "things to do the week before the exam", "things to do during the week of the exam," etc.
Be sure that assignment books are checked regularly by a parent, teacher or peer partner.

Breaking Activities Into Steps (Staging) Help students efficiently stage or break down long term activities. For example, a history report may be broken down into the following steps: Monday: Go to the library to collect sources, Tuesday: Write first draft, Wednesday: Proofread, Thursday: Revise to final copy, Friday: Take to school.

Create a large classroom wall calendar that shows an outline of the stages and time frame for completing long-term projects. Note important steps and dates with color cues.

Review the calendar regularly. Provide students with a written schedule of daily and weekly deadlines, such as reminders of tests and important long-term due dates, that they can keep in their notebooks or at home.

Assign long-term projects one step at a time, and check students' progress before moving them on to the next step. Emphasize the use of checklists for students to keep track of multi-step assignments and activities.

Teach students how to set their own landmarks, or goal points, that will mark their progress towards finishing an assignment. Encourage students to write down long term goals (related to class requirements) on a calendar, short term goals (related to weekly assignments, immediate tests and projects) on a schedule or "goals" sheet, and daily goals (related to homework, study related tasks) on a "to do" list.

Creating Schedules Help students understand the place and importance of schedules in daily activities and with regard to long term success. Help students learn how to work within schedules both at home and at school.

Do scheduling activities with students. For example, plan the day, the week, or even the year together. Keep daily schedules on the board, and announce transitions or activity changes in advance.
Use your own experiences as models for students. Discuss ways you schedule your daily activities, how long you allow for certain tasks, etc.
Provide concrete examples, such as your schedule book, a peer's activity book, etc., and examples using specific academic tasks, e.g. taking a timed test, etc. Have students practice budgeting time and planning ahead, particularly when they must prioritize, or fit several tasks into a certain time period.
For example, have students come up with a plan for one or more scheduling scenarios, e.g., "How should I plan to study for next week's test, when I have a book report due the day before the exam?"

To aid students in their own time management, have them create personal schedules for study time, after school activities, etc. Help students learn to set goals that emphasize the important tasks they need to accomplish

8) **Describe for me the organization that goes into your planning for a lesson. .I'm sitting in the back of your classroom; in some detail tell me what I see as you implement the lesson just described.**

A lesson plan is the instructor's road map of what students need to learn and how it will be done effectively during the class time. Then, you can design appropriate learning activities and develop strategies to obtain feedback on student learning.
Having a carefully constructed lesson plan for each 3-hour lesson allows you to enter the classroom with more confidence and maximizes your chance of having a meaningful learning experience with your students.

A successful lesson plan addresses and integrates three key components:
Learning Objectives
Learning activities
Assessment to check for student understanding

A lesson plan provides you with a general outline of your teaching goals, learning objectives, and means to accomplish them, and is by no means exhaustive. A productive lesson is not one in which everything goes exactly as planned, but one in which both students and instructor learn from each other. You may refer to an example of a 3 hour lesson plan.

BEFORE CLASS: STEPS FOR PREPARING A LESSON PLAN

Listed below are 6 steps for preparing your lesson plan before your class.
1. Identify the learning objectives Before you plan your lesson, you will first need to identify the learning objectives for the lesson.

A learning objective describes what the learner will know or be able to do after the learning experience rather than what the learner will be exposed to during the instruction (i.e. topics). Typically, it is written in a language that is easily understood by students and clearly related to the program learning outcomes.
The Bloom's Revised Taxonomy of Educational Objectives (link) is a useful resource for crafting learning objectives that are demonstrable and measurable.

2. Plan the specific learning activities When planning learning activities you should consider the types of activities students will need to engage in, in order to develop the skills and knowledge required to demonstrate effective learning in the course. Learning activities should be directly related to the learning objectives of the course, and provide experiences that will enable students to engage in, practice, and gain feedback
on specific progress towards those objectives. As you plan your learning activities, estimate how much time you will spend on each. Build in time for extended explanation or discussion, but also be prepared to move on quickly to different applications or problems, and to identify strategies that check for understanding. Some questions to think about as you design the learning activities you will use are:
What will I do to explain the topic?
What will I do to illustrate the topic in a different way?
How can I engage students in the topic?

What are some relevant real-life examples, analogies, or situations that can help students understand the topic?
What will students need to do to help them understand the topic better?
Many activities can be used to engage learners. The activity types (i.e. what the student is doing) and their examples provided below are by no means an exhaustive list, but will help you in thinking through how best to design and deliver high impact learning experiences for your students in a typical lesson.

3. Plan to assess student understanding
Assessments (e.g., tests, papers, problem sets, performances) provide opportunities for students to demonstrate and practice the knowledge and skills articulated in the learning objectives, and for instructors to offer targeted feedback that can guide further learning.
Planning for assessment allows you to find out whether your students are learning.

It involves making decisions about: the number and type of assessment tasks that will best enable students to demonstrate learning objectives for the lesson Examples of different assessments

Formative and/or summative the criteria and standards that will be used to make assessment judgements.

Rubrics
• student roles in the assessment process o Self-assessment o Peer assessment
• the weighting of individual assessment tasks and the method by which individual task judgements will be combined into a final grade for the course o information about how various tasks are to be weighted and combined into an overall grade must be provided to students
• the provision of feedback o giving feedback to students on how to improve their learning, as well as giving feedback to instructors how to refine their teaching

4. Plan to sequence the lesson in an engaging and meaningful manner Sequencing a lesson in an engaging and meaningful manner involves carefully organizing the content and activities to maximize student understanding and retention. Here's a general framework you can use:

1. Engagement (5-10 minutes): Start with a hook or an engaging activity to grab students' attention and activate their prior knowledge related to the topic.

2. Introduction (5-10 minutes): Provide an overview of the lesson objectives and explain why the topic is important or relevant to students' lives.

3. Direct Instruction (10-15 minutes): Present new information or concepts using a variety of methods such as lectures, videos, or demonstrations. Keep this segment concise and interactive to maintain student interest.

4. Guided Practice (10-15 minutes): Engage students in activities that allow them to apply the new concepts with guidance and support. This could include group work, discussions, or hands-on activities.

5. Independent Practice (10-15 minutes): Give students an opportunity to work independently to reinforce their understanding. This could be in the form of worksheets, reading assignments, or online activities.

6. Closure (5-10 minutes): Summarize the key points of the lesson and provide closure. You can also use this time for a brief assessment to check for understanding.

7. Extension (5-10 minutes, optional): Provide an extension activity for students who finish early or want to explore the topic further. This could be a challenge question, a creative project, or additional reading.

8. Reflection (5-10 minutes, optional): End the lesson with a reflection activity where students can think about what they have learned and how it connects to their own experiences or the world around them.

By sequencing your lesson in this manner, you can create a cohesive and engaging learning experience that helps students understand and retain the material.

5. Create a realistic timeline A list of ten learning objectives is not realistic, so narrow down your list to the two or three key concepts, ideas, or skills you want students to learn in the lesson. Your list of prioritized learning objectives will help you make decisions on the spot and adjust your lesson plan as needed. Here are some strategies for creating a realistic timeline:

• Estimate how much time each of the activities will take, then plan some extra time for each
 • When you prepare your lesson plan, next to each activity indicate how much time you expect it will take

• Plan a few minutes at the end of class to answer any remaining questions and to sum up key points
 • Plan an extra activity or discussion question in case you have time left
 • Be flexible – be ready to adjust your lesson plan to students' needs and focus on what seems to be more productive rather than sticking to your original plan.

6. Plan for a lesson closure Lesson closure provides an opportunity to solidify student learning. Lesson closure is useful for both instructors and students.

You can use closure to:
• Check for student understanding and inform subsequent instruction (adjust your teaching accordingly)
• Emphasize key information
• Tie up loose ends
• Correct students' misunderstandings
• Preview upcoming topics

Your students will find your closure helpful for:
• Summarizing, reviewing, and demonstrating their understanding of major points
• Consolidating and internalizing key information
• Linking lesson ideas to a conceptual framework and/or previously-learned knowledge
• Transferring ideas to new situations

There are several ways in which you can put a closure to the lesson:
• state the main points yourself ("Today we talked about…")
• ask a student to help you summarize them
• ask all students to write down on a piece of paper what they think were the main points of the lesson.

DURING THE CLASS: PRESENTING YOUR LESSON PLAN
Letting your students know what they will be learning and doing in class will help keep them more engaged and on track. Providing a meaningful organisation of the class time can help students not only remember better, but also follow your presentation and understand the rationale behind the planned learning activities. You can share your lesson plan by writing a brief agenda on the whiteboard or telling students explicitly what they will be learning and doing in class. Click on link here for tips and techniques to facilitate an interactive lesson.

AFTER THE CLASS: REFLECTING ON YOUR LESSON PLAN

Take a few minutes after each class to reflect on what worked well and why, and what you could have done differently. Identifying successful and less successful organization of class time and activities would make it easier to adjust to the contingencies of the classroom. If needed, revise the lesson plan.

9) What are some of the considerations you make when planning your lessons? How do you go about planning a unit?

Each lesson is an opportunity to reach your students. Considered:
• What students need to know before you start teaching it?
• How will students show you the lesson was effective?
• What will students be doing?

See if this template helps

• INSTRUCTIONAL GOAL (outcome that students should be able to demonstrate upon completion of the entire unit)
• PERFORMANCE OBJECTIVE (use an action verb in a description of a measurable outcome)
• RATIONALE (brief justification — why you feel the students need to learn this topic)
• LESSON CONTENT (what is to be taught).

• **INSTRUCTIONAL PROCEDURES**
1. Focusing event (something to get the students' attention) 2. Teaching procedures (methods you will use) 3. Formative check (progress checks throughout the lesson) 4. Student Participation (how you will get the students to participate) 5. Closure (how you will end the lesson)
• EVALUATION PROCEDURES (how you will measure outcomes to determine if the material has been learned)
• MATERIALS AND AIDS (what you will need in order to teach this lesson)

The Importance of Lesson Planning This section is about the importance of planning and some considerations to keep in mind when beginning a lesson. Let us check them up.
Defining Goals for Every Lesson Planning helps you define goals for every lesson you are going to teach.
The defining goal of every lesson is to provide students with the knowledge they need to succeed.

A lesson plan is a sequence of planned activities for students to complete. Every lesson plan has an introduction, a lesson, and a conclusion.

When planning a lesson, you consider three things: the content, the level of difficulty, and the goal.

The content has relevance to what students are learning in class and is meaningful for what they're trying to teach.

You also determine the level of difficulty for the lesson by identifying what skills you want students to learn during that time.

Finally, you decide on the outcome or purpose of the lesson, so it can guide you through each step of the process.

For example, if your objective is to have students understand how to use technology safely, then you would need to know which specific technologies will be used as well as when those technologies should be introduced into lessons.

Selecting the Right Resources to Achieve Goals
Lesson planning helps you select appropriate resources and materials to achieve the goals of your lessons.

You may already have a list of required books for your course, but this does not mean they are all equally effective in achieving your objectives. Some textbooks are more suitable than others, depending upon the subject matter being taught.

For example, if you were teaching about the history of science or mathematics, you would likely want to teach from an introductory textbook rather than one written by experts on these subjects.

The same goes for any other type of resource, such as videos, websites, etc.

If you do not know which book will be most useful for your students, then you should consider using a variety of different sources so that you can find out what works best with each group of learners.

Identifying Potential Obstacles Planning lessons can help you identify the potential challenges you will encounter when teaching your lessons.

For example, if you are planning to use a video in class, you may need to make sure that all computers have access to the internet and that there is enough bandwidth available.

You might also need to plan ahead to ensure that you have sufficient time to prepare before classes begin.

If you want to teach an online lesson, it's important to think about how you'll communicate with your students during this process.

Will they receive instructions via email or text message? How do you expect them to respond? What tools will you provide to support their learning?

It Improves Quality of Your Lessons Lesson planning helps you to deliver your lessons effectively and efficiently.

It allows you to focus on the most relevant aspects of a topic while avoiding unnecessary details. This means that you can spend more time teaching rather than writing out long lists of information for each student.

You also have greater control over what is covered in class because you know exactly which topics are being discussed at any given point.

Making Learning Easier for Your Students
When you plan your lessons before delivering them, you make learning and understanding easier for students.
They will be able to understand concepts better if you deliver well-thought-out lessons. It further helps improve students' achievement. That is why you need to engage in lesson planning.

Lesson Planning Reduces Behavior Problems during Lessons Not all lessons are created equal. Some lessons go well, while others do not.

Lesson planning is essential to ensure that teachers are prepared for any situation, no matter how inevitable the problem may be.

You should consider various factors before planning a lesson, some of which include the following: age range of students, desired goals of the lesson, and available resources.

Planning ahead can reduce problems that often arise during lessons- such as behavior problems or lack of understanding. When you plan your lessons, you also have time to prepare the materials needed for the lesson. This allows you to focus on teaching rather than spending extra time searching for supplies.

Factors to Consider When Planning a Lesson Today's teachers are asked to do more than ever before, with less time and fewer resources. How can educators reduce their stress levels?

Consider the following tips for successful lesson planning: Have Clear Goals A lot can be learned from research done on goal setting. One particular study found that people who had clear goals were more convinced of the outcomes they could achieve and less likely to give up.

These results suggest that when teachers plan a lesson, it's important to set goals such as what skills they want their students to master and how they will know if these skills have been achieved. Goals also allow teachers to measure their success, which is essential for refining plans in the future.

What Objectives Can Help You Meet Your Goals?

You must consider the objectives to be achieved to help you meet the goals of your lessons. For example, if one objective is "to learn about the different types of animals on Earth" then this would mean that all other learning activities should revolve around this topic.

If another goal was "to understand why some people are more intelligent than others" then this could lead to an investigation into IQ tests or even brain research.

The key here is to make sure that each activity contributes toward achieving at least one of the goals.

What are the Demands of the Content? You must determine the demands and expectations of the topic or subject you are going to teach.

This will help you know what type of content you need to prepare for a lesson. For example, if your students have been studying about dinosaurs in science class, they may be interested in knowing how many species there were during their time.

You can use this information as part of your preparation by creating a timeline with pictures and facts from different sources.

If your students want more details on the history of dinosaurs, then you should create an outline using these resources. The key is to find out what the needs of your learners are so that you can provide them with relevant learning materials.

What Are Your Resources? Many teachers spend a lot of time planning their lessons, but not all teachers take the time to make sure they have the resources to teach these lessons.

If you are about to start lesson planning for your class and realize that you don't have any of the necessary resources, it is important to know what types of resources you need and where you can find them. Below we will discuss some different ways in which you may be able to get access to teaching tools such as books, videos, websites, etc.

1) Books: You should always try to use books when possible because they tend to be more comprehensive than other forms of media. However, if there isn't an appropriate book available on the topic or concept being taught then you might want to consider using another form of media instead.

2) Videos: If a video would work better for your student's learning needs, then by all means go ahead and use one! There are many great online sources out there that offer free educational content including Khan Academy, TED Talks, YouTube, Vimeo, PBS Learning Media, etc.

3) Websites: The internet is full of amazing resources for teachers looking to find quality materials related to their teaching topics. Many times, these sites will have links to additional information about how to implement them in class.

Time for the Lesson You must consider the time available for you to deliver each lesson. You may need to plan accordingly so as not to overwhelm or bore your students with too much material at once.

If possible, try and break up a large amount of content into smaller chunks over several lessons. This way, it's easier for both you and your students. It also allows you to focus more attention on one topic per week rather than trying to cover everything all at once.

The Abilities of Your Students What are the levels of your students? Their levels will determine how you plan and deliver the lesson. If you don't know what level your students fall into, try asking their teachers or parents.

You can use this information when planning out your curriculum. For example: if you have an intermediate student who is struggling in math, then perhaps you should start by teaching them basic addition before moving on to multiplication.

Consider the things that can be achieved by the lowest-ability students. What do they need to learn first? How much time does it take for a low-level learner to master something?

Can they understand concepts without being able to explain why those concepts work? Are there any skills that would help these learners succeed more quickly? If so, what are some of their strengths and weaknesses?
Take these questions into consideration when planning your lessons. When planning your lessons, also consider things that will challenge the highest-achieving students.
Do you have enough challenging material available in your curriculum or is this an area where you could use additional resources?
Is there anything about your current lesson plan that might not be working well with certain types of learners?
Think about how you can make adjustments to improve learning outcomes for all students.

Practical Exercises Prepare practical exercises for students to perform during the lesson.

They could be paper-based or oral, done individually or in groups.

The purpose of these activities should be to help them practice what they've learned and reinforce it through real-life experience.

These are great ways to get students thinking critically about their own work and others' work. You may want to have some examples ready so that students don't need to spend too much time on preparation.

If you're doing this with an online course, make sure your assignments can be completed within one week.

This will give students enough time to complete the assignment before the next lesson starts. In essence, class exercises must be as practical as possible and must be doable.

Extra Supporting/Practice Materials Plan supporting exercises to keep students who finish their work early busy.

Don't let them sit idly, or else they will engage in disruptive activities.

Extra practice materials help students practice more of what they have learned in the classroom. Remember the saying, "practice makes better." On the other hand, it can help reduce behavior problems in the classroom. If a student is having trouble with an exercise, give him extra support material so he doesn't feel left out.

This also helps prevent boredom from setting in.

The political ramifications of the lesson you are going to teach In today's politically charged climate, when planning a lesson, it is important to consider how the lesson you are going to teach will affect the students and school.

In order to do this, there are a few things you can do in advance of your lesson plan. The first is to have a conversation with your principal or other administrators who may be involved in your lesson plan.

Ask them what they think about teaching certain topics such as gun control, abortion, homosexuality, etc. If possible, ask for their input on how best to approach these issues. You should not assume that just because something has been taught before, it does not mean it needs to be repeated again.

Your Familiarity with the Topic You must know what you are going to teach. This means having some familiarity with the topic itself. For example, if you were planning to talk about guns, then you would need to understand firearms and ammunition. It also means knowing where the information comes from so that you can cite sources appropriately. In this case, your source could be a book or magazine article, an online resource, or even another teacher's lecture notes. The more familiar you become with the material, the easier it will be to prepare and deliver the lesson.

Conclusion Lesson planning is an essential part of teaching. Without proper planning, teachers can fail to reach their students and their lesson will not be as effective. This article has provided some tips on what to consider to plan your lessons effectively.

10) How much homework will you assign? How do you know how long it will take your student?

The amount of homework young people are given varies a lot from school to school and from grade to grade. In some schools and grades, children have no homework at all. In others, they may have 18 hours or more of homework every week. In the United States, the accepted guideline, which is supported by both the National Education Association and the National Parent Teacher Association, is the 10-minute rule: Children should have no more than 10 minutes of homework each day for each grade reached.

In 1st grade, children should have 10 minutes of daily homework; in 2nd grade, 20 minutes; and so on to the 12th grade, when on average they should have 120 minutes of homework each day, which is about 10 hours a week.

It doesn't always work out that way. In 2013, the University of Phoenix College of Education commissioned a survey of how much homework teachers typically give their students. From kindergarten to 5th grade, it was just under three hours per week; from 6th to 8th grade, it was 3.2 hours; and from 9th to 12th grade, it was 3.5 hours.

There are two points to note. First, these are the amounts given by individual teachers. To estimate the total time children are expected to spend on homework, you need to multiply these hours by the number of teachers they work with.

High school students who work with five teachers in different curriculum areas may find themselves with 17.5 hours or more of homework a week, which is the equivalent of a part-time job. The other factor is that these are teachers' estimates of the time that homework should take.

The time that individual children spend on it will be more or less than that, according to their abilities and interests. One child may casually dash off a piece of homework in half the time that another will spend laboring through in a cold sweat.

Do students have more homework these days than previous generations? Given all the variables, it's difficult to say. Some studies suggest they do. In 2007, a study from the National Center for Education Statistics found that, on average, high school students spent around seven hours a week on homework.

A similar study in 1994 put the average at less than five hours a week. Mind you, I [Robinson] was in high school in England in the 1960s and spent a lot more time than that—though maybe that was to do with my own ability.

One way of judging this is to look at how much homework your own children are given and compare it to what you had at the same age.

There's also much debate about the value of homework. Supporters argue that it benefits children, teachers, and parents in several ways:

- Children learn to deepen their understanding of specific content, to cover content at their own pace, to become more independent learners, to develop problem-solving and time-management skills, and to relate what they learn in school to outside activities.
- Teachers can see how well their students understand the lessons; evaluate students' individual progress, strengths, and weaknesses; and cover more content in class.
- Parents can engage practically in their children's education, see firsthand what their children are being taught in school, and understand more clearly how they're getting on—what they find easy and what they struggle with in school.

PROFESSIONAL EXPERIENCE

1) Discuss your student teaching experience. What you liked/disliked? Changes you would have made?
Teachers in the 21st century need to be good at many different things. They are, of course, expected to know their subject well or to have a wide range of knowledge if they are teaching one grade many different subjects, but as well as this, teachers need to be technologically savvy, they need to be caring and patient, and, perhaps above all, they need to be organized. Just what is it that is so important about organization for teachers that makes it something they all need to be able to do? Read on to find out.

Beginning Of the School Year There are basic principles and ways of operating to get yourself off to the best start at the beginning of the school year. Revisiting at any time during the year is a great idea also. Take a look at our series where Marie Amaro walks through these principles in a fantastic step-by-step practical guide.

No Wasted Time The school day is full – very full – of lessons, breaks, sports, and lunch, as well as additional activities depending on the student's own choices. This means that, in order to offer the best education to each child, a teacher will need to be highly organized because, in this way, there will be no wasted time.

A disorganized teacher, one who doesn't know where their class notes are or who hasn't checked they know how to use the equipment they need for the lesson, will waste a lot of time getting ready. Even a few minutes can mean that an entire topic can be lost.

If you organize your files online, if you have your handouts pre-printed, if you have checked that you have everything ready before the lesson begins, you can make the most out of the time you have with your class, even if it's a single period. If you are organized as a teacher, you can make great use of your time. You don't want to waste any of your precious class time by being unprepared or not knowing where things are located in your classroom.
If you know exactly where everything is located within your room, then you won't waste valuable minutes looking around for something.
This will allow you to get right into the lesson without wasting time searching for items. It's much better to have all materials ready before starting than to find yourself running late because you couldn't locate an item quickly enough.

Important Life Habits As well as ensuring that students get their full lesson quota by being organized, an organized teacher will also be able to help students develop good life habits now and in the future.
They will learn the difference between having everything they need with them and being able to enjoy a smooth and interesting lesson, and not having what they need, in which case they will be stressed and tense and won't learn so well. The earlier this can start, the better.
A child who can emulate an organized, punctual teacher from when they are very young will keep these lessons with them well into the future, including when they start work.

Fewer Discipline Problems It might be surprising to learn that a more organized teacher is a teacher who has fewer discipline issues in their classrooms, but it's true.
Students will know that this teacher is ready to start teaching, and they need to be prepared to start learning; there is no time for messing around and playing games because work begins right away. When the work begins immediately – thanks to the teacher's organizational skills – the children in the class will have much less opportunity to talk among

themselves and disrupt the rest of the class.
Even those who might want to act up won't have the chance to, and soon enough, they will learn that it's not worth even thinking about. Plus, an organized teacher will gain a reputation for being aware of everything that is happening around them as they won't be distracted by their lack of organization. Again, this means that anyone attempting to be disruptive will be stopped much sooner.

Improves Personal Relationships Teachers work hard, and they don't just work in the classroom –

there are lessons to plan and papers to grade, and this all has to happen after or before school hours. This can have an impact on personal relationships, as there isn't much time for anything other than work. However, the more organized the teacher is, the more time they can save overall, and the better their relationships with friends and family will be.

Students and their parents will expect teachers to meet their deadlines and keep their promises. Being organized and therefore saving time by not searching for books and papers and other important items means this can happen and you can still find time to relax and enjoy your time with others or by yourself, depending on your preference.

Better Health We've mentioned that teaching is hard work, and that can also sometimes be stressful work as there is a lot to do and a lot of responsibility. Being disorganized on top of all this can certainly have a negative effect on the body and mind and potentially make your stress levels even higher.

If you are organized, no matter what the job might throw at you, you will always be able to stay calm and focused, and you should be less stressed, improving your health and helping you become a calmer, more focused teacher overall.

It Reduces Stress How much stress is usually thrust onto the shoulders of a teacher? It often feels like we're juggling balls in the air, just waiting for one to fall and break. When teachers get stressed out, they tend to become less effective at their jobs. Being organized helps reduce this stress by making sure everything has its place.

This means fewer things on our desks or shelves, which makes us feel better about ourselves and our work. We also have time to focus on what's important instead of worrying about where something went when it was supposed to be somewhere else.

It Improves Students' Learning Getting organized as a teacher can be difficult. There are many tasks that need to be done, and you might not have the time to think about organization.

However, being organized as a teacher can help students learn better because they will have a sense of order. Getting organized, as a teacher, can help you improve learners' learning. It is important for teachers to keep track of what needs to be done in class. If there is too much work to do, then it could cause stress among students.
Students should know where things stand at all times.

They should understand what has already been completed and what still needs to be finished. You must also make sure that your lesson plans are well-organized. The best way to organize your lessons is by using an outline or schedule.
You may want to use different colors depending on whether something is due today, tomorrow, next week, etc.

It Improves Your Teaching Being organized helps improve your teaching efforts. It makes you more efficient because you can easily find the information you need when needed. When teachers have a clear understanding of how they will teach each day's material, they can better prepare for classes.

This means less time spent preparing materials and more time spent actually teaching. In addition, it also allows students to focus their attention on learning instead of having to spend extra time trying to figure out what lesson activities they should be doing that day.

It Makes You Confidence Organized teachers always have confidence in themselves. This is because they are able to achieve much within the limited time in school.
They can easily organize their lessons and make sure that students understand what they need to learn.
When a teacher has organized his/her class, he/she knows how long it takes him/her to teach each subject or topic.

He/She also knows which subjects or topics require more attention from other classes. Therefore, when teaching any given lesson, he/she will be confident of its success.

It Teaches Life Lessons to Students learn to be organized, responsible, and accountable from organized teachers. When a teacher teaches his/her class in an orderly manner, he/she will also teach life lessons such as being organized, responsible, and accountable.

These three things are very important for people who want to succeed in life because these traits make it easier for someone to achieve success. For example, if you have good organizational skills, then you won't forget anything when preparing to teach a lesson.

If you're responsible, then your schoolwork is always done on time or before the deadline. And lastly, if you're accountable, then you'll know that

you must do something about any mistakes that you made during teaching.

Have a Purpose Both in and out of the classroom, the very best teachers and the happiest people have a clear sense of purpose.
On a grander scale, they have a dream, a vision, and a view of their world as they would like to see it become. Thus, have a goal of how you want to be organized, both in and out of your classroom. It will help keep you focused on what is important for yourself and your students.
You can also use this list as an outline or guide when planning lessons, projects, etc. This way, you won't get lost in all the details that go into teaching. Instead, you'll focus on the big picture.

Plan for Success Whether teaching a lesson or building a house, a good plan helps us get things done efficiently, effectively, and correctly. A good plan stimulates creativity. Plan the process of making decisions about what to do, when to do it, and how to do it. Make sure your plans include all aspects of the lessons, so nothing is left out.

When planning your lessons, think through every step in detail before starting. It will save time later if something goes wrong. Also, make sure you have enough supplies available to deliver the lesson. If not, don't start a topic or lesson until you can deliver it with everything on hand.

Discover Your Prime Time Don't waste your most creative time doing menial tasks like photocopying, stapling, cleaning, filing, or grading objective tests.

Safeguard those precious hours when you are at your intellectual peak to do the most cognitively challenging tasks: writing, planning, and creating. You may be surprised at how much more productive you become during this prime time than at any other period of the day.

Set Up a Schedule for Yourself It takes discipline to stick to a schedule, but it pays off big-time.

The key is to set up an efficient system that works best for you. For example, if you have trouble getting started in the morning, try waking up early so you can get some work done before others wake up.

If you're not sure what's going on with your life right now, use a calendar app such as Google Calendar to keep track of important events.

It will help you stay organized and avoid missing out on anything significant.

Get Rid of Distractions If you find yourself constantly distracted by social media or email notifications, turn them off completely until after you've finished working. This way, you won't be tempted to check those apps while trying to focus on something else. You'll also save time because it takes less effort to ignore distractions than it does to actually complete tasks.

Use the Pomodoro Technique The Pomodoro technique is an effective method for getting things done in short bursts. The idea behind this approach is that if you break down large projects into smaller chunks, then you can work more efficiently without feeling overwhelmed. It's a simple concept: set aside 25 minutes of uninterrupted, focused work and take breaks every four hours.

If you're not sure how long your task will take, estimate about 20% longer than you think it should take. This way, when you get stuck on something or feel like giving up, you'll have some buffer room before you start working again. You might even find yourself finishing early!

Keep a Personal Calendar A daily calendar is the single most valuable time management tool. It doesn't matter which kind you use, as long as it meets your needs.

If you don't have one already, try using Google Keep or Evernote instead of pen and paper. They're free, easy-to-use tools with built-in reminders. And they sync across all devices, so you won't lose any information when switching between them.

You'll also be able to see what's coming up next on your schedule at a glance. This will help keep you organized and avoid getting distracted by unplanned events that pop up during the day.

Lead a Balanced Life First, lighten up a little!

Grab a little gusto. Live each day as though it might be the last. The second part of my guiding philosophy is a commitment to do at least one thing each day that will make for a better tomorrow—for my family, my community, and myself.

I believe in balance because life isn't fair; we can only control what happens today. But if we are going to live our best lives, we must commit ourselves to live well every single day.

We need to take care of ourselves physically, emotionally, spiritually, mentally, financially, socially, and environmentally. It's not always easy, but it's worth it.

I am committed to being an advocate for those who have been left behind by society.

My goal is to help others understand how they too can find their way back home.

I want to be the kind of person who makes people feel good about themselves when they look at me. I don't want to just talk about things or give advice. I want to inspire people with my actions.

I want to show them that there is hope after all. Find Time for Really Important Things No matter how well organized we may be, unanticipated tasks occasionally demand our attention.

It may be a report requested by an administrator, a favor for a friend, a school or personal crisis, or simply something important we just didn't have time to get done earlier. When these interruptions occur, it's easy to let other priorities slide and put off what really matters until later.

But if you're like most busy professionals, your schedule will never allow you to do everything on your list in one day. So, when the unexpected happens, don't panic! Instead of letting yourself become overwhelmed with too many things at once, take some time out from your daily routine to focus on those truly important items.

You'll find they are easier to accomplish than you thought possible.

2) What do you include in your daily lesson plans?
The daily lesson plan is the most detailed standards-based plan that a teacher will develop. It outlines the purpose and activities of what will be done on a specific day or across several days.

Unit plans help to turn year-long plans into daily plans. Standards-based daily lesson plans are composed of objectives and activities that are based on the unit plans.

The standards-based daily lesson plan allows the teacher to make academic learning relevant to students by intertwining content knowledge, information-processing skills, and life experiences. The daily lesson plan includes the following components:

Lesson Information The teacher begins to plan each lesson by considering the students' characteristics as well as the learning context.

This consideration entails a deep understanding of what he or she is to teach (content standards, standards-based curriculum, and guidelines), what students should be able to do, and what performance will look like when instruction has been completed.

Lesson information includes not only the content but also the learning and developmental needs of the students.

The teacher must consider the time he or she has to complete the lesson and other resources available, and should decide whether or not the lesson should take one class period or several. Questions to ask include:

Am I planning the right amount of activities for the time I have?

Is the scope of the lesson too ambitious for the time allotted?

Will students be able to stay on task, or will they become disengaged because they're spending too much time on one small aspect of work?

Success in the lesson depends on how appropriate the focus, time frame, activities, and assessments are for the students.

It also depends on the skill with which the teacher is able to match instructional strategies to student learning needs.

Lesson Topic The lesson should begin with a topic derived from the adopted standards-based curriculum for a school or district.

Because it relates to specific information the teacher is trying to impart, the topic should be part of the larger curriculum (such as unit instruction) required at your grade level.

However, the specific topic for the lesson may emerge from student questions or interests (e.g., a lesson about the environment or space exploration), from community resources

Intended learning outcomes "When first planning for instruction, teachers frequently focus on the selection of content, teaching method, and instructional materials. These are all important elements of instructional planning, but the entire process is more effective if attention is first directed toward instructional objectives"

Intended learning outcomes:
• Are tied specifically to the standards or benchmarks addressed in the lesson.

• Clarify intended learning outcomes for both the teacher and the student
• Provide a focus for instructional planning
• Set the stage for teaching, learning, and assessment
• Identify specifically how learning will be evidenced

In the lesson plan, state your intended learning outcomes using the following language: By the end of the lesson, students will be able to… (e.g., recognize the leaves of piñon, aspen, and juniper trees; create a timeline of nineteenth-century New Mexico.)

Clarify the intended learning outcomes for students by writing them on the board or through some other visual format.

Instructional Resources In your planning, carefully consider the resources that will support student learning during the lesson.
These might include:
• Textbook or other reading materials
• Websites
• Word processors or other specific computer software
• Movies, CDs, of other media
• Guest speakers
• Project supplies, including posters, paper, markers, or tape.

Arrangement of the Environment Arranging the environment is a decision closely related to the ways in which students will complete components of the lesson.

Questions to consider:
• Will students work in cooperative groups or independently?
• Will several activities take place during the lesson or require more than one desk arrangement? How will transition between activities take place?
• Will students move among learning centers that are set up in the classroom?
• What arrangement will best support movement among these centers?
• Will accommodations for special needs students need to be made to support movement among centers or any other activities?
• Will students need to focus attention on a screen or guest speaker at one point in the room?
• Where will supplies be located for easy access?

Instructional Activities

A good daily lesson plan will include at least the following:

Introduction The beginning of the lesson should engage the students' attention and focus on the topic. Remember, activities should be based on the standards-based curriculum.
Activities might include a challenging question, a quick survey of attitudes or beliefs about the topic, or a movie clip or other short media device to stimulate discussion. Reviewing what the students know or have previously experienced is key to the activity and would be an appropriate introduction, as well.

Lesson development Teachers should make students aware of the intended learning outcomes of the lesson. Your description of each activity should include a discussion of what you will do as the teacher and what the students will do, as well. It is important for students to employ higher order thinking skills so they may apply and synthesize new content.
Explain what modifications will be made for special needs students. Remember that the time frame you have established for this lesson.
How long will each activity take to complete? How many activities can students realistically engage in during the time allotted?

Assessment activities During the lesson, you should monitor student learning.

Describe specifically and in measurable terms how you will determine whether students have met the intended learning outcomes. For example, your description of the assessment process might include statements such as the following: All students will actively participate in each activity. All students will complete a timeline that includes the important events discussed during the lesson. All students will write a statement at the end of the class about what they learned during the lesson.

Wrap up: End class with a restatement of the intended learning outcomes. Decide on a way to close the activities. Will students reflect on what they have learned? Will they turn in their work or complete it as homework? Have you clearly defined expectations for their homework assignment (if applicable)? Does the homework assignment extend or complete the intended learning outcome?

Teacher Reflection When you have actually taught each lesson, write a reflection on what occurred during the process. Did students meet the intended learning outcomes of the lesson? Why or why not? Consider your part in their success.

Was the timeframe appropriate? Were your directions clear? Did the activities you planned

actually, support the intended learning outcomes or were they somehow off-track? Were activities adequately modified for special needs learners in your class? What activities would you do again? What would you do differently next time?
It is important to recognize and incorporate students' cultural and linguistic differences while developing standards-based lessons.

Write a standards-based lesson plan that includes the elements described in this module. You should include at least the following:

I. Lesson information: content area, grade level of target group of students, and timeframe of the lesson
II. Lesson topic
III. Standards, benchmarks, or performance standards addressed in the lesson
IV. Intended learning outcomes for students
V. Instructional resources
VI. Arrangement of environment (e.g., independent seat work, cooperative groups, work on projects or presentations, specific modifications)
VII. Instructional activities:
VIII. Introduction to lesson
IX. Lesson development (be sure to include lesson adaptations for students with special needs)
X. Assessment activities (be sure to include adaptations for students with special needs)
XI. Wrap up
XII. Teacher reflection

3) Do you prefer to do long term or short-term plans? How do you plan for instruction?

I think both short term and long-term plans are equally important and necessary. I start long-term planning over the summer months to really think through what I want my students to have learned after the course of a year.

For long-term planning, I think broadly about concepts and ideas I want students to gain. I formulate units in various subjects around those big ideas.

I get much more specific for short-term planning and consider which skills I want students to master within a unit or even within one lesson.
I backwards plan my short-term plans to ensure that my assessment at the end of a week or a unit aligns with my daily lessons and objectives. I enjoy planning with a team because of the value of added contributions."

The long-term plan will: • provide a forward vision of the range, content and curriculum coverage, and focus over a longer period of time

• provide a shared, agreed pathway through the years of the key stage for the cohort, group, year, etc.
• link to the medium-term plans and, by implication, the short-term plans
• provide a form of curriculum 'road-map' that may draw on wider departmental, school and local events, processes, timetabling and links
• be adaptable and evolve according to changing circumstances and needs
• draw on broader strands of progression that can be traced and linked across the timescale of the plan
• be evaluated through feedback to see that it matches the needs of the learners.

The short-term plan A successful medium-term plan will result in a range of possible formats and ideas for what a short-term plan or resource might be.
For example, while the short-term plan may still in many cases provide a clear, structured lesson plan with starter, introduction, development and plenary session, this will be one of a range of pedagogies and learning designs chosen because of the stage pupils have reached in their learning.
Other plans may more appropriately begin, for example, with investigation and group discussion, leading to presentation and peer review. Alternatively, they may start with experiences outside the classroom and lead to independent research followed up by direct teacher-led instruction on how to interpret or process findings or responses for specific purposes and audiences.
Whatever the format, style or content of the resource that will guide short-term work, it will need to have personalization at its heart and,

alongside it, an understanding of how the short-term plan will aid progression.

Above all, the detail of the plan will ensure a rich and engaging learning experience that will build upon what has happened previously in a teaching sequence, and link into what is to happen thereafter – guided by the medium and long-term planning. The following set of principles may assist you in the short-term planning process.

There are three areas against which to reflect on your plans and processes:
• building, practising and applying skills
• the learning process
• progression through levels and leading to independence.

BELOW ARE 8 WAYS TO INCREASE STUDENT MOTIVATION THROUGH GOAL SETTING
a) Identify a Goal
b) Visualize the Results
c) Plan Backward with a SMART Goal-Setting Plan

d) Identify Motivation
e) Overcome Obstacles
f) Find a Support System
g) Avoid Procrastination by Increasing Accountability
h) Plan for the Future.

4) How closely do you follow your plans?

Sticking to the plan is good when it's reviewed, and thought through. Consistency is good most of the time. There are two dangers, however:
I. It's bad to stick to a plan that was based on assumptions that have since changed. It happens far too often.
II. The idea that having a plan means being locked in, forced to stick to it, confuses the daylights out of people. They start to argue against having a plan because of it.

As if having a plan doesn't help you navigate better when there are changes. As if having a plan reduces your freedom to change course, which is simply not true.

Follow these tips to increase your chances of successfully following your plans.
Write it down Write down your career plan so that you will remember it and can track your progress. You are more likely to commit to your plan that is specific, measurable, achievable, realistic, and timely (SMART).
Put a copy of your plan some place where you can see it often such as on your bedroom mirror or the refrigerator door.

Set deadlines Make one of two goals that you can achieve within a few days or a week. Then make other short-term goals that only take a few months to complete.
Over time you will see how many tasks you have completed and how much closer you are to accomplishing your long-term goals.
Reward yourself Working toward your goals is hard work. Think of small rewards to give yourself when you accomplish something big or small.
These bonuses will help you stay motivated.
Have an accountability partner It's important to not try to complete your goals alone. Find one or two people who will help you stick to your plan. This can be a friend, a job coach, or your supervising agent (or corrections agent). Your partner will remind you of deadlines and give you encouragement when you face setbacks.

5) How do you feel when you don't meet a deadline as a teacher?
While missing a deadline can feel overwhelming, it happens even to the most experienced professionals.

Whether you missed a deadline due to an emergency or other obligations, there are some steps you can take to explain yourself and ask for an extension. If you recently missed a deadline, then you might be wondering what you can do to remedy the situation. In this article, we discuss the benefits of addressing a missed deadline, provide instructions to help you explain the situation to your supervisor and provide tips to help you get your work back on track.

Benefits of addressing a missed deadline Addressing a missed deadline can make you seem more professional, especially if you're proactive.

Taking the initiative to start a conversation with your supervisor or client to explain the situation can also show you respect them and care about making things right. Some other ways addressing a missed deadline can benefit you include by helping you:

➢ Regain trust ➢ Formulate a solution ➢ Take responsibility for your actions ➢ Protect your reputation in the workplace ➢ Decrease stress ➢ Improve communication.

How to tell a supervisor you missed a deadline If you recently missed a deadline, it's important to let your supervisor know.

By handling this situation professionally, you can likely develop a solution to help both of you move forward.

Here are some steps you can take to tell your supervisor you missed a deadline:

1. Address the situation as soon as possible
While the deadline may have already passed, addressing the situation as soon as possible is still important.
This can give your supervisor the time they need to make necessary adjustments to keep the rest of your department or your project on track. If possible, notify your supervisor in person.
However, if a phone call is the quickest way to contact them, this may be your best option. If you're unable to contact your supervisor via phone, leave a brief message and follow up with an email to show you're doing your best to notify them.

2. Provide a brief explanation Offer a brief explanation of why you were unable to meet the deadline.
While you don't have to share personal details, letting your supervisor know if there was an emergency you needed to take care of or there was another reason for the delay can help them understand the situation.

Instead of making excuses, be honest and admit if there's something you could have done to prevent the situation.
Explaining that you understand why you were unable to meet the deadline can show your supervisor you know what steps to take to make sure you complete future tasks on time. For example, if you missed a deadline because you were waiting on a key piece of information from another team member, you might share that you understand you could have followed up with that team member earlier in the week to ensure they were on track and prepared to deliver their portion of the project on time.

3. Apologize for the delay While it may seem like a small act, simply apologizing for the delay can improve how your supervisor reacts to the news. Try to understand how missing this deadline may impact their job, your team's workflow or the organization.
For example, if your supervisor was waiting on you to share a data analysis report so they can finish a slide show presentation to share with the rest of your team, let them know you understand how important the project is and apologize for delaying their portion of the project. Showing you understand the impact of your actions can make your apology seem more sincere.

4. Propose a new timeframe Consider what other priorities you have on your list and whether you can move some of them around to make sure you can finish the project you need to complete. Then propose a new timeframe that works for both you and your supervisor.
Make sure you agree to a deadline you can meet this time to help you rebuild trust. If you're overwhelmed with the amount of work you currently have, you might suggest moving another task to a different team member or delaying a less important project so you can focus. This can show your supervisor you're dedicated to finding a solution to remedy the situation.

5. Show your appreciation Finally, make sure to thank your supervisor for understanding your situation and working with you to find a solution. Let your supervisor know you're grateful for the extension and reassure them that you can meet the new deadline.

While you can keep your statement of appreciation brief, try to be specific about what you're thanking your supervisor for and why it means a lot to you. Taking the time to show your appreciation can help you end your conversation on a positive note.

Tips for handling a missed deadline Here are some additional tips to help you handle missing a deadline and prevent it from happening again in the future:
Be proactive If you notice that a project is taking you longer to complete than expected, let your supervisor know ahead of time.

Requesting an extension before the due date can reduce stress and give other members of your team time to adjust their schedules or priorities. If you miss a deadline due to unforeseen circumstances, you can still be proactive by reaching out to your supervisor before they notice the delay.

This may involve sending an email during hours outside of work, especially if there's an emergency situation. Being proactive can show your supervisor and your team members that you care about your work.

Take responsibility for your actions Instead of placing the blame on another coworker, your current workload or a faulty computer program, take responsibility for the missed deadline. While there may have been other extenuating circumstances at play, it's important to show your supervisor that you understand where you may have been able to mitigate these challenges.
For example, if you were unable to meet a deadline because you took on too many responsibilities, you could share that you understand you need to prioritize your work more effectively in the future.

This can show your supervisor that you're responsible and capable of improving your workflow in the future.

Provide frequent updates as you work toward your new deadline, provide frequent updates to let your supervisor know you're on track.
This can alleviate some of the stress they may be feeling and help you ensure you complete the project by the upcoming due date.
For example, if you're working on a large report, you might let your supervisor know when you're halfway finished and ask if they would like you to send them the information you have completed so far.
If they need this information to complete another task, it may be helpful and allow them to continue working while you finish the rest of your report. Improving your communication can also help you rebuild trust with your supervisor.
Take steps to prevent missing future deadlines Identify what steps you can take to prevent missing future deadlines. This might involve working ahead during slower periods, being more selective about the projects you take on or maintaining a more organized to-do list.

Another great option is to give yourself a soft due date for future projects.
For example, if you have a report due on March 14, you might make it a goal to have a rough draft finished by March 7. This can help you break large projects into smaller, more manageable pieces that you can make regular progress on to ensure you meet your deadline.
Once you've identified a few steps you can take to improve your performance, share them with your supervisor. This can show them that you're committed to taking actionable steps to prevent missing future deadlines.

6) What do you do when students do not meet their deadlines?

Any reluctance shown by a student in meeting a deadline has two aspects. One is the laziness of the student and the other some short comings of the teacher.

The first one is very clear but the second aspect needs clarification. When we say short comings of the teacher it includes failing to make your student understand enough the given task., loose command and indiscipline.

Certainly it is a matter of disappointment for a good teacher but we have to remove the hurdle after proper analysis and encourage the student to proceed with confidence. Time Management and accountability should be taught at a young age.

Working for a specific target teaches this to a child. Not meeting a deadline should not be left unchecked even at elementary level because it conveys a wrong message that it is alright not to be punctual. That is why an adult or a teacher should be strict in this issue.

It is best to reduce points for late assignments proportionately.
If you do not want to be strict with marks you can ask the child to do some extra work because he was late with the assignment. Or you can give pair work and ask them both to motivate each other and see that they stick to the time. This enhances team work and punctuality. Always compliment punctuality and encourage it openly in the class.
This helps as reinforcement. It also increases peer estimation which again helps in motivation to the student.

6) Describe for me the organization that goes into your planning for a lesson. I'm sitting in the back of your classroom; in some detail tell me what I see as you implement the lesson just described.

A lesson plan is the instructor's road map of what students need to learn and how it will be done effectively during the class time.
Then, you can design appropriate learning activities and develop strategies to obtain feedback on student learning. Having a carefully constructed lesson plan for each 3-hour lesson allows you to enter the classroom with more confidence and maximizes your chance of having a meaningful learning experience with your students.

A successful lesson plan addresses and integrates three key components:
Learning Objectives
 Learning activities
Assessment to check for student understanding

A lesson plan provides you with a general outline of your teaching goals, learning objectives, and means to accomplish them, and is by no means exhaustive.

 A productive lesson is not one in which everything goes exactly as planned, but one in which both students and instructor learn from each other. You may refer to an example of a 3 hour lesson plan.

STEPS FOR PREPARING A LESSON PLAN

Preparing a lesson plan involves several key steps to ensure that the learning objectives are met effectively. Here is a general outline of the steps involved:

1. Identify Learning Objectives: Determine what you want students to learn or be able to do by the end of the lesson. Objectives should be specific, measurable, achievable, relevant, and time-bound (SMART).

2. Assessment: Decide how you will assess whether the learning objectives have been met. This could include quizzes, discussions, projects, or other forms of assessment.

3. Gather Materials: Gather all the materials you will need for the lesson, such as textbooks, handouts, multimedia resources, and any other materials or equipment.

4. Design Instructional Activities: Plan the activities and methods you will use to teach the content. This could include lectures, discussions, group work, demonstrations, or hands-on activities.

5. Sequence the Activities: Arrange the activities in a logical sequence that builds on students' existing knowledge and skills.

6. Consider Differentiation: Plan how you will differentiate instruction to meet the needs of diverse learners, including students with disabilities, English language learners, and gifted students.

7. Allocate Time: Estimate how much time each activity will take and allocate time accordingly. Be sure to leave some extra time for transitions and unexpected interruptions.

8. Plan for Engagement: Include strategies to actively engage students in the learning process, such as asking questions, facilitating discussions, or incorporating interactive activities.

9. Incorporate Technology: Determine how you will incorporate technology into the lesson, if applicable, to enhance learning and engagement.

10. Plan for Closure: Plan a closing activity that summarizes the key points of the lesson and allows students to reflect on what they have learned.

11. Reflect: After teaching the lesson, reflect on what worked well and what could be improved. Use this feedback to inform future lesson planning.

12. Modify for Future Use: Make any necessary modifications to the lesson plan based on your reflections and feedback from students, and save it for future use.

By following these steps, you can create a well-organized and effective lesson plan that helps students achieve their learning objectives.

7) What are some of the considerations you make when planning your lessons? How do you go about planning a unit?

Each lesson is an opportunity to reach your students. Considered:

• What students need to know before you start teaching it?
• How will students show you the lesson was effective?
• What will students be doing?

See if this template helps

• INSTRUCTIONAL GOAL (outcome that students should be able to demonstrate upon completion of the entire unit)

• PERFORMANCE OBJECTIVE (use an action verb in a description of a measurable outcome)

• RATIONALE (brief justification — why you feel the students need to learn this topic)
• LESSON CONTENT (what is to be taught)

• INSTRUCTIONAL PROCEDURES
1. Focusing event (something to get the students' attention)
2. Teaching procedures (methods you will use)
3. Formative check (progress checks throughout the lesson)
4. Student Participation (how you will get the students to participate)
5. Closure (how you will end the lesson)
• EVALUATION PROCEDURES (how you will measure outcomes to determine if the material has been learned)
• MATERIALS AND AIDS (what you will need in order to teach this lesson).

The Importance of Lesson Planning This section is about the importance of planning and some considerations to keep in mind when beginning a lesson.

Let us check them up. **Defining Goals for Every Lesson Planning** helps you define goals for every lesson you are going to teach.

The defining goal of every lesson is to provide students with the knowledge they need to succeed. A lesson plan is a sequence of planned activities for students to complete. Every lesson plan has an introduction, a lesson, and a conclusion.

When planning a lesson, you consider three things: the content, the level of difficulty, and the goal.

The content has relevance to what students are learning in class and is meaningful for what they're trying to teach.

You also determine the level of difficulty for the lesson by identifying what skills you want students to learn during that time. Finally, you decide on the outcome or purpose of the lesson, so it can guide you through each step of the process.

For example, if your objective is to have students understand how to use technology safely, then you would need to know which specific technologies will be used as well as when those technologies should be introduced into lessons.

Selecting the Right Resources to Achieve Goals
Lesson planning helps you select appropriate resources and materials to achieve the goals of your lessons.

You may already have a list of required books for your course, but this does not mean they are all equally effective in achieving your objectives.

Some textbooks are more suitable than others, depending upon the subject matter being taught. For example, if you were teaching about the history of science or mathematics, you would likely want to teach from an introductory textbook rather than one written by experts on these subjects.

The same goes for any other type of resource, such as videos, websites, etc. If you do not know which book will be most useful for your students, then you should consider using a variety of different sources so that you can find out what works best with each group of learners.

Identifying Potential Obstacles Planning lessons can help you identify the potential challenges you will encounter when teaching your lessons. For example, if you are planning to use a video in class, you may need to make sure that all computers have access to the internet and that there is enough bandwidth available.

You might also need to plan ahead to ensure that you have sufficient time to prepare before classes begin.

If you want to teach an online lesson, it's important to think about how you'll communicate with your students during this process.

Will they receive instructions via email or text message? How do you expect them to respond? What tools will you provide to support their learning?

It Improves Quality of Your Lessons Lesson planning helps you to deliver your lessons effectively and efficiently. It allows you to focus on the most relevant aspects of a topic while avoiding unnecessary details.

This means that you can spend more time teaching rather than writing out long lists of information for each student. You also have greater control over what is covered in class because you know exactly which topics are being discussed at any given point.

Making Learning Easier for Your Students
When you plan your lessons before delivering them, you make learning and understanding easier for students.

They will be able to understand concepts better if you deliver well-thought-out lessons. It further helps improve students' achievement. That is why you need to engage in lesson planning.

Lesson Planning Reduces Behavior Problems during Lessons Not all lessons are created equal. Some lessons go well, while others do not. Lesson planning is essential to ensure that teachers are prepared for any situation, no matter how inevitable the problem may be.

You should consider various factors before planning a lesson, some of which include the following: age range of students, desired goals of the lesson, and available resources.

Planning ahead can reduce problems that often arise during lessons- such as behavior problems or lack of understanding. When you plan your lessons, you also have time to prepare the materials needed for the lesson. This allows you to focus on teaching rather than spending extra time searching for supplies.

Factors to Consider When Planning a Lesson
Today's teachers are asked to do more than ever before, with less time and fewer resources. How can educators reduce their stress levels? Consider the following tips for successful lesson planning:

Have Clear Goals A lot can be learned from research done on goal setting.

One particular study found that people who had clear goals were more convinced of the outcomes they could achieve and less likely to give up.

These results suggest that when teachers plan a lesson, it's important to set goals such as what skills they want their students to master and how they will know if these skills have been achieved. Goals also allow teachers to measure their success, which is essential for refining plans in the future.

What Objectives Can Help You Meet Your Goals? You must consider the objectives to be achieved to help you meet the goals of your lessons. For example, if one objective is "to learn about the different types of animals on Earth" then this would mean that all other learning activities should revolve around this topic.

If another goal was "to understand why some people are more intelligent than others" then this could lead to an investigation into IQ tests or even brain research. The key here is to make sure that each activity contributes toward achieving at least one of the goals.

What are the Demands of the Content? You must determine the demands and expectations of the topic or subject you are going to teach. This will help you know what type of content you need to prepare for a lesson. For example, if your students have been

 studying about dinosaurs in science class, they may be interested in knowing how many species there were during their time. You can use this information as part of your preparation by creating a timeline with pictures and facts from different sources. If your students want more details on the history of dinosaurs, then you should create an outline using these resources.

The key is to find out what the needs of your learners are so that you can provide them with relevant learning materials.

What Are Your Resources? Many teachers spend a lot of time planning their lessons, but not all teachers take the time to make sure they have the resources to teach these lessons. If you are about to start lesson planning for your class and realize that you don't have any of the necessary resources, it is important to know what types of resources you need and where you can find them.

Below we will discuss some different ways in which you may be able to get access to teaching tools such as books, videos, websites, etc.

1) Books: You should always try to use books when possible because they tend to be more comprehensive than other forms of media. However, if there isn't an appropriate book available on the topic or concept being taught then you might want to consider using another form of media instead.

2) Videos: If a video would work better for your student's learning needs, then by all means go ahead and use one! There are many great online sources out there that offer free educational content including Khan Academy, TED Talks, YouTube, Vimeo, PBS Learning Media, etc.

3) Websites: The internet is full of amazing resources for teachers looking to find quality materials related to their teaching topics.

Many times, these sites will have links to additional information about how to implement them in class.

Time for the Lesson You must consider the time available for you to deliver each lesson.

You may need to plan accordingly so as not to overwhelm or bore your students with too much material at once. If possible, try and break up a large amount of content into smaller chunks over several lessons.

This way, it's easier for both you and your students. It also allows you to focus more attention on one topic per week rather than trying to cover everything all at once.

The Abilities of Your Students What are the levels of your students? Their levels will determine how you plan and deliver the lesson. If you don't know what level your students fall into, try asking their teachers or parents.

You can use this information when planning out your curriculum. For example: if you have an intermediate student who is struggling in math, then perhaps you should start by teaching them basic addition before moving on to multiplication.

 Consider the things that can be achieved by the lowest-ability students. What do they need to learn first? How much time does it take for a low-level learner to master something? Can they understand concepts without being able to explain why those concepts work? Are there any skills that would help these learners succeed more quickly? If so, what are some of their strengths and weaknesses? Take these questions into consideration when planning your lessons.

When planning your lessons, also consider things that will challenge the highest-achieving students.

Do you have enough challenging material available in your curriculum or is this an area where you could use additional resources? Is there anything about your current lesson plan that might not be working well with certain types of learners? Think about how you can make adjustments to improve learning outcomes for all students.

Practical Exercises Prepare practical exercises for students to perform during the lesson. They could be paper-based or oral, done individually or in groups. The purpose of these activities should be to help them practice what they've learned and reinforce it through real-life experience.

These are great ways to get students thinking critically about their own work and others' work. You may want to have some examples ready so that students don't need to spend too much time on preparation.

If you're doing this with an online course, make sure your assignments can be completed within one week. This will give students enough time to complete the assignment before the next lesson starts. In essence, class exercises must be as practical as possible and must be doable.

Extra Supporting/Practice Materials Plan supporting exercises to keep students who finish their work early busy. Don't let them sit idly, or else they will engage in disruptive activities.

Extra practice materials help students practice more of what they have learned in the classroom. Remember the saying, "practice makes better." On the other hand, it can help reduce behavior problems in the classroom. If a student is having trouble with an exercise, give him extra support material so he doesn't feel left out. This also helps prevent boredom from setting in.

The political ramifications of the lesson you are going to teach In today's politically charged climate, when planning a lesson, it is important to consider how the lesson you are going to teach will affect the students and school.
In order to do this, there are a few things you can do in advance of your lesson plan.

The first is to have a conversation with your principal or other administrators who may be involved in your lesson plan. Ask them what they think about teaching certain topics such as gun control, abortion, homosexuality, etc.

If possible, ask for their input on how best to approach these issues. You should not assume that just because something has been taught before, it does not mean it needs to be repeated again.

Your Familiarity with the Topic You must know what you are going to teach. This means having some familiarity with the topic itself.

For example, if you were planning to talk about guns, then you would need to understand firearms and ammunition. It also means knowing where the information comes from so that you can cite sources appropriately. In this case, your source could be a book or magazine article, an online resource, or even another teacher's lecture notes.

The more familiar you become with the material, the easier it will be to prepare and deliver the lesson. Conclusion Lesson planning is an essential part of teaching.

Without proper planning, teachers can fail to reach their students and their lesson will not be as effective. This article has provided some tips on what to consider to plan your lessons effectively.

8)How much homework will you assign? How do you know how long it will take your student?

The amount of homework young people are given varies a lot from school to school and from grade to grade. In some schools and grades, children have no homework at all.

In others, they may have 18 hours or more of homework every week.
In the United States, the accepted guideline, which is supported by both the National Education Association and the National Parent Teacher Association, is the 10-minute rule: Children should have no more than 10 minutes of homework each day for each grade reached.

In 1st grade, children should have 10 minutes of daily homework; in 2nd grade, 20 minutes; and so on to the 12th grade, when on average they should have 120 minutes of homework each day, which is about 10 hours a week. It doesn't always work out that way. In 2013, the University of Phoenix College of Education commissioned a survey of how much homework teachers typically give their students. From kindergarten to 5th grade, it was just under three hours per week; from 6th to 8th grade, it was 3.2 hours; and from 9th to 12th grade, it was 3.5 hours.

There are two points to note. First, these are the amounts given by individual teachers. To estimate the total time children are expected to spend on homework, you need to multiply these hours by the number of teachers they work with. High school students who work with five teachers in different curriculum areas may find themselves with 17.5 hours or more of homework a week, which is the equivalent of a part-time job. The other factor is that these are teachers' estimates of the time that homework should take.

The time that individual children spend on it will be more or less than that, according to their abilities and interests. One child may casually dash off a piece of homework in half the time that another will spend laboring through in a cold sweat.

Do students have more homework these days than previous generations? Given all the variables, it's difficult to say. Some studies suggest they do. In 2007, a study from the National Center for Education Statistics found that, on average, high school students spent around seven hours a week on homework.

A similar study in 1994 put the average at less than five hours a week. Mind you, I [Robinson] was in high school in England in the 1960s and spent a lot more time than that—though maybe that was to do with my own ability. One way of judging this is to look at how much homework your own children are given and compare it to what you had at the same age.

There's also much debate about the value of homework. Supporters argue that it benefits children, teachers, and parents in several ways:

- Children learn to deepen their understanding of specific content, to cover content at their own pace, to become more independent learners, to develop problem-solving and time-management skills, and to relate what they learn in school to outside activities.
- Teachers can see how well their students understand the lessons; evaluate students' individual progress, strengths, and weaknesses; and cover more content in class.
- Parents can engage practically in their children's education, see firsthand what their children are being taught in school, and understand more clearly how they're getting on—what they find easy and what they struggle with in school.

QUESTIONS FOCUSED ON STUDENTS

1) Are you willing to sponsor any extra-curricular activities?

I have always been a person who is involved in extracurriculars. From the time I was three until I graduated from college, I was in something extra. At the end of my freshman year of college, I knew I wanted to be a teacher after what felt like a long process of soul searching.

I wanted to do something that was important, I loved working with youth, and I knew my talents in connecting with people could help me in contributing to a positive school culture one day, which I knew was incredibly important.

While I was excited to share my passion for reading and writing with students, I also knew right away that I wanted to be a teacher who did more than lead classes.

I knew I wanted to get involved and do all that I could to positively impact a school's culture. Extracurriculars and fostering a positive school climate are two things that are very important to me. You can include your extra-curricular skills which is related to school.

2) How would your students describe you as a teacher? How do you want students to view you?

This question is used to learn more about your personality and self-awareness. Employers may compare your answer to how your references described you. A thorough and thoughtful answer can show strong interpersonal skills and perceptiveness. Use anecdotes and examples from your experience to support your answer.

How to Answer Think of three to five qualities you have or some words that your students have used to describe you in the past.
What would your students say about you? What kind of teacher do you want to be? Highlight some of the top qualities that make you a great teacher that the students will appreciate.

Example answer: "My peers and students would describe me as encouraging, creative and inspiring. I love planning fun activities for my classroom and involving other classrooms as well. For example, last year I organized 'Pi Day' on March 14 for the whole six-grade class. I planned scavenger hunts, relay races and trivia all based on math. It was great to see all the students work together, have fun and learn." "I developed some strong connections with my students during my 12-week practicum.

I believe they would say that I am a good listener, fair at giving feedback, and dedicated to their success." "My students say I'm tough but fun.
I try to create a positive learning environment, so I can be strict about enforcing rules. I care about my students, and I want the best for them. I stay positive and give them projects that allow them to use their creativity." "My students and faculty would describe me as a dedicated teacher with current lesson plans and the ability to crack open the struggles of even the toughest students.

I want everyone to succeed in my classroom and will go over and above my job description to make that happen." Being fair, understanding, and nurturing are very important traits for a teacher to have; it's wonderful that your students described you in this way! Your ability to put students first really shines through.

3) Do you want pupils to like you? Why?

The answer is yes, but with a qualifier. It matters why you want your students to like you. If they like you because you genuinely like them and show a real interest in their growth, then they will also respect you and work hard for you.

Students do not learn because of teachers, they learn for teachers."

Why it Matters that Your Students Like You:
The Research

The brain is a social organ and close relationships, such as a positive student teacher relationship, encourage learning, in part, because they promote a positive learning environment.

From birth, we learn from our interactions with other people; this includes, family, friends and yes, teachers.

Positive teacher- student relationships in the school setting have positive implications not only for students, but for teachers and the school climate as a whole. For this reason, students who are in classrooms with teachers that they like and have a close relationship with may learn more.

For teachers, teaching students who like you makes their job easier. Teachers who experience close relationships with students report that their students have better attendance, cooperate more, are more engaged and are more self-directed.

These little things can make a big difference Students performed faster when they were shown a picture of a teacher they had a close relationship with before solving the problem versus a teacher they didn't have a relationship with.

While this study shows the direct effect of students thinking about teachers that they are close to prior to solving a problem, it also gets at a deeper message. When students have positive relationships with their teachers, it affects how they view school and how engaged they are.

Students who have these kinds of relationships have more positive feelings about school, are more engaged, and in turn, are often higher achievers. Think for a minute about any high achieving student you know.

More than likely, this student enjoys school, or at least likes it. Now, think about that students' relationship with his/her teachers.

I'm sure at least one teacher that student has a positive relationship with will come to mind. While positive student teacher relationships can result in more engagement, and higher grades among students, negative relationships can have the opposite effect.

Positive student-teacher relationships also have the power to positively improve school climate, something that can affect everyone involved in a school. School is, in a very general way, student and staff perception of their school.
We can think of it this way: Students who have positive relationships with their teachers tend to be more engaged. Students who are more engaged typically are more likely to succeed. Being successful in school leads

to positive educational experiences which in turn, creates a positive perception of school. Of course there are exceptions and limitations to this logic and not all students, teachers, and schools are the same – but the research suggests it's worth paying attention to.

Teachers play a huge role because they can very well shift the climate of their school by building stronger relationships with their students.

Note: These tips are rooted in my personal experiences, not peer-reviewed research.

1. Sincerity When building a relationship with your students it's important to be sincere. Ask yourself why you want to have a better relationship with the student. If your reason is simply because you have him/her in your class and you don't want it to be a miserable experience for both of you all year, be honest about that. In my experience, students have an amazing ability to detect when someone is not genuine.

Keep in mind that even if you are approaching a student with sincerity, he/she may have his/her defenses up, especially if he/she has not had many positive relationships with adults. Keeping your intentions pure and being honest with the student about why you want to get to know him/her and conveying that you truly care are important first steps.

2. Consistency This may be the most important factor. In any relationship, consistency is key. Showing your students that you are going to show up and be there for them every day by actually doing it says a lot.

Conveying the message that you care over and over again may eventually reach even the most stubborn students.

3. High Expectations A hard lesson I learned in my early years of teaching is the importance of having and keeping high expectations. If you truly care about your students, you hold them to a high standard because anything less would be a disservice to them.

I used to think that taking it easy on my students by accepting excuses when they didn't do their homework, or turning a blind eye when they occasionally misbehaved, was showing that I cared. I've learned that in holding high expectations of my students I'm conveying the message that I believe

you are capable of doing something great and so, I'm not going to accept anything less than greatness from you.

Where to Go from Here While there are great implications for having a positive relationship with your students, the fact of the matter is that it's not possible to have a great relationship with every student.

As teachers, what's most important is that we hold every student to high expectations and put forth an honest effort to show support and genuine interest in as many of our students as we can. While we may not have amazing relationships with every student, the ones we really take the time to nurture can make all the difference in the world.

4) As a teacher, should you intentionally try to build rapport with your students? How?

How do we get the best out of our students? By building a rapport with them. We hear that over and over again, but do we really know what that looks like or what that means?

It's not about preaching to them or trying to make them better people. It's about learning who they are, accepting and celebrating their uniqueness, and really listening to them.

STRATEGIES FOR GETTING TO KNOW YOUR STUDENTS BETTER

Getting to know your students better is essential for building rapport and creating a positive learning environment. Here are some strategies you can use:

1. Icebreaker Activities: Use icebreaker activities at the beginning of the school year or semester to help students feel more comfortable and get to know each other. This can also help you learn more about your students' interests and personalities.

2. Student Surveys: Administer surveys to your students to gather information about their interests, hobbies, learning preferences, and goals. This can help you tailor your instruction to meet their needs.

3. One-on-One Meetings: Schedule one-on-one meetings with each student to discuss their goals, challenges, and interests. This can help you build a stronger connection with each student and better understand their individual needs.

4. Classroom Discussions: Encourage classroom discussions where students can share their thoughts, ideas, and experiences. This can help you learn more about your students' perspectives and interests.

5. Interest Inventories: Use interest inventories to gather information about your students' interests, hobbies, and passions. This can help you incorporate topics that are meaningful to your students into your lessons.

6. Learning Profiles: Create learning profiles for each student that include information about their learning styles, strengths, weaknesses, and preferences. This can help you tailor your instruction to meet their individual needs.

7. Attend School Events: Attend school events such as sports games, concerts, and plays to show your support for your students outside of the classroom. This can help you build stronger relationships with

your students and their families.

8. Use Technology: Use technology to connect with your students, such as through email, social media, or online discussion forums. This can help you stay connected with your students and learn more about their interests and concerns.

By using these strategies, you can get to know your students better and create a more positive and supportive learning environment.

10 Ways to Build Positive Relationships with Students

In order to build a positive rapport with a student, you have to intentionally carve out time for the student. If you are busily running around the room and trying to talk with the student it, you will not be fully engaged and it will come off as insincere.
Once you have the time carved out for your specific student(s), here are some ways to build rapport with your students

Smile– Be genuinely happy to see your students each day. This could be the thing that brightens their day!
Be Respectful- Give students time and space to problem solve issues if needed. Let them know you are there for them when they are ready to talk.
Know their Hobbies and Interests- Take some time, even just in passing to talk about what your students like to do for fun. Share what you like too!
Play a Game– Go out for recess or spend a few minutes playing games with students. They love having their teachers playing with them!
Lunch with a Student- Invite a student or two in for lunch sometime. This provides a quiet time to get to know your students better.

Greet Students at the Door- You can tell a lot by a student's body language when they enter the room. Stand outside of the door and shake their hand in the morning or at each class period.

Attend Student's Activities– Get a sports or performance schedule from your students who are in extra-curricular activities. They love it when you come to an event!

Look for the Positive in Your Students- Try to find one or two affirmations to say to your students each day. The ones who really struggle will need to be built up daily!

Be Sincere- When you are talking with students, put down your computer, and be an active, sincere listener. Students will know when you are not being genuine.

Believe in Your Students- Tell them, especially when things are hard, that you believe in them. Show them as well by being there for your students when they need extra support with an assignment or a listening ear for them during a tough time.

We all want to have great relationships with our students. Sometimes the busyness of our work and teaching can be a barrier to building rapport with our students.

As I return to school this week, I will work harder at becoming more intentional with more of my students. Building up your students and taking time to be there for them will bring a lifetime of great results.

5) How can you get students to be excited about learning?

How You Get Students Excited About Learning In pedagogy (the science of teaching), this is called an "anticipatory set." It's the part that builds anticipation, and, thus, interest. Virtually anything can be used as an anticipatory set.
Keep your eyes open for things that you see in your everyday life that can be adapted for class.
You must make sure that the connection to the topic is clear. It should feel smooth, not disjointed. Having a list of ideas in your toolbox is helpful because you aren't trying to come up with something out of the clear blue sky.
You can simply scan your list and choose something that will work.
You may wish to create digital files or paper files for ideas you come across, so you have a place to save that cool picture or object for the perfect lesson.

Ideas for Getting Students Excited About Learning ➢ Play a short version of a game like charades, Password, Taboo, Pictionary, etc. ➢ Show a piece of art or architecture and make a comparison or observation ➢ Have a guest share a story (or lead any one of these ideas) ➢ Display a powerful quote, with or without an accompanying image ➢ Use senses of smell or sound ➢ Show a clip of a video ➢ Tell a story (make sure to disclose if it is fiction) ➢ Share an item from a news story ➢ Have a mystery box or item or sound ➢ Use an object or prop ➢ Draw a picture or have class members draw a picture ➢ Ask class members to agree or disagree with a series of statements ➢ Do a simple magic trick ➢ Show a comic ➢ Play a reveal game, slowly uncovering sections of a quote or image ➢ Show a picture and have the class think of captions ➢ Do a scavenger hunt ("Find a word in the text that is a synonym for …" or "What is the third word in the first sentence of the ….") ➢ Tell a riddle or a joke ➢ Give a case study and have the class share suggestions ➢ Have class complete a short, small task or questionnaire/survey➢ Dress up/come in character (I've done this as Shakespeare's granddaughter!) ➢ Delve into a vocabulary word from the lesson ➢ Share statistics or have students make predictions

Final Thoughts on Getting Students Excited About Learning Remember: classes are like mirrors. They reflect the teacher's attitude and energy. Give to them what you would like from them. If you have a high energy lesson, give a high energy anticipatory set. If you have a more mellow lesson, have a more mellow anticipatory set.

6) What do you value most in a child?

Now more than ever, it is vital to teach your child important values to make the world a better place. In order for a child to succeed and excel in life, parents need to educate their children. As they age, they will learn many important principles; however, there are many values that we must teach explicitly. Why You Should Teach Your Child Values With the world changing so fast, it is essential to teach your children values so they can influence the world for the better.

Parents are the best examples to teach their children. We teach our children values to help them become the best version of themselves.

How Children Learn Values Children mainly learn values by watching their parent's example, hence why it is so important to set a good example for them. One of the best ways to ensure you are setting the right example is to practice what you preach. Live your values, don't just talk about them with your kids.

When Is the Best Time to Teach Morals and Values? The younger you start to teach your children values the better. Some argue that preschool is too young to teach moral values; however, it is best to teach them as pre- schoolers, so it becomes a natural part of their personality.

The 10 Most Important Values for Children Here are ten values to teach your child as early as possible:

1. Honesty For your children to develop honesty, you must be honest yourself. Your children are very perceptive and will take cues from you. If they see you lying, they will understand that lying is okay. If your children lie to you, sit them down, and communicate the importance of being honest. Try not to overreact as children become fearful when yelled at. Each time your children are honest, tell them how much you appreciate their honesty. Positive reinforcement of good behaviors helps the behavior to continue. Explaining the consequences of lying is also an important step. They need to know what happens when they lie and what happens if they tell the truth. Doing so will show them that it is always better to tell the truth.

2. Manners Having good manners is another essential value to teach your children. When they have good manners, they can better interact with people on a daily basis in a considerate and thoughtful way. The more you practise and use good manners, the more your children will as well. Teaching manners can be as simple as always using please and thank you. You can even start that from the time they are born. Even though they cannot speak early on, they still learn from your actions and will imitate them as soon as they start to communicate.

3. Responsibility When teaching values to your children, responsibility is one of the top values to include. As soon as your children grow up, you want them to be dependable, keep commitments, and be accountable. If you do not instil in them a sense of responsibility from an early stage, they will have a harder time in the future. The world needs children to be responsible more than ever before.

It will help them to find jobs and be successful in school as well as in their adult life. Again you start by showing responsibility for your actions. Start by having them make their bed each morning. As they get older and can complete more tasks, have them do more chores around the house. Whether you give an allowance is up to you; the important part is making them feel responsible for things around the house.

4. Respect Respect is another vital value to teach your children from a very early stage. Many parents focus so much on respecting their elders, they sometimes forget about the rest.

However, make sure to teach your children to respect everyone, no matter what age, race, religion, or status they may be. Teaching respect helps them to be kind and thoughtful to strangers they will encounter daily.

It will also help them be kind to you no matter what stage in life they are at. Starting early will help them to be consistently respectful, even as the world goes astray.

5. Love You can never give a child too much love. It is one of the basic emotional needs of a child. Children are natural in giving love; however, if it is not reciprocated, it may not always last as they age. Start by always saying, "I love you" to your children.
Let your children see your love for them as well as others in your life. Display some affection to your spouse when they are around. Share your love both verbally and physically.
Never let a day pass without expressing your love to your children. Show love in unusual ways as well, not just saying, "I love you." Leave a note in their lunch if they go to school or put a heart on their bedroom door.
The more you give and show love, the more your children will as well. Soon it will become a regular part of their day. It is also important to teach your children to love people for who they are.
This will also show them respect for others as well. Love can be present no matter if you agree with the person or not.

6. Consideration Being thoughtful and kind to others will always be a value to teach your children. You can brighten someone's day just by being kind. When you are kind and thoughtful, you are more aware of others' feelings and can better help someone.
Talk about a small problem with your children and let them think of ways to overcome it. If someone you know is sick, ask them what they believe will help them to feel better.

Doing these problem-solving situations will help them learn to always be on the lookout to help someone in need.

7. Perseverance Rewarding your children is a vital part of teaching values. But, if you reward them for everything they do, whether they try or not, they will lose their sense of perseverance.

Encourage your children to do something challenging. Encourage them to try their absolute best. When you praise your children, praise their effort rather than the finished result.

This will teach them to try their hardest. Help your kids to overcome something challenging and praise them when they do.

8. Courage If you do everything challenging for your children, they will have a harder time developing courage. Even though you want to protect your children no matter what, you will not always be there in situations they may need courage.

Teaching them to face their fears helps them conquer hard things with courage. Teach your children to stand up for themselves. In today's world, this is especially important.

Teach them to speak up if they are not comfortable or if something is bothering them. This will help them to ask questions when they are confused in school as well as gain confidence and self-esteem.

9. Justice It is essential to teach children to express their feelings; however, it is also equally important to help them learn about consequences.

Instead of merely making your child say she's sorry when she has done a wrong, teach her to find a way to help make it right again.

Teaching justice will help them to see the right and wrong in the world as well as help them fix the mistakes they will inevitably make. Teaching them to set a wrong with action helps them develop an ethical, strong moral compass.

10. Happiness Everyone ultimately wants happiness. However, children can perceive when something is wrong.

Try to remain positive despite the challenges that arise in your life. If something is challenging, communicate the trial with your children and that you are trying to stay cheerful despite it.

When you focus on the positives, so will your children. Then they will learn to see the good in everything, including people.

Something as little as saying five things they are grateful for each day can help children understand the good in life.

This will also teach them resilience amidst trials and help them to overcome them better. These are just ten values to teach your children; however, the list can go on and on.

Making it a priority every day to teach through your actions rather than your words can help children develop strong values they will use throughout the rest of their life.

7) Should a teacher intentionally use humor in the classroom? How do you use humor in the classroom?

Researchers agree that children who laugh in the classroom develop strong communication and critical thinking skills, become more creative, and easily cope with stress. When children laugh together in group settings, they build a sense of team comradery, creating a strong bond with their classmates and teachers.
Humor is a natural icebreaker that helps connect children regardless of their differences. All of this reduces classroom conflict and increases student attention and participation.

Sound too good to be true? It's not! Infusing humor into your classroom is simple and easy to do. Here are some ways I have found to easily bring some giggles into our day.

1) Laugh during morning meeting Morning meeting is the perfect time to sneak in some humor and let the morning giggles out! You can start with funny ways to greet each other once a week.
Sharing funny quotes is a great way to increase student reflection and encourage meaningful discourse. By choosing different quotes, you can informally "measure" what students in your class find funny.
Periodically allow students to share funny stories that have recently happened to them. On days that there are no stories to share, we take out our class "Humor Log" and revisit a time something funny happened in our classroom.

2) Keep a humor log Don't the funniest things happen in your classroom? Keep a log about it! Our class humor log helps us to capture the funny memories of our year together.

Students complete a form that simply asks, "What happened, and why was it funny?" Students record the date and their name and add it into our log. This book is perfect to pull from the shelf when a student needs a good chuckle! This simple task encourages writing, even for the most reluctant writers, as they all want to add a page to the humor log.

3) Joke of the day If you ask my class, they will tell you that our daily joke is the highlight of their day and what they miss the most when they are absent! Students enter the room in complete anticipation to read the day's joke. I keep a small basket on my shelf labeled Joke of the Day.
Inside, there are enough copies of the joke for each student. Students use critical thinking to try to "solve" the joke. Jokes and riddles promote non-conventional thinking, as they encourage multiple acceptable responses.
As the year progresses, students love to find many "answers" for the joke, encouraging and supporting their classmates with each new answer shared. Students are motivated to participate in the joke's discussion, so in turn they complete their morning responsibilities in a timely manner.
As students begin to understand more complex humor in jokes, they are encouraged to find and share jokes related to the content we are studying, as well as to create their own.

4) Read aloud funny poetry and literature What better way to model appropriate humor than to incorporate funny poetry and literature into your read aloud time? The list of funny children's poetry and literature is endless.
Grab a book and read it. If you giggle as you turn the page, chances are your students will, too! If you are thinking that there is not enough time to read funny books, try squeezing in a few funny poems during dismissal time. Need some suggestions to get you started?
Try A Bad Case of The Giggles by Bruce Lansky, Where the Sidewalk Ends by Shel Silverstein, Those Darn Squirrels by Adam Robin, Amelia Bedelia series by Peggy Parish, and the Ramona Quimby series by Beverly Cleary. An extra perk of reading humorous literature with your students is that you will notice humor and wit developing in your students' writing pieces.

5) Play with words Playing with words is a higher-order thinking skill. The witty humor in puns promotes retention of new vocabulary words and can increase the connection between new and previous learning. Think about the statement, "Teddy bears are never hungry because they are always stuffed."

After you finish giggling, you realize the clever play on words. Reading a pun like this requires students to understand the multiple meaning of the word stuffed, to construct meaning from context, to visualize to understand the humor, and then to giggle a bit at its connotation.
That's a lot of learning from one sentence! Word play can be used to teach multiple meaning words,

homophones, synonyms, and alliteration.

Humor Strategies to Use Even if you are what Ed calls "humor challenged," there are things you can do to lighten the load and dissipate the clouds in your classroom. Just remember, above all, that sarcasm has no place in the school. Only "no hurt" humor is acceptable.
• Laugh at yourself -- when you do something silly or wrong, mention it and laugh at it.
• Add humorous items to tests, homework or class assignments -- even at the University, one of my favorite options when I give multiple choice exams requiring students to identify pairs of psychologists is Calamari and Endive. It always gets smiles, and helps to break exam tension.
• Keep a quotable quotes bulletin board or corner in your room -- look for humor quotes and post them and encourage your students to do the same.
• Keep a cartoon file, and have an area where you can display one or two a day on a rotating basis, with students making the choice.
• Have Joke Friday -- ask students to bring in jokes to share, either to start the day on Friday, to make a transition between lunch and the following class, or at the end of the day (be sure to screen the jokes in advance, of course).
• Ask students to try to build humor into occasional writing assignments -- that will start a conversation about what it funny, how they know something is funny, why different people find some things funny but some things are funny to almost everyone.
• Have a funny hat day, or mismatched socks day, or some other funny dress-up time.
• Build creative and humorous thinking by showing cartoons and picture without captions and asking students to create them -- individually, in pair-shares, or small groups.
• Ask students to bring in books they think are funny. Ask them to talk about why, and to use examples from the book.

8) Have you developed any new ideas about teaching in the past few months? Describe one or two of them.

Innovative teaching strategies don't always mean introducing the latest and greatest technology into the classroom. Instead, innovative teaching is the

process of proactively introducing new teaching strategies and methods into the classroom. The purpose of introducing these new teaching strategies and methods is to improve academic outcomes and address real problems to promote equitable learning.

Jump to: • How Innovation Can Help You Become Better at Teaching • 10 Innovative Teaching Strategies for Better Student Engagement • The Future of Innovative Teaching • Summary

How Innovation Can Help You Become Better at Teaching In many ways, applying innovative teaching strategies to the classroom is a tacit understanding that our teaching methods can be improved.
 It accepts the need to grow and develop, which is exactly what we ask of our students. What better way to lead than by example? So, innovative teaching strategies start with a growth mindset. We identify room for improvement. We invest our time in researching and thinking of better strategies to teach our students.
We create something new or adapt existing methods. We take risks. We may fail. We try again. We iterate and by doing so establish a culture of innovation and creativity in the classroom that inspires our students to do the same. In this post, we talk about popular innovative teaching strategies that help drive better student outcomes. These strategies often focus on student engagement. After all, students that are actively engaged in their learning are less likely to be absent from the class and more likely to succeed academically. It is important to take a student-centric approach to our methods.
As a student, do we gain more from class by sitting passively in our seats for a 45-minute lecture? Or, are we more likely to learn by actively participating in the class by asking questions, collaborating on projects, and problem-solving?
Let's look at ten innovative teaching strategies that teachers use in their classrooms to improve student engagement and academic outcomes.

The Future of Innovative Teaching The shift over the last couple of years of brick-and-mortar students to digital students accelerated a trend that was already developing. Believe it or not, by 2019 nearly 60% of all students in the US used digital learning tools. Virtual academy enrollment numbers have seen steady growth well before the pandemic serving hundreds of thousands of students each year in the US.
Though many school districts happily reopened in 2021, it is unlikely that schools will completely abandon their digital experiences.

Offering digital programs provides students flexibility with greater access to teachers and classes as well as the opportunity to take more control over their learning. As Plato wrote, "our need will be the real creator" or as we say today, "necessity is the mother of invention".

Introducing innovative teaching strategies into the classroom may have been a niche academic practice conducted by a few bold educators previously, but these strategies are becoming more commonplace today as schools look to make up for learning loss and our new reality.

We can expect to see more blended learning, hybrid learning, and bold initiatives to address the challenges schools and students face today. This trend goes beyond the classroom as the workplace also faces these challenges and figures out how to approach their own hybrid learning experiences.

9) If I were a child why would I want to be in your classroom?

If you are a student in my classroom. You can see such things in my classroom.

I inspire my students by building trust and understanding. I fulfil my promises by real practice, and behavior. Hence they know that I am sincere for their academic progress, and I care about them for their future lives.

I pay individual attention to polish their abilities and capacities.

I integrate new technologies into my teaching such as the computer, internet, DVD, smart board etc.

I put students' assignments, tests reviews, students' awards on the web pages developed by me for them.

I use tests as teaching tools. My students were so inspired that they arranged math fairs/exhibits to show their class projects to inspire the learning communities.

10) Do you have a specific grade level/age that you prefer to teach? Why?

Share your own answer

What Grade Should You Teach? It Depends on Your Preferred Age Group The first step to deciding what grade you should teach is deciding on a preferred age group. You have three basic choices: young children (preschool and elementary school), adolescents (late elementary school, middle school, and early high school) and teens who are nearing adulthood (high school).

Part of this choice depends on what you love to do as a teacher. If you enjoy directing children in guided play, younger kids are the best to work with.

If you want to teach kids how to develop their higher thinking skills, adolescents are probably the group for you. And if you want to teach serious academic content that prepares students for college and work, you'll likely enjoy teaching high school aged teens.

You should also consider the job market before choosing an age group. Sure you might prefer teaching younger children, but maybe your city or state has a greater need for middle or high school teachers. Doing what you love is very important in your career. But if you can be flexible to meet the needs of your preferred job market, that can be good for your career in the long run too.

So What Grade Should You Teach Within Your Preferred Age Group?

Once you've decide on a preferred age group, you're ready to choose a specific grade. Again, the kind of teaching you want to do is an important factor. If your really love helping young learners grow and play, preschool, kindergarten, or grades 1 through 3 are great. If you're more interested in helping children develop good thinking skills as they mature, grade 4 is a good place to start. And opportunities to teach college-style academics really increase from the sophomore year of high school onward. The job market also plays a role in your decision here of course. Maybe you really want to teach first grade, but only kindergarten or second grade jobs are open to you at the moment. In cases like this, I strongly recommend choosing the next nearest grade to your preferred one. Starting your teaching career sooner rather than later will open up a lot of doors to you in the future. When it comes to age groups, there's no sense in waiting for a completely "perfect" teaching job.

What to Do if You're Not Sure What Grade You Should Teach

A lot of people aren't sure what age or grade they would really prefer to work with. And they may not be sure which grades have the most teaching jobs. If you're studying to be a teacher and you're not sure which grade is best for you, you'll have chances to decide while you do your teacher training.

Seek out field experiences in many different classrooms during your studies. And start keeping an eye on the job market now–read school district job postings and teacher job boards.

If you're not sure how to find varied fieldwork and good job boards to review, check with an adviser. Your academic advisers may be able to give you some additional advice about this important decision as well.

If you're still not sure what grade you should teach, even after you graduate, consider substitute teaching. Subbing is a really good way to feel out the kinds of teaching work you'd like to do full time.

And most school districts love to hire licensed subs for teaching positions.

Here's how to decide what grade to teach:
1. Explore different curriculums.
2. Consider the salaries being offered.
3. Think about job prospects.
4. Think about potential teaching challenges.
5. Understand your personal teaching style.
6. Decide on the type of relationships you want to form.
7. Consider market trends.
8. Explore with teaching experiences.

11) What do you feel is important for you to know about the students with whom you work? How do you go about gathering this information?

Development of a student's postsecondary goals requires professionals, students with disabilities, and their families to view assessment as an ongoing process.
However, this does not mean that new methods and models of assessment are needed. Rather, it is necessary to determine what information is currently available, what additional information is needed and, what methods of assessment would be most effective.
Critical transition points for individuals with disabilities, along with relevant assessment information, need to be identified to make appropriate planning and placement decisions.

There is a wealth of information collected in a variety of ways in the general education and special education system that can be used to help plan for transition.
However, more specific information, especially in planning for employment, usually needs to be gathered.

FORMAL ASSESSMENT Formal transition assessments usually involve using standardized instrument for administering, scoring, and interpreting an assessment. This allows a student's score to be interpreted compared to other students (e.g. norms). However, not all standardized assessments are norm-referenced. Although these assessments provide useful data in determining aptitudes, skills and abilities, usually, further assessment in "real" environments needs to be done.

Advantages of Formal Assessments include:
• Provide norming process, validity and reliability
• Compares student to others his/her age
• Is often a starting point for determining career development activities
• Is usually enjoyable for students – hands on tests.

Disadvantages of Formal Assessments include:
• Can be costly
• Lack of availability
• May be time consuming to give and take
• May be limited to use by a professional with a requisite qualification. Examples of Formal

Assessments: • *Self-Directed Search Form R or E*

• Armed Services Vocational Aptitude Battery (ASVAB)

• Brigance Transition Skills Inventory

• Wechsler Intelligence Scale for Children

• The Vineland – II • Woodcock Johnson Test of Achievement

• ACT Plan (grade 10)

• Reading Free Vocational Interest Inventory

• Enderle-Severson Transition Rating Scales (ESTR-R and ESTR-III)

INFORMAL ASSESSMENT

Informal assessments provide measures of student performance over time and are useful in determining the effectiveness of instructional interventions.

However, they do not allow for comparison to other students.

Information accumulated and documented by observing the student as he/she participates in various academic and work experiences, talking with the student about likes and dislikes, and setting up experiences that will allow the student to try something that he/she thinks may be of interest provides a wealth of informal data.

Advantages of Informal Assessment:
• Inexpensive/sometimes free
• Seldom have professional qualifications for use

• Provides good, usable information especially when used on an ongoing basis by more than one

person (increases validity)
• Information can be easily attained from questionnaires, interviews, observations, etc.

Disadvantages of Informal Assessment:

• May be time consuming to arrange and/or set up try outs.
• Some careers cannot be "tried out"- like therapists.
• Expressed interests can be narrow and only reflect the student's limited experiences
• Lack formal norming process, and reliability or validity information Examples of Informal

Assessments: • Behavior Checklists
• Transition Planning Inventory
• Curriculum Based Assessments
• Situational Assessments
• Interest Inventories
• Environmental/ecological Checklists
• Job Try Outs
• Interviews and Surveys

HOW DO I DECIDE WHICH INSTRUMENTS AND METHODS TO USE?

1. Become familiar with the various types of transition assessments available including their characteristics remembering that you need multiple assessments that are ongoing viewed through a transition lens.
2. Choose assessments that assist students with answering the following questions:

a. Who am I?
b. What are my unique talents and interests?
c. What do I want in life, now and in the future?
d. What are some of life's demands that I can me now?
e. What the main barriers to getting what I want from school and my community? And f. What are my options in the school and community for preparing me for what I want to do, now and in the future?

3. Select assessments that are appropriate for your students considering the nature of the disability, the students' post-school goals, and opportunities in the community.

Whichever assessments are chosen, the data should inform your decisions in developing realistic and meaningful transition IEPs, guide instructional programming decisions, assist students in making connections between their post-school goals and their academic plan, and finally, inform the Summary of Performance.

Interest Inventories Interest inventories can provide valuable information regarding a student's interests. However, particularly with career/vocational interest inventories, the information must be considered with caution. The validity of the results is only as accurate as the student understands the world of work. Because students assessed are often teenagers, their understanding is limited to their own job experiences and the jobs they have seen others perform like teachers, lawyers, doctors, professional athletes, police officers, firefighters, waiters, and store clerks – to name a few. Even though these jobs are visible jobs, what the public sees is not necessarily a complete look at the job. The only way to really understand a job is to spend time job shadowing or participating in a try out of that job.

As an example: A student who struggles with reading and does not like to read and write wants to be a lawyer.

This student sees lawyers as people who argue verbally in court, have power and perhaps help people and/or society. It is the assessor's job to determine what it is about this job that is appealing. If this student really understood that lawyers spend a great deal of time researching, reading and writing, this career may not be as appealing.

However, one can learn important information about the kinds of careers a student identifies as interesting from these inventories. The student may be saying that prestige or good salaries are important. He/she may be saying that helping people is important. The student may be saying that moving around, physical work is important. Acknowledging this and considering environments which provide for these values are critical in helping students discover and define interests.

Even if a student is interested in a specific job that seems to be a poor match, a job in that environment may fulfill the student's work values and needs. For example: John wants to be a doctor, but because of cognitive and physical limitations, this is probably not realistic. But other jobs within hospitals and nursing homes exist that would allow John to work in the medical field.

There are a wide range of interest inventories available on the market today. Many address the needs of non-readers, students with low reading skills and students who are fluent readers. Several are computer based and provide the student with a video description of various jobs that may be difficult to visit in the community. Further, there are several that are posted on the internet and students can take them online.

Refer to the Resources section of the kit for specific inventories and publishers. There are also some examples of student inventories provided for you in the Tools and Templates section.

Situational Assessment The most useful strategy for gaining meaningful information about a student's strengths, limitations and interests is to perform an assessment in an actual environment, doing real work tasks. This can be accomplished by defining specific tasks, teaching a student to perform them, and then observing the student while completing them.

This must be done in the actual work environment. Another way to accomplish this type of assessment is to evaluate a work environment based on requirements of the job such as hours, dress and grooming, communication with the public, physical skills, etc. Then, evaluate a student's ability to meet these requirements by observing him/her for a period of time working in the environment. This can sometimes by accomplished by setting up a try out or unpaid work experience with the employer. Then, if the student is able to meet the requirements, with or without accommodations, he/she may have an opportunity to be hired for pay.

The Job/Student Match worksheet included in Tab 7, Tools and Templates section of the kit provides a template for doing an environmental assessment and setting up a situational assessment.

Environmental Assessment Like situational assessment, evaluating an environment and then matching a student's skills and interests to that environment and the job tasks required, provides an excellent means for gathering useful information. Often, a student may express interest in a specific career or in a particular type of environment. In looking at other assessment information, it may be determined that the student would not be able to perform the desired career, but may find great success and interest in working in that environment. Other jobs in that environment should be evaluated with the skills of the student in mind. If an apparent match is found, the student should have an opportunity to participate in a situational assessment. Students are involved in activities at home, in school, and in the community that provide ready assessment opportunities. At these times, parents or the school staff accompanying the student(s) should determine specific skills to be assessed during the activity. Whether the environment is in the school building, at home, in a grocery store or at the mall, a variety of skills and behaviors related to work can be evaluated. Use these opportunities to learn about the student. Observations in classrooms and student's reports of their abilities to advocate for the accommodations needed in general education classes can also provide assessment information related to work. The ability to advocate and explain needs to an employer is necessary skills for success. More information and activities to help you consider jobs in different environments are provided in the Career Development section of the Toolkit.

Job/Vocational Program Tryouts Try outs are assessments based on a specific occupation and occur in the actual environment of a job. Students complete a series of hands-on tasks that are required to do a particular job.

Tryouts are one of the best ways to assess a student's interest in a particular job and his or her skills to perform the job.

The assessor has the opportunity to witness the student's abilities and attitudes about the work while performing various tasks in the actual work environment. The following list of components should be included in a tryout assessment:

• *Analysis of knowledge, academic skills and thinking skills required.* Include opportunities for the student to perform some of the academic tasks required in this job. For example, if forms need to be filled out, the student should complete a sample form. If math calculations are required, the student should have toperform calculations on paper, using a calculator or in their heads in order to complete the task(s).

• Hands on activities that are actually done in a particular job or program. The assessor will be able to evaluate the student's speed in learning new information, frustration tolerance when faced with new material, ability to perform the task, and most importantly, the student's actual interest in the job.

• Task analysis of the hands on tasks that will be performed. These tasks should be broken down into step-by-step directions.

6• Self-evaluation Students should have the opportunity to evaluate their own abilities to do the job and their interest in the job and the environment.

• Assessor's evaluation The person assessing the student records the student's abilities, work tolerances, observed behaviors and interests. This can be done in the form of a short narrative report, completion of a checklist or a pre-made evaluation form.

SUMMARIZING, REPORTING AND DOCUMENTING THE DATA

Summarizing the Data All information available should be used to help students develop plans which will help them define or achieve future goals. This includes records, reports from teachers, employers, family members and the student, and formal and inform al assessment. The content of the career/vocational assessment summary should include a description of the student's current skills, the student's goals and suggestions for steps which will help the student achieve the goal.

Reporting the Data Results of transition assessments should be included in the Transition IEP so that the student and family have access to the information. It should be easy to read and understand, and have recommendations for steps to be taken to achieve the student's goals. Comments about accommodations that will be necessary should also be included.

Documenting the data It is important that all assessment information be documented in the IEP and/or other portfolio collections of student transition activities.
This information should be included in the assessment portion of the IEP, and can also be mentioned in strengths and needs, in development of goals and objectives and in related services .In addition, school staff should have a way of documenting transition skills learned within general education, job shadowing experiences, paid job experiences, volunteer activities, attendance at job or college fairs, participation in recreation and leisure activities both in school and in the community, and other experiences a student has during their years in school. This information can be recorded as part of the Transition Portfolio included with this kit's materials.

EXAMPLES USING FORMAL AND INFORMAL ASSESSMENTS FOR TRANSITION PLANNING

A student with specific learning disabilities A student may participate in a formal career/vocational assessment in the 11th grade that indicates that she is interested in becoming an auto mechanic and that she has the eye-hand coordination and tool use skills to perform the job.

A review of academic grades indicates that she received mostly C's in academic subjects with B's in art and music. She has not taken any mechanical courses. She started Algebra and dropped after the first three weeks when she felt it became too difficult. Her attendance is good and her behavior is generally appropriate.

Given the assessment information we have so far, she should actually try out her interests and skills in an auto mechanic environment while teachers, as well as potential employers assess her potential for work in the field of auto mechanics.

This could be accomplished by trying a variety of activities that reflect the skills needed to be an auto mechanic. The activities should occur in a technical program or in an auto shop. Sometimes, students get paid jobs working in the environment.

Their interest and skills can be assessed while they are working. Sometimes employers will allow a student to spend a short period of time observing and trying various tasks in the environment

A student with developmental disabilities

A student, who participates in a special education program designed for students with developmental disabilities, has no idea what he or she is interested in pursuing as a career.
Because of ongoing medical difficulties, this student will not be able to work full time. In fact, it is questionable whether he or she will be able to participate in competitive employment. Currently, the student is a sophomore in high school and is 16 years old.
Formal skills assessment may not be appropriate, as it will not reflect true skill or interest. However, an interest inventory that requires no reading, or work try outs, may offer some ideas about career opportunities that may have various job options in different environments. At this point, the options provided by volunteer experiences would be

appropriate for this student. Through these informal assessments (try outs) interest and ability can be

determined. Then a volunteer or paid job can be pursued based on the information gathered.

Combining formal and informal assessments to ensure appropriate career/vocational planning

A student has stated that he is interested in working in the field of auto mechanics. An informal interest inventory supports his interests. However, further information is needed regarding specific vocational skills that apply to this field.
A formal skills assessment or work sample may be given to help determine his abilities to perform tasks requiring work with his hands and with tools, his mechanical reasoning, and problem-solving skills.

The results suggest that the student has the motor and reasoning skills to perform the tasks. Further evaluation or data gathering should be done to assess academic ability as it applies to auto mechanics.

To be sure the student is truly interested in this field, based on actual knowledge of the tasks performed and the work environment, he should participate in a job shadow or tryout.

Teachers and parents can develop a wide variety of performance tasks that simulate "real-world" job tasks that students can perform to assess their knowledge, skills, and aptitudes as well as reveal interests in career areas. Some examples might include:

• classroom messenger • office assistant • copier assistant • technology monitor • cafeteria worker • snack bar • coaches assistant • jobs at home • community volunteer

Many of these opportunities can be developed in the school for younger students or when it is difficult to make arrangements for students to be away from the school building. In addition to helping students develop important work place skills through these activities, parents and teachers can use the assessment data collected in this way throughout the transition planning process.

FAMILY / PARENT INVOLVEMENT IN THE ASSESSMENT PROCESS

Parents are an integral part of the assessment and transition planning process from the very beginning.

They have an important part to play before, during, and after the evaluation. Just as each professional assesses the student's functioning and prepares an

assessment report, so should parents. Providing them with a worksheet that asks them to note their child's strengths and areas of difficulty at home and in the community can facilitate their involvement. Questionnaires, checklists and inventories provide parents with a structured way to think about their child's strengths and needs.

Use the following letter and the questionnaire designed for parents in Tab 7, Tools and Templates, (Parents – Sample Questionnaire) as examples and tools to assist you: Dear Parents, In order for us to get a better understanding of your child's strengths and areas of difficulty, it would be helpful if you and your family would provide the information listed on the attached questionnaire.

Your child may function differently at home than he or she does in school, and it is important that we know and understand these differences. Please complete the questionnaire and bring it with you to the meeting so that your information is included as we discuss your child's current level of functioning and needs.

Thank you for taking the time to participate with us in this important step in the planning process. We look forward to working with you. It is important that parents have the opportunity to think through and record their thoughts on their own and not through an interview process with a professional. It becomes particularly critical that the meeting be structured in such a way as to encourage and support parents to contribute their thoughts and observations. Parents report that there is nothing more degrading and humiliating than to have a professional report for them.
Providing parents with an assessment structure accomplishes several things.

First, recording their specific observations may help them conceptualizing the reality of their child's abilities. It also facilitates communication among family members.

Second, it gives credibility to parent's perceptions during the meeting when assessments and observations are discussed. Often when a parent disagrees with a professional observation, professionals may interpret this as parent denial of reality or an emotional reaction. However, when parents have been involved in the data collection process, the information they contribute is seen as more credible. Finally, any of these parent reports should be included in the student's profile in conjunction with the professional assessment reports

QUESTIONS FOCUSED ON PARENTS

1) Describe your approach with a parent who is upset with you – and you know you are right.

Idea:1 All teachers, no matter how experienced, will face a time when parents are frustrated with them. In most cases, it may not be because the teacher has done anything wrong. Frustration is often the result of unmet expectations or misunderstanding.
No matter the reason, there are a few things teachers can do to help ease the tension.

Seek First to Understand

In 7 Habits of Highly Effective People, Stephen Covey coined Habit 5 as "seek first to understand, then to be understood." Stephen Covey himself stated that it was one of the most challenging habits to master.
When meeting with a parent, don't try to defend yourself or your methods, at least not at first. Your first job is to listen, not with intent to respond, but with the intent to understand the parents' perspectives.

So what does active listening look like? It means two things: You should be able to restate (or reflect), in your own words what the parents are saying.

You should be able to state the emotion the parents are demonstrating. For example: "You sound frustrated and confused because I haven't communicated about..."

If you practice reflecting both their statements and emotions, most people will trust that you have heard them and they will likely even affirm that you are hearing them. Listen for it. You may surprise yourself in that you will also begin taking on a new perspective.

Don't forget about the second half of Habit 5: seek first to understand, then to be understood. After the parents believe that you understand them, you can then make your case and offer ideas. At this point, you can politely help the parents understand your perspective. Be sure you come prepared with examples and data supporting your case. Parents might slip back into previously voiced frustration. If they do, be prepared to return to listening mode. Sometimes, you may not get a chance to be understood, so don't try to push being understood.

Be Open to Ideas It's easy to get stuck in your own way of doing things or believe that your perspective is the right one.

Be aware of this tendency in yourself and notice if you slip into usual patterns. The parents know their child better than the school and they may provide some innovative ways to work with their student. If you and the parents are both stuck for ideas or can't agree, it may be time to seek help from others.

Ask for Help When you're stuck or need assistance, another teacher, the principal, counselor, or school psychologist can be excellent partners in thinking through the situation.
The principal can be especially helpful if you reach an impasse with the parents and can't come to an agreement.

The principal can bring forth resources that you may not have thought of and can provide the parents reassurance of follow through. School psychologists and counselors can be helpful in thinking through and supporting behavioral or emotional challenges.

Communicate the Positives This one is so important. Always communicate positive attributes about the student to the parents and show them that you care about their student's success. If your communication is primarily about negative behavior or lagging academics, don't be surprised if the parents react negatively or defensively. Tell them, specifically, what you love about their student. Demonstrate how excited you are when the student makes good choices and experiences success. Parents will begin to assume that you have good intentions if they know you care. Occasionally, you will encounter a student who is a significant challenge to your abilities as a teacher. See this as a learning opportunity. The difference between a good teacher and a great teacher is being willing to take on the challenge of learning how to work with even the most challenging students. When parents see this willingness to learn and to help their student, they will see how much you care.

Idea:2 Types of complaints No matter how experienced you are, all school leaders receive complaints from time to time. These can range from informal, verbal comments up to formal, written complaints; from minor to major concerns. They may come from students, staff, parents, or even members of the public.

They could be about students, teaching or non-teaching staff, you, the board, your school policies, or school events. Some you might be ready for, others will come out of the blue and surprise you. Complaints may escalate rapidly unless they are well managed.

It is better to have processes in place and rarely need them than to have nothing in place and end up with an issue that has the potential to flare up. One principal suggests you "deal with the complaint at the lowest level possible.
An escalated complaint is like a hurricane; the more emotional the heat, the more ferocious it becomes."
Is it a complaint? It is not always obvious when someone is making a complaint, so be alert to the possibility.
Ask, "Are you making a complaint?" Find out whether they have seen your school's complaints policy.
Make a note of the response you receive. Complaints can be made in the form of softly presented expressions of concern about something or someone.
These can often be missed by busy principals and grow in seriousness. If this happens, a complainant could justifiably say, "I asked you to do something about this 6 months ago!"
However, you don't want to be over-reactive, so seeking clarification at an early stage is important.
If it seems tricky, don't hope it will just go away. It won't. Involving the board If the complaint is made to you, use your judgment.
Try to achieve resolution at the lowest level possible. Don't involve the board unless you feel you are going to need help. If you think things might escalate, advise the board chair of the measures you're taking so that he/she will not suddenly be surprised by what has become a major concern. You may also need to alert the school's insurer if the complaint is "high level" - for example, if it could become a personal grievance case. If a complaint is addressed to the board, it must go to the board. When a complaint is made to the board, it's not your decision.
You will play whatever role the board requires of you. For example, you might be asked to gather and pass on the evidence.
If you collect and present the evidence, natural justice says you should not be involved in any judgment – let the board make the decision. If the complaint is about you, the board must handle it without your involvement, but with your knowledge.

Being prepared Check your school policy You need a process ready to follow that follows the principles of natural justice and is respectful. If you're new to the school, check whether there's a policy for dealing with complaints and when it was last reviewed – every three years is an ideal goal. If there is no policy, develop one with your board of trustees. When checking your policy, ask:
• Does it conform to best practice and is it open to legal scrutiny?

• Has the board of trustees ratified the policy?
• Does it include a flowchart of the process which is easy to follow?
• Is it inclusive? Does it reflect our community?
• Is it available in the languages used in our community?
• Have we given copies to parents or whānau?
• Is it easy to find on our school website?

Check employment agreements and rules Be familiar with the requirements and processes set out in the employment agreements of teachers and other staff members. Know what you must report to the Education Council and how to do that. Employment agreements - Ministry of Education Reporting a concern – Teaching Council

Seek advice If in doubt always seek advice. Contact the advisory service or your sector representative group. They are always there to provide advice and guidance and it's better to talk with them than to try and handle things on your own, especially if you are inexperienced or unsure in the particular situation. *Advisory and support center*

When you receive a complaint Listen Let the complainant have their say.

Make it clear that you have heard the complaint. Say something like, "Thanks for letting me know. I'll follow this up and get back to you by ..." Name a time that is easy to achieve and contact the complainant with your progress report towards resolution of the issue.
Make the complainant feel that you value their coming to you. Do this even if they are angry. Remain calm even if what is being said seems unfair.
You are the one in control of the situation. Write down the specifics of the complaint. You might need to get the complainant to pause while you gather things to write with.
Check back that you have the details right. If it seems appropriate, ask them to write down the complaint as well, so that you can compare what you have written with what they said.
Keep this written documentation safe, as you may need it later.

Investigate Depending on the nature of the

complaint, you will probably not need to respond straight away, other than to thank the complainant for letting you know.

However, if you deem the complaint to be serious, for example if it involves the safety of a child or staff member, you may need to take immediate

action before you can begin an investigation. This may involve the removal of a person, or contacting external support. Do not assume blame on anyone's part until you have gathered all the facts.

Make a judgment call about the time you need to deal with this complaint. Is it something that you can leave for a little while, or something that requires nipping in the bud now?

Ask yourself what the consequences of not dealing with the complaint immediately are likely to be. It is possible that the complainant will want an instant response.

Reassure them that you will give them a response as soon as you have had time to consider it. Use this time to assess the gravity of the complaint, and then you can priorities it.

Don't leave dealing with it for too long, though. Small issues can grow out of all proportion if they are not dealt with smartly. The priority scale you might use will probably be: now, later today, tomorrow or the day after, rather than next week.

Inform where necessary Let everyone who needs to know, know what is going on. Any staff member who is the subject of a complaint must be told about it and any likely investigation of it as soon as the complaint is received. Tell all parties that discussions are confidential.
Keep those who are affected informed about what is happening, especially if the investigation takes longer than expected. Clear communications will help people to feel confident that you are handling the situation appropriately.
Procedure must be strictly followed or you might find yourself in an employment-related situation. There has been at least one case where a person was not told of a serious accusation until several weeks later, after an investigation had been carried out to determine whether an offence had occurred. Because of this procedural omission, the person was found not guilty in court and the board was required to pay the person $40,000.
You should call on the assistance of your sector representative group to help you follow this procedure correctly. Taking too long to act invites speculation and encourages those who don't need to know to become involved.

When you have the evidence Seek to resolve the issue Keep a record of everything. Consider all possible resolutions and possible unintended outcomes.
You might want to discuss these with a trusted colleague, your sector representative group.

Meet with the complainant to convey your decision or to discuss the options for resolving the issue. If the complaint involves two parties, that is, one person complaining about another person, you might need to decide whether to bring the parties together to try to achieve a resolution.

Depending on the seriousness of the complaint, you might need assistance to plan and manage this process. Again, use one of the services available to you. However, in more difficult cases this may not be an option. Make a decision.
Acknowledge any errors made, if necessary. Ask the complainant whether he/she is happy with the outcome. If not, offer further options that may be taken. Follow up with a letter to the complainant detailing the discussion, the agreement, if any, you have reached, and the intended actions.
If the complaint involves an employee of the school, then you may need to put copies of the complaint, letter and resolution on the employee's file.

2) What are some methods of communicating student progress to parents other than report cards?
It's challenging for a teacher to find the time to make parent phone calls after a long day in the classroom, with grading and lesson planning still left to do.
There is often no opportunity during the day to write notes home and update charts with individualized grades for each child.
But communicating with parents is an important component of the learning experience. When multiple people are involved in a student's learning, the student is more likely to be successful.
Building a team to support a student starts with trust and open lines of communication.
Communication is the foundation of parent and teacher relationships.
Teachers must find efficient and creative ways to communicate with parents. Parent involvement connects parents to classroom teachers across all grades and ultimately supports learning for all children.
To communicate effectively and efficiently, teachers can use different tools to structure their

feedback to parents.

Why parent-teacher communication is important Teacher-parent communication is critical for a student's academic and social success. Parental involvement requires teachers and parents to connect regularly, allowing parents to be involved in school learning while teachers can gather information about the student outside the

classroom. Parent involvement is also a key element in advancing school culture and helps parents and teachers develop a relationship in and out of the classroom. Open communication lines help teachers share good feedback and constructive suggestions with families.

Parent-teacher communication strategies Students feel supported when both their parents and teachers are involved in their education, which in turn encourages positive school behavior. This intentional support for students also has an impact on academic achievement. Building parent-teacher relationships takes work and can be time-consuming. That's why we've gathered some efficient and effective ways for teachers to communicate with parents so that both parties are knowledgeable about a student.

Verbal and written communication Effective communication is the most important point between parent and teacher relationships. The classroom teacher can leverage parental involvement to connect parents to their child's education. Here are some ways parents and students can begin to build their relationships with the teacher by relying on verbal and written forms of communication.
Annual open houses—This annual school event allows for parents to meet teachers and learn about classroom structures, homework, and behavior expectations. During this time, parents can learn more about their student's classroom environment and begin to develop an understanding of the experience of being in class.
Parent-teacher conferences—These meetings between guardians and teachers are a great way to report student progress and allow time to ask student-specific questions.
Parent-teacher conferences can be set up during different times of the year or centered around grade level milestones like report cards or testing.
 Parent-teacher association group—These groups connect parents and children to the school community. They serve as support for school leadership, and they work towards facilitating positive relationships between parents and teachers.
Pro tip: Create parent-teacher groups that welcome all families and are thoughtful and inclusive about ways to keep families engaged.
Phone calls and emails—Phone calls and emails are a quick and convenient way to connect parents and teachers. Calls and emails can be scheduled for extended conversation or can be good for a quick connection. Pro tip: Don't always make calls or send emails for negative behaviors. Reward students by complimenting their positive behaviors or contributions to the class.

Digital communication Communication tools and apps like Unified Classroom® Behavior Support offer a few ways for teachers to communicate student progress with parents. Digital parent-teacher communication uses technology in education spaces to share information.
Family Portal—This portal provides parents with student reports in real-time. Teachers can share student information and exchange messages via computer or mobile devices.
Social media classroom page—Having a social media page allows teachers to post announcements and content for parents to access on their own. Teachers can present important documents or materials and communicate with families.
Student behavior reports—This digital document can be used to update parents on student behaviors and progress. It is consistent with the PBIS incentives for students. Each school staff person with access to the reports can add details about the student throughout the day. Parents then know what is going on with their child or children and can monitor behavior and progress.
Student agendas—Student agendas can be digital tools that are emailed to parents weekly so that parents stay current with their student's workload. This agenda also provides structure to student learning. Elementary school teachers use agendas or lists so that students are clear about what to expect for the day, helping to manage behavior and classroom expectations.
Classroom website—Classroom websites can connect students and families with information. Social media websites, student agendas, and other key information can be shared and visible to all. Teachers can communicate to individuals on classroom progress, projects, and school information. Some websites also include a parent-teacher communication portal for direct communication access.
Recording a podcast—This audio platform will inform parents about grades, homework, and class projects and will benefit families who want to learn from each other. Parents will not have to wait for their kids to share their lessons because they can hear about it on the podcast. The podcast can also include school announcements and updates on

student work.

Strive to create a relationship When planning actual communication strategies or ways to increase family involvement in elementary school programs, parent partnerships are important for supporting classroom work.
These partnerships might include volunteer hours, contributing supplies, or even supporting class learning by participating in a lesson.

Most parents are very interested in their child's education, and regular communication between the educators and parents is a great benefit. If a student is having a challenge in school, teachers and parents can work together because they have already developed a relationship that allows them to collaborate on interventions.
Educators can set an example of communication strategies that will positively impact student learning, class behavior, and academic achievement (including homework and lessons) through effective communication.
School leaders can champion this communication work by also engaging with families. School leaders who are thoughtful about the school culture and climate can leverage some of these practices to engage families.
Six Tips for Communicating Student Progress to Parents Mumble the words "report card" and watch teachers shudder with dread. When report cards are due, we dash madly to our school-issued computers to compile weeks' worth of data into a single number or letter. We work into the night. Afterward, we struggle with the feeling that it wasn't enough. The truth is that it's rarely enough.
Report cards typically don't paint a complete picture of a student's progress. Parents often want and appreciate more. And they deserve more. When parents and teachers work together, the impact on student progress can be significant. But the parent-teacher partnership, like any other, won't work without communication.

3) How do you feel about parent contact?

Parent benefits Positive parent-school communications benefit parents. The manner in which schools communicate and interact with parents affects the extent and quality of parents' home involvement with their children's learning. For example, schools that communicate bad news about student performance more often than recognizing students' excellence will discourage parent involvement by making parents feel they cannot effectively help their children.

Parents also benefit from being involved in their children's education by getting ideas from school on how to help and support their children, and by learning more about the school's academic program and how it works.

Perhaps most important, parents benefit by becoming more confident about the value of their school involvement. Parents develop a greater appreciation for the important role they play in their children's education.

When communicating with parents, consider your remarks in relation to the three categories that influence how parents participate.
For example, are you communicating about: • Classroom learning activities? • The child's accomplishments? • How the parents can help at home with their child's learning?

Student benefits Substantial evidence exists showing that parent involvement benefits students, including raising their academic achievement.

There are other advantages for children when parents become involved — namely, increased motivation for learning, improved behavior, more regular attendance, and a more positive attitude about homework and school in general. Teacher benefits Research shows that parental involvement can free teachers to focus more on the task of teaching children.

Also, by having more contact with parents, teachers learn more about students' needs and home environment, which is information they can apply toward better meeting those needs. Parents who are involved tend to have a more positive view of teachers, which results in improved teacher morale.

Good two-way communication Good two-way communication between families and schools is necessary for your students' success. Not surprisingly, research shows that the more parents and teachers share relevant information with each other about a student, the better equipped both will be to help that student achieve academically.

Opportunities for two-way communication include: ➢ Parent conferences ➢ Parent-teacher organizations or school community councils ➢ Weekly or monthly folders of student work sent home for parent review and comment ➢ Phone calls ➢ E-mail or school website ➢ Communication strategies ➢ Personal contact, including conferences, home visits, telephone calls, and curriculum nights or open houses, seems to be the most effective form of communication and may be among the most familiar.

However, the establishment of effective school-home communication has grown more complex as society has changed.

The great diversity among families means that it is not possible to rely on a single method of communication that will reach all homes with a given message. It is essential that a variety of strategies, adapted to the needs of particular families and their schedules, be incorporated into an overall plan. Some strategies to consider include:

➢ Parent newsletters ➢ Annual open houses ➢ Curriculum nights ➢ Home visits (where applicable) ➢ Phone calls ➢ Annual school calendars ➢ Inserts in local newspapers ➢ Annual grandparents or "special persons" days ➢ Board of Education spokesperson or communications officer at PTA meetings ➢ Homework hotlines ➢ Annual field days ➢ Notices and handouts in local markets, clinics, churches, mosques, temples, or other gathering sites ➢ Website for the school ➢ Workshops for parents ➢ Communications that are focused on fathers as well as mothers.

Effective communication strategies involve:
Initiation: Teachers should initiate contact as soon as they know which students will be in their classroom for the school year. Contact can occur by means of an introductory phone call or a letter to the home introducing yourself to the parents and establishing expectations.
Timeliness: Adults should make contact soon after a problem has been identified, so a timely solution can be found. Waiting too long can create new problems, possibly through the frustration of those involved.
Consistency and frequency: Parents want frequent, ongoing feedback about how their children are performing with homework.
Follow-through: Parents and teachers each want to see that the other will actually do what they say they will do. **Clarity and usefulness of communication:** Parents and teachers should have the information they need to help students, in a form and language that makes sense to them.
Surprise a parent Parents are not accustomed to hearing unsolicited positive comments from teachers about their children, especially in a phone call from the school. Imagine how you would feel, as a parent, if you were contacted by a teacher or the school principal and told that your son or daughter was doing well in school, or that your child had overcome a learning or behavior problem. When you make calls to share positive information with parents, be prepared for them to sound surprised-pleasantly surprised.
Research shows that school-home communication is greatly increased through personalized positive telephone contact between teachers and parents. Remember, when a phone call from school conveys good news, the atmosphere between home and school improves. When you have good news to share, why wait? Make the call and start a positive relationship with a parent.

Phone guidelines Sometimes, as a new teacher, it's difficult to make the first call to a parent or guardian. Preparing for the call will make it easier. Before making a call, write down the reasons for the call. One reason can be simply to introduce yourself to the parent or guardian.
Here are several guidelines you can use as you prepare:
• Introduce yourself
• Tell the parents what their child is studying
• Invite the parents to an open house and/or other school functions
• Comment on their child's progress • Inform them of their child's achievements (e.g., "Student of the Week")
• Inform them of their child's strengths or share an anecdote.

4) Write a letter to a parent explaining why you will not recommend moving the child to a higher grade for your subject grouping.

What is an academic letter of recommendation? An academic recommendation letter is a document that details a student's academic achievements, character and goals.

Teachers, guidance counselors, school administrators, club organizers and coaches often have ample evidence of a student's capabilities.

They are often the most qualified sources to write academic letters of recommendation that suggest how the student will fit into the new university or career.
Academic letters of recommendation can supplement a student's transcript to help organizations better understand who the student is and what they aspire to.
They can also complement a student's resume and cover letter to a company to provide more insight into their school-related accomplishments.

An academic recommendation includes several types of letters, including:
➢ College recommendation letters ➢ Graduate school recommendation letters ➢ Job application recommendation letters ➢ Letters to gain financial aid ➢ Letters to gain teaching assistant employment at a university

The student may request a general letter of recommendation to be used for several university admissions or job applications. Otherwise, it's best to address the letter to a specific person or a university admissions office or a company's human resources department.

How to write an academic recommendation letter
These steps will help guide you as you write an academic letter of recommendation.

Include the following information to help ensure your academic recommendation letter sets your student apart from other applicants:

1. Address the letter. 2. Include a brief introduction. 3. Outline the student's qualifications. 4. Describe a time that the student impressed you. 5. End the letter with a particular endorsement. 6. Provide your contact information.

1. Address the letter It's important to understand who will be reading your letter so you can provide appropriate information tailored to their program or company in your letter. Ask your student who to address the letter of recommendation to. If they're applying to a specific position or school, then address the letter to the hiring manager or admissions director. If the student is applying to several programs, then address the letter "To Whom It May Concern."

2. Include a brief introduction In the first paragraph of the letter, introduce yourself by explaining who you are, your profession, expertise and your relationship to the student. Consider including how many years you've known the student and your impressions when you first met. Be sure to also state why you are writing by mentioning the position or program you recommend the student for. Detailing your qualifications and your intention at the beginning of your letter can help the reader trust your recommendation.

3. Outline the student's qualifications Next, an academic letter should include specific details of your student's time in school to prove their academic abilities. You should ask the student to provide you with a list of achievements and activities as well as their transcript or GPA so you can have a comprehensive perspective of their qualifications.

You can discuss the following areas to give the reader your endorsement:

Extracurricular activities: The student may be involved in a number of clubs, sports or other activities that make them a well-rounded individual. Consider selecting one or a few of these activities and expressing the skills and character traits the student has developed through them. Awards or recognitions: Your student referee may participate in academic or creative competitions or show consistent academic excellence. Discuss the awards they've won or the impressive grades they've maintained to illustrate the student's ability.

Academic specialties: Include your student's area of expertise or which subjects they're most passionate about.
This will help persuade your reader that your student is genuinely interested in the position or program they're applying to. Attitude and perspective: Include details about your student's positive character traits.
Workplaces and universities often value people who bring a positive attitude to their environment because it helps boost morale and improve working environments or academic relationships. Demonstration of improvement:
Describe your student's ambitions, and discuss how they improved in your class or finished a big project successfully. These items can demonstrate that your student works toward goals that will help the company grow or the university grow.

4. Describe a time that the student impressed you
As you highlight your student's character and skills, use specific anecdotes to help the university or company understand more details about the student's personality, drive and abilities.
Describe the student's situation, the actions they took to succeed and the results of the student's actions. By providing an objective and a result, you can demonstrate your student referee's ability to identify an opportunity and take steps to complete the task or improve the situation.

5. End the letter with a particular endorsement
You can make your recommendation letter more effective by directly relating the student's qualifications to the university or company to which they're applying.
In the final section of the recommendation letter, state specifically that you recommend the student, and highlight their potential contributions to the position or program.
To complete this element of the letter, consider also

asking the student for more information about the school or company and why they chose to apply. This valuable information can also be paired with your own research of the company or school to properly outline the student's compatibility.

6. Provide your contact information At the end of the recommendation letter, include your contact information and offer to provide any additional information the recipient may ask for. This allows your reader to gain a better understanding of the student, and it gives you an opportunity to be an even better advocate for the student. Do you need help with your resume? Academic recommendation letter examples Here are two examples of academic recommendation letters from teachers. The first example gives you a guide to writing a general letter of recommendation that a student could use for several applications. You can use these to help you write your letter of recommendation:

Example 1: *General letter of recommendation for a college student To Whom It May Concern:* I have had the pleasure of working closely with Shirley Rodriguez for the past three years as she pursues her undergraduate degree in health science. My name is Jameson Quall, and I am Shirley's academic advisor.

I can wholeheartedly recommend Shirley and confidently say that she will make a great addition to your company. From the first time I met Shirley in my Anatomy Foundations course, she has impressed me with her knowledge and ambition.

She participated in every discussion and performed exceptionally well on all of her assignments. Our sports trainers were so impressed with Shirley that they chose her as a lead student aide for the sports training program.

I've watched her work with injured college athletes with compassion and care. She understands the holistic approach it takes to keep injured players positive during their recovery. I believe she has the drive to be a successful physical therapist or sports physiologist, and your work placement program will help her pursue this goal. She ranks in the top 5% of our sports science program at James Clever University. She is one of the brightest students I've advised in several years, so I am convinced that Shirley will prove to be a pivotal asset to your company.

I would be happy to further discuss Shirley's skills and charismatic nature with you.
Feel free to call me at 456-345-7778, or email me at jameson.quall@jcu.edu.
Sincerest regards,

James Quall Program Director,
Health Sciences
James Clever University

Sample:2

Dear Admission Committee, I am pleased to recommend Anita School, who has been a student in my math class for the past three years. During that time, I have come to know her as a strong student and a role model for her peers. Anita is a rare type of student who combines exceptional natural ability with a willingness and eagerness to learn. Anita is able to help her peers with difficult mathematical concepts, but does so in a way that is both practical and non-condescending. Although she is aware of her natural ability in the area of mathematics, Anita is constantly challenging herself. She is part of the

school's Mathletics Team, which challenges local college/university students in mathematical competitions.
She is also active in the community of the school by being a member of Greenpeace, and a cheerleader, while also playing defense on our school's soccer team. Anita would make an excellent candidate for early admissions.
I recommend her without hesitation. Should you have any questions, please feel free to contact me.

QUESTIONS FOCUSED ON PERSONAL QUALITIES

1) Why have you selected teaching as a profession?

I can provide some common reasons why people choose teaching as a profession:

1. Passion for Education: Many individuals are passionate about education and see teaching as a way to make a positive impact on the lives of students.

2. Desire to Make a Difference: Teachers have the opportunity to shape the future by helping students learn and grow academically, socially, and emotionally.

3. Love of Learning: Teaching allows individuals to continue learning and exploring new ideas while sharing their knowledge with others.

4. Influence of Role Models: Positive experiences with teachers or mentors can inspire individuals to pursue a career in education.

5. Job Satisfaction: Teaching can be a rewarding profession that provides a sense of fulfillment and satisfaction from seeing students succeed.

6. Work-Life Balance: Some people are attracted to teaching because of the relatively stable work hours and vacation periods, which can provide a better work-life balance compared to other professions.

7. Creativity and Innovation: Teaching offers opportunities for creativity and innovation in lesson planning, instructional strategies, and curriculum development.

8. Community Impact: Teachers play an important role in their communities and have the opportunity to contribute to the growth and development of future generations.

These are just a few reasons why individuals may choose teaching as a profession. Each person's motivations may be unique and influenced by their personal experiences, values, and goals.

2) Tell us about yourself and why are you interested in this school district and/or position?

I can provide some general information on why someone might be interested in a particular school district or position:

1. Alignment with Personal Values: Individuals may be drawn to a school district or position that aligns with their personal values and beliefs about education.

2. Professional Growth Opportunities: Some may be interested in a school district or position that offers opportunities for professional growth and advancement.

3. Community Impact: Others may be attracted to a school district or position that allows them to make a positive impact on the local community.

4. Innovative Practices: Individuals may be interested in a school district or position that embraces innovative teaching practices and approaches to education.

5. Supportive Work Environment: Some may seek a school district or position that offers a supportive work environment and opportunities for collaboration with colleagues.

6. Student Population: Others may be interested in a school district or position that serves a particular student population, such as diverse or underserved communities.

7. Location: The location of the school district or position may also be a factor, with some individuals preferring urban, suburban, or rural settings.

8. Professional Challenge: Some may be motivated by the challenge of working in a school district or position that presents unique challenges and opportunities for growth.

These are just a few reasons why someone might be interested in a specific school district or position. Each individual's motivations may vary based on their background, experiences, and goals.

3) What do you consider to be your major strength you bring to the classroom?

As a teacher, one major strength I bring to the classroom is my ability to connect with students and build positive relationships. I believe that establishing a supportive and trusting relationship with each student is essential for creating a conducive learning environment. This allows me to better understand their individual needs, motivations, and learning styles, enabling me to tailor my teaching approach to meet their needs effectively. Additionally, my enthusiasm for the subject matter and dedication to student success help to inspire and motivate my students to achieve their full potential.

List of 15 Strengths & Qualities of a Good Teacher

1. Strong Communication Skills and Interpersonal Skills
2. Active Listening
3. Collaborative
4. Adaptability
5. Engaging and Exciting
6. Empathetic
7. Patience
8. Real-World Learning is Prioritized
9. Great Teachers Share Their Best Practices
10. Never Stop Learning
11. Organizational Abilities
12. Passion for Teaching
13. Problem Solving
14. Ability to Simplify Concepts
15. Creativity

4) What do you believe is the one area you want to work on improving?

As a teacher, one area I want to work on improving

is my ability to effectively differentiate instruction to meet the diverse needs of all students in my classroom.

While I strive to create inclusive learning environments, I recognize that there is always room for improvement in this area. I am committed to exploring new strategies and techniques to better support students with varying learning styles, abilities, and backgrounds, ensuring that all students have the opportunity to succeed.

What can teachers improve on?

Self-evaluation Change and evolution require self-awareness. Educators must cultivate the ability to see themselves clearly and objectively through reflection and self-analysis. This way, they see what is happening around them, learn from the situation, and can be able to make the necessary adjustments.

We can divide this process of self-evaluation into three fundamental phases:
• First, a teacher must recognize there is a need for change, both within and around them. Detecting that something goes wrong it is the first step towards improvement;
• Secondly, they have to determine what areas of their teaching need the most attention. Before setting their goals, they have to figure out which are their strengths and weaknesses;
• Thirdly, they must decide on key areas of growth and commit to them. When it comes to reflecting on the classroom experience, the students' small clues and positive feedback is a rich source of information.

That is, paying attention to what students comment in class is an effective way to find out strengths. Usually, we can find that there are recurring themes of conversation which can help identify what is working well or not.

Finding the positive in the students' daily evaluations is a sure way to:
• Pinpoint which strategies are the best to engage their attention and interest;
• Consider the implementation of small progressive changes.

In conclusion, self-evaluation is a critical step in any process of growth and change. Generally, the path towards improvement becomes clearer when a teacher is willing to admit mistakes and put their students' needs first.

Pedagogical learning Teachers' efficacy is, arguably, the product of three aspects:
• Deep knowledge of the subject-matter or content area;
• Professional experience;
• Development of teaching skills. Consequently, due to the fast changes in technology and society, an educator must brush up on their pedagogy to stay relevant.

Those changes greatly affect the way students learn and the way teachers teach, so there is always room for pedagogical improvement. As a result, learning "how to teach" and "how students learn" become priorities in a teacher's journey towards significant growth.

In order to improve the way they teach, an instructor can focus on these tasks:
• Brush up on the basics; that is, come back to what they once learned but it is now partly forgotten, and renew those skills;

• Learn about new theories which can provide useful information about how people learn best;
• Learn about new teaching strategies and techniques which can be actually implemented in the classroom;
• Improve the way they differentiate instruction in order to meet the individual learning needs of each student.

This way, all students have the same opportunities to reach the common learning goals. We can safely affirm that methodology is at the core of the success of the learning and teaching process; so, studying the best approaches and adapting them effectively to their classroom's idiosyncrasies is a course of action worth being taken by any committed teacher. Find more about how teachers can improve their lessons by reading our blog article.

What communication skills are required to grow as a teacher?
An educator willing to improve their performance in class should master these communication skills:
• Active listening;
• Speaking clearly and concisely;
• Non-verbal language (keep eye contact, smile, energetic body language to transmit enthusiasm);
• Consistent constructive feedback;
• Deliver instruction in a way that lessons keep students involved and engaged;
• Management of the classroom in an observant and empathic way.

5) **What characterizes required for innovative teacher?**

An innovative teacher is characterized by several key traits and practices that set them apart in the field of education. These include:

1. Creativity: Innovative teachers are creative in their approach to teaching, finding new and engaging ways to present information and inspire learning.

2. Adaptability: They are adaptable and willing to try new strategies and technologies to meet the evolving needs of their students.

3. Collaboration: Innovative teachers collaborate with colleagues, students, and parents to enhance the learning experience and share best practices.

4. Critical Thinking: They encourage critical thinking and problem-solving skills in their students, challenging them to think beyond the textbook.

5. Flexibility: They are flexible in their teaching methods, adjusting their approach based on student feedback and learning outcomes.

6. Lifelong Learning: Innovative teachers are **committed to lifelong learning, continuously** seeking out new ideas and approaches to improve their practice.

7. Risk-taking: They are willing to take risks and try new things, even if they may not always succeed.

8. Empathy: They demonstrate empathy and understanding towards their students, recognizing and addressing their individual needs and challenges.

9. Reflective Practice: They engage in reflective practice, regularly evaluating their teaching methods and outcomes to identify areas for improvement.

10. Technology Integration: They effectively integrate technology into their teaching to enhance student learning and engagement.

Overall, an innovative teacher is someone who is passionate about education, open to change, and dedicated to creating dynamic and meaningful learning experiences for their students.

6) What distinguishes you from another candidate?
1. Unique Teaching Approach: Your approach to teaching, including any innovative methods or strategies you use, could set you apart from other candidates.

2. Specialized Knowledge or Skills: If you have specialized knowledge or skills in a particular area, such as technology integration, special education, or language instruction, that could distinguish you from other candidates.

3. Experience and Track Record: Your experience and track record of success as a teacher, including any awards, recognition, or accomplishments, could make you stand out.

4. Passion and Enthusiasm: Your passion for teaching and enthusiasm for your subject matter could make a strong impression on employers.

5. Commitment to Professional Development: Your commitment to ongoing professional development and learning could demonstrate your dedication to being the best teacher you can be.

6. Strong Interpersonal Skills: Your ability to connect with students, parents, and colleagues could distinguish you as a candidate who is easy to work with and effective in building relationships.

7. Involvement in the Community: Your involvement in the school community or broader community through volunteer work, extracurricular activities, or other initiatives could demonstrate your commitment to making a difference.

These are just a few examples of factors that could distinguish you from other candidates in a teaching job application or interview. Each candidate is unique, and it's important to highlight your own strengths and qualities that make you a great fit for the position.

7) Who influenced your choice to become a teacher? How?

Answer your own words!

I can share some common influences that may lead individuals to choose a career in teaching:

1. Teachers or Mentors: Many people are influenced by the positive experiences they had with teachers or mentors who inspired them and made a difference in their lives.

2. Family Members: Family members who are teachers or who value education may influence someone to pursue a career in teaching.

3. Personal Values: Some individuals are drawn to teaching because they value education and see it as a way to make a positive impact on society.

4. Passion for a Subject: A passion for a particular subject or field of study may inspire someone to

become a teacher and share their knowledge and enthusiasm with others.

5. Desire to Make a Difference: Many people choose teaching because they want to make a difference in the lives of students and contribute to their personal and academic growth.

6. Career Satisfaction: The satisfaction that comes from seeing students learn and grow can be a strong motivator for individuals to pursue a career in teaching.

These are just a few examples of influences that may lead someone to become a teacher. Each person's journey to teaching is unique, and there may be multiple influences that play a role in their decision.

8) What are your career goals, short term and long term?

As a teacher, my short-term career goals are to continue developing my teaching skills and classroom management techniques to create a positive and effective learning environment for my students. I also aim to build strong relationships with my students, colleagues, and parents to support student success.

In the long term, I aspire to take on leadership roles within the education field, such as becoming a department head, curriculum coordinator, or mentor teacher. I also hope to pursue further education and professional development opportunities to stay current with best practices in teaching and learning. Ultimately, my goal is to make a lasting impact on the lives of my students and contribute to the advancement of education as a whole.

Short term goals for teachers:

6 Most Common Improvement Goals for Teachers

- Classroom Organization.
- Self-development.
- Improve Student Learning.
- Inspiring Students.
- Personal Organization.
- Become a better teacher.

Long term goals for teachers: 10 Professional Development Goals for Teachers

- Advocating for Continuous Lifelong Learning.
- Earning National Board Certification.
- Sharpening Your Presentation Skills.
- Improving Classroom Management.
- Expanding the Role of Parents.
- Finding a Mentor.
- Adjusting Your Mindset.
- Taking Professional Development Courses

9) What do you bring to the community besides your educational background?

Besides my educational background, I bring a range of skills, experiences, and qualities to the community as a teacher. These include:

1. Leadership: I can serve as a leader and role model for students, demonstrating positive behaviors and values.

2. Communication Skills: I can communicate effectively with students, parents, and colleagues, fostering strong relationships and promoting collaboration.

3. Creativity: I can bring creativity to the classroom, developing engaging lesson plans and activities that inspire and motivate students.

4. Problem-Solving Skills: I can help students develop critical thinking and problem-solving skills, which are valuable both inside and outside the classroom.

5. Empathy and Compassion: I can show empathy and compassion towards students, helping them feel understood and supported.

6. Community Engagement: I can engage with the community through volunteer work, extracurricular activities, and partnerships with local organizations, enhancing the school's connection to the community.

7. Cultural Competence: I can promote cultural competence and diversity in the classroom, helping students develop a respect for different cultures and perspectives.

8. Commitment to Lifelong Learning: I can model a commitment to lifelong learning, showing students the importance of continued growth and development.

Overall, I strive to be a positive and active member of the community, contributing to the well-being and success of students, families, and the broader community.

10) Reason for leaving current school?

➢ I want to find new ways to advance as a professional educator. The position you have available includes responsibilities in line with how I'd like to develop my teaching skills.

➢ I'm looking for a bigger challenge to grow in my education career, and I couldn't job hunt part-time while working. It didn't seem ethical to use my former school's time to work on my own personal career goals. I left that position on excellent terms to devote the time needed to find an ideal new work situation.

➢ I'm relocating to this area due to personal circumstances and left my previous teaching position to make a move.

➢ After several years in my last teaching position, I'm looking for a school to contribute and grow in a team-oriented and collaborative environment like this campus.

➢ I am inspired to seek a new career challenge and an opportunity to use my technical skills and experience in a different capacity than I have in the past.

➢ As a recent graduate of my administrative leadership degree, I want to use my next position's educational background.

➢ Securing a role with more responsibility is my goal. I am ready and eager for a new teaching challenge.

11) Describe yourself as "the teacher"? What makes you an effective teacher?

As "the teacher," I see myself as a facilitator of learning, dedicated to nurturing the academic, social, and emotional growth of my students. My effectiveness as a teacher stems from several key qualities and practices:

1. Passion for Teaching: I am deeply passionate about education and committed to inspiring a love of learning in my students.

2. Student-Centered Approach: I prioritize the needs and interests of my students, tailoring my teaching to accommodate diverse learning styles and abilities.

3. Clear Communication: I communicate clearly and effectively, ensuring that students understand the material and feel comfortable asking questions.

4. Engaging Instruction: I use a variety of instructional strategies and resources to keep students engaged and motivated.

5. High Expectations: I set high expectations for my students and provide the support and guidance they need to meet and exceed those expectations.

6. Positive Classroom Environment: I create a positive and inclusive classroom environment where students feel safe, valued, and respected.

7. Reflective Practice: I regularly reflect on my teaching practices and seek feedback from students and colleagues to continuously improve.

8. Collaboration: I collaborate with colleagues, parents, and community members to support student learning and well-being.

9. Adaptability: I am adaptable and open to trying new approaches and technologies to enhance student learning.

10. Lifelong Learner: I am committed to my own professional development and lifelong learning, staying current with best practices in education.

Overall, I strive to be an effective teacher by creating a supportive and stimulating learning environment where every student has the opportunity to succeed and thrive.

12) What do you enjoy most about teaching?

What I enjoy most about teaching is the opportunity to make a positive impact on the lives of my students.
I love seeing the growth and development of each student, both academically and personally, throughout the school year. It's incredibly rewarding to witness the "aha" moments when students grasp a new concept or overcome a challenge.
I also enjoy the creativity and variety that comes with teaching, as each day brings new opportunities to engage with students and explore different teaching strategies. Overall, the joy of teaching comes from knowing that I am helping to shape the future by empowering and inspiring my students to reach their full potential.

These are just six of the reasons I love being a teacher:

1. Every child is different You learn quickly that children don't fit into stereotypes – the sporty one, quiet one, high achiever etc. It doesn't end up like that.

They all have different backgrounds and you get to see the children grow in all sorts of ways. You can support them with their home life and relationships with peers as well as their academic work – you just have to find a way in with each individual.

I had a girl who wouldn't read but I found out she likes cats so I found her a book with cats in and she loved it! Her dad then started buying her more cat books. Other children have specific needs. When I was at school there were only a few children with recognized special educational needs. Now there's much more awareness, you can have 10 pupils in a class with different needs that you need to support in some way to help them make progress.

2. You learn from teaching One of the things
I like about teaching in primary schools is teaching the range of subjects. I've never had one subject that I loved or excelled at more than the others, so primary teaching has allowed me to develop in all the subject areas I have to teach. This is what I try

to pass one to the children; you don't want them to think they're only good in one subject. It also means I never get tired of a curriculum area and that I'm developing my knowledge in a range of areas all the time.

You can't be an expert in everything all the time so you have to go away and research things before you teach it to the children. Teaching also keeps my technology skills up-to-date as schools are using new technology all the time.

For example, the children sometimes use iPads for tests now, which is helpful in making tests less scary – plus I get instant data back to see how they're doing. One of the schools I was in during my first year even has a 4D classroom!

3. You really do make a difference You get wins with both individuals and the whole class all the time but sometimes you can really transform a child's life. During one placement, a child had just joined the school from an African tribe.

He didn't speak much English and communicated by pointing. He was in Year 5 but was being given phonics classes with much younger children, which really upset him. The school were doing it so he learnt the basics but it wasn't helping due to the way he felt.

I started working with him on a one-to-one basis (when I was supporting the class teacher) and made sure the work I gave him was at his level but still related to the lesson (when I was teaching), rather than a separate activity. He also got sent in from playtime regularly because he was frustrated with not being able to communicate with his classmates so I also did extra reading with him.

These small changes had a big impact and his mum even started asking for extra work for him to do at home. By the end of my placement two months later, he was speaking and writing in full sentences and made progress in maths. When I left he gave me handshake and said, "Thank you very much, Miss." It was so lovely.

4. The children can surprise you! You cannot smile when you're working with children. The comments they come out with can amuse and surprise you!

They range from being told I'm like someone's mum, pupils who think I'm really young, those who ask how many children I have even though I'm only 20, to those who tell me they love me and bring in cards.

I even had one girl who would actively give me feedback on my lessons – for good and bad! But feedback from their point of view is actually really useful to help me to reflect on why a particular lesson was or wasn't successful.

The children are pretty open and honest generally as I also get compliments (and criticism) about my outfits!

5. Every day is different As the children are all different and we teach a variety of subjects, every day is different. For example, you could be working on a cross-curricular project about the rainforest, which might cover skills and knowledge in English, science, art, geography and history, but you equally might have a parent helper in for the day, take the children swimming or even have an external visitor in, such as a sports agency or supermarket to engage the children about healthy lifestyles.

We get involved in things like World Book Day and even had a maths day at my first placement school. We all dressed up as a number on the side of a die and did fun activities that related to real life. Maths can be a subject they either love or hate but the day really helped to them understand why it's useful and definitely improved their perception.

6. Schools are communities' Primary schools are usually small so everyone knows each other. You work as a team and can support each other.

In larger primary schools I've seen the teachers work as team, having the one who is strongest in English, for example, take the higher achievers in that subject; this plays to the teachers' strengths and helps the pupils' progress. If you're a community it's not like work.

For me it's more like going back to school myself as we're learning from each other and learning from the senior leadership team. You share ideas and can work together to implement them rather than being competitive like some industries. This follows all the way from the Head to teaching assistants; everyone has a valuable role to play in the school community.

13) If I were to contact your references, what do you think they would say about you?

If you were to contact my references, I believe they would say that I am a dedicated and passionate teacher who is committed to the success of my students.
They would likely mention my strong communication skills, my ability to connect with students and colleagues, and my willingness to go above and beyond to support the learning needs of all students.
They may also mention my creativity in lesson planning, my adaptability in the classroom, and my commitment to ongoing professional development.
Overall, I believe my references

would speak positively about my abilities as a teacher and my contributions to the school community.

Some ways that your references may describe you:

- High-integrity
- Accountable
- Reliable
- Punctual
- Accepting of feedback
- Confident
- Well-educated
- Honest
- Results-driven

14) What is your mission as a teacher?

As a teacher, my mission is to inspire and empower my students to become lifelong learners who are curious, critical thinkers, and compassionate members of society.
I aim to create a positive and inclusive learning environment where all students feel valued, supported, and challenged to reach their full potential.
My goal is to instill a love of learning in my students and equip them with the knowledge, skills, and mindset they need to succeed academically, personally, and professionally.
Ultimately, my mission is to make a meaningful and lasting impact on the lives of my students, helping them to become the best versions of themselves.

Achievement of my mission will lead to my students becoming independent and critical thinkers. Following after the teachers who have made a positive impact on my life, I will be a catalyst for academic and character development in my students. My mission as a teacher is to raise up students who will become future leaders by instilling morals so that they can create for us a better future. For me, this means that I may need to step aside at times and adjust my curriculum to what students enjoy learning. Projects will be student oriented and much of my lesson planning will be done around class time discussion.

I believe a student should enjoy learning and learn about practical, life-changing scenarios. However, there will be a structure in my classroom and a daily schedule that we follow along with basic rules which will be laid out for students during the beginning of the year. In my opinion students, if applicable, should be keeping up with recent times in the news, show more content.

As a teacher, this may mean stepping aside in the classroom and letting the students' become leaders in small group settings. I am a tool for students and will be prepared to help them in any way I can. Class discussions that go on should be thought provoking and relatable; students are always more likely to remember something when they can relate the topic back to themselves.

I will help bring up topics and subjects that should be focused on and allow my students to choose what kind of project or learning opportunity should go on to help them better understand and remember the subject matter. Stepping into the real world and showing students how what we are learning relates to adulthood is important as well

15) What are your beliefs about the significance of education?

I believe that education is one of the most powerful tools we have for transforming individuals and society. Education not only provides individuals with the knowledge and skills they need to succeed academically and professionally, but it also helps them develop critical thinking, problem-solving, and communication skills that are essential for navigating the complexities of the modern world.

Education is also key to promoting social mobility and reducing inequality. By providing all individuals with access to quality education, we can help level the playing field and create a more just and equitable society.

Furthermore, education plays a crucial role in fostering a sense of community and belonging. It helps individuals develop an understanding and appreciation of different cultures, perspectives, and ways of life, leading to greater empathy, tolerance, and respect for others.

Overall, I believe that education is a fundamental human right and a powerful force for positive change. It has the potential to empower individuals, strengthen communities, and transform the world for the better.

16) Tell me three things you believe about teaching.

Three things I believe about teaching are:

1. Teaching is a noble profession: Teaching is not just a job; it is a calling that requires passion, dedication, and a genuine desire to make a difference in the lives of others. Teachers have the

power to inspire, motivate, and empower students to reach their full potential.

2. Teaching is a lifelong learning process: Effective teaching requires continuous learning and growth. Teachers must stay current with best practices in education, adapt to the changing needs of students, and seek out opportunities for professional development.

3. Teaching is about more than just academics: While academic learning is important, teaching is also about fostering social, emotional, and ethical development in students. Teachers play a critical role in helping students develop empathy, resilience, and a sense of social responsibility.

17) what gives you pride as a teacher?

What gives me pride as a teacher is seeing my students succeed and grow both academically and personally. It is incredibly rewarding to witness the progress they make, whether it's mastering a difficult concept, achieving a high grade on a test, or demonstrating kindness and empathy towards others.
Knowing that I have played a role in their development and helped them become more confident, independent, and compassionate individuals fills me with pride and reaffirms my commitment to teaching.

18) Describe your fears of being a teacher.

Like other professions, teachers have their fair share of worries.

The most common worries teachers have are:
• The fear that your students may know more than you do
• Your student's welfare
• Your teaching quality
• The fear of making mistakes
• The fear of coming back to work after a holiday.

What are the Top Things Teachers Worry About

The Students' Welfare First, most teachers worry about their students' education and general welfare.

The primary reason why you are a teacher is that you have the passion to teach, you want your students to learn from your wealth of knowledge and experience. Irrespective of the fact that we are hired to teach, most of us find ourselves assuming the role of a disciplinarian, counsellor, and even

advocate. While students may appear to have very similar challenges, the truth is that everyone in your classroom has a unique set of attributes; peculiar to only them.
You can help fix some of these challenges, however, a lot of them likely occur outside your jurisdiction making it hard for you to help.

This, in turn, can affect your state of mind and leave you unduly troubled. Fortunately, most schools have school psychologists and guidance counsellors; they are best suited to handle such challenges.
Some of the other worries that teachers face are particularly related to 'learning.' Several teachers have adapted the use of culturally responsive and differentiated instruction teaching methods to deal with some of these challenges.

You too can adopt these methods and see how far it goes with your students.

Your Teaching Quality

Most teachers spend their working hours working with their students and delivering lessons.

We do research on the topic we want to teach our students, make lesson notes on it, and revise with the students to help them understand it and possibly, commit it to their memory.

Even with all this, it is not uncommon to see a lot of teachers worrying about their method and quality of teaching.

You must be able to do a self-evaluation about 'what' you teach your students. Are your lessons up-to-date?
Do you use the right methods to deliver your lessons? What were the reactions of the students to your lessons?
An in-depth consideration of these questions will help you fix some loopholes in your teaching method.
The Fear of Boring Your Students For a fact, you may think you're not very interesting. But, what should be important to you as a teacher is delivering excellent and interesting lessons to your students.

Engagement is (always) the key!

To begin with, make sure that the topic is of interest to you too. If it does not interest you as their teacher, the chances that it will interest your students are slim. Humans are creatures that learned how to read even before the introduction of alphabets and words. We knew how to read sensations and emotions; we take in information with our ears, eyes, and skin, which we send directly to the brain to process it for us. For a second, imagine that yourself pacing around your class, worrying that your students will be bored by your lesson. The resultant effect can be a less engaging classroom.

Your actions and inactions (other than speech) go a long to determine if your students end up bored.

When though you have the best of intentions, you've detached from your students. Now, what they are rather focused on is the nervousness that you are exuding with your futile attempt to appear interesting.
If you are not putting the right amount of energy into your practice to deliver noteworthy lectures, there is a high chance that your communications with your students will be boring.

On the flip side, if you think your lessons have (and they are) high value then there's a good chance that they do. The burning question that you should seek to answer is; what does your student consider valuable?

You'll begin to see a new world of possibilities opened before you when you find the right answer to this question.

The solution to this problem is simply to value all that you teach them! Genuinely try to get yourself interested. Understand why the lessons you are about to teach your students are important and constantly remind yourself of it while teaching.

As they are also humans, your students will perceive that you believe in what you are teaching them and see your interest.

Students May Know More Than I Do Ask yourself for a minute;
do you expect yourself to know all there is to a topic you are about to teach your students?

No doubt, every teacher in teaching a subject, will always want to deliver like an expert in the field. They also want their students to perceive that they have a thorough comprehension of what they are teaching.
The finest teaching method is one that helps students employ something they already understand or know and correlate it to what you are currently teaching them.

It is a gradual process as opposed to a whole seamless one.

Teaching ought to be a two-way affair where you are making inputs and your students are there to receive them and make outputs by asking for clarifications on things they don't understand and asking questions.
But, this feeling is quite different from imposing on yourself the expectation that you'd know and understand every concept in the topic more than any other person in the classroom.
The blatant truth is, you can't know everything there is to a topic. And also, when you don't have an immediate answer to a particular problem, don't pretend that you do.

Letting your students know you don't know and then finding out is much better than pretending. They'll appreciate it much more.

When you unnecessarily assume the role of a genius in the topic you are teaching, you rob yourself of two things. Stress-free lessons and optimum learning opportunities for your students.
Students who are always exposed to teachers who act like they are a supreme authority in a certain topic will not appreciate the fact that it is okay to make mistakes, find solutions, and seek the opinion of others.

Fear of Forgetting what You are Supposed to Know It is quite normal to forget some things

occasionally. Right?

In every lesson there's a lot of things to think about; how your lessons are progressing, your teaching methods, the names of your students, the right teaching materials to use, etc.

You can become distracted at any point; a student may disturb the class when they shift their desks, the back-benchers may decide to disturb just when you turn your back to write on the chalkboard, a favorite student appears to be troubled and that could bother you.

Scenarios like these will affect even the best teachers, and when they happen, it may lead to forgetfulness.

Don't put yourself under unnecessary pressure.
It is simply irrational to think that you'll be everything and remember everything, fill all the gaps, have the attention of all your students at the same time.

There are still other explanations as to why forgetfulness may set in. Psychologists say that sometimes, it can be a consequence of information overload. Or maybe trying to remember so many things at the same time i.e. there're so many things you want to communicate that you don't know which to say first.

How can you help yourself?

Plan your lessons to be as simple as possible. Know the topic you intend to teach and ensure that you simplify the most complex concepts for easy assimilation.

Lack of control

Most people heading a group would not feel comfortable if they can't wield a level of control over it.

Teachers are no different.

It is doesn't mean you're a control freak, rather it is the desire to have an organized environment that would facilitate learning and assimilation.

• What are your expectations for an organized class?
• Do you feel like you need to have complete control of your class?
• Does an unorganized class hamper your thought process thereby interfering with your teaching?

When you don't feel in control, you should start by asking yourself 'Why?' Are they genuine concerns or are they self-imposed thoughts that you can do away with by changing your thought patterns?

These are very important questions that make you understand why you are having these feelings and what you should do to fix them.

If you are too lenient with your students, try setting clear expectations next lesson. A good place to start is our managing misbehavior article.

The Fear of Making Mistakes Don't forget to remind yourself that it is human to err. No one is perfect!
Even the brightest minds may find it difficult to remember the right formula to solve simple arithmetic

Go out of your way and devise a method of taking challenges in stride without allowing your pupils to see you break a sweat.

For instance, you may decide to reward a student who pointed out an embarrassing mistake, instead of taking it personally: The old "congratulations for spotting my deliberate mistake" strategy! This makes it look more like an act of teaching and your students will surely appreciate you for it.

Conclusion We've covered some of the regular worries that teachers or prospective teachers have about their students and themselves.

19) Describe your heroes.

Points to Emphasize In properly answering questions about your heroes, there are a few points that you should emphasize.
• Clearly describe your heroes and your relation to them.
• Explain why they are your heroes.
• Share how they have influenced your life, decisions, career path, etc.
• Make a correlation between your heroes and the job you are applying for.
• Give a clear and concise answer and show a genuine connection.
Mistakes You Should Avoid

Properly answering this question can be tricky. Here are a few mistakes to avoid.
• Do not cut your answer short by just stating a name.
• Do not go into too great of detail about your heroes and explanations.
• Stay away from sharing a laundry list of heroes;

give one or two and share their correlating characteristics.
• Do not focus on several characteristics that cannot be related to the position. I'm sure that you've seen some concerns that you thought were pertinent to just you but now you know that it is something that troubles other teachers like yourself.

20) Would you describe yourself as a team player or individual achiever?

During a typical job interview, you'll most likely be asked many different questions related to the job and your qualifications. Some are straightforward, such as: "Why do you want to work for this company?"
And some are seemingly silly: "Do you believe in Bigfoot?" But from the practical questions to the just plain oddball ones, there is one that can stump a potential candidate—the preference of teamwork vs individual work. Now, the reason why this question is tricky is because there really isn't one "right" answer to give.
Does the employer want you to be a team player, and work with a group of employees, or do they prefer individuals who are more autonomous?
When it comes down to it, inquiring about a candidates preference in teamwork vs individual work seems to really be asking if you're an introvert or an extrovert. Chances are, you probably know which one you are.
Extroverts enjoy working with others, are oftentimes outgoing, and are energized when they're around others. Introverts, on the other hand, crave quiet time and solitude, and are at their best when they are alone While it may seem like there's only one choice that would satisfy a potential boss, in reality, there really are positives and negatives to working on a team and individually. We asked the FlexJobs Career Coaching team to unpack this topic with us, and provide tips on how to handle this tricky question.

Successfully Answering "Would you rather work on a team or alone?"

If you answer: "Work on a team."

The pros to working on a team: This might seem like the obvious answer to give. After all, collaboration is a key part of a successful team, and you might assume that your boss wants a new hire who can work well with other coworkers.
They don't want someone who is going to be antisocial or sit silently during meetings, you reason. Extroverted people can be exciting to be around, and their outgoing nature can make them quite likeable and amenable in a group setting.

The cons of working on a team: All that aside, stating that you prefer to work on a team could potentially be misconstrued by a hiring manager. They might think that you need other people's input and advice in order to make decisions. They could think that being on a team is a way to help you to get your own work done. And if you're applying for a remote job, it could be counted against you, since you'll need to know how to work independently in order to be successful.

If you answer: "Work alone."

The pros of working alone: Being able to work independently is a soft skill that many employers look for in potential new hires. So whether you're working in a regular office space or remotely, you're going to have to be able to work on your own at various times. Stating that you prefer to work alone conveys to an employer that you don't require much hand-holding to get the job done (which is a big bonus!). It shows that you're a good self-manager and most likely able to meet your deadlines without the interference of other team players.

The cons of working alone: Even if you prefer to work by yourself, you might be hesitant to admit it.

By stating that you enjoy working solo, you might imagine that your boss-to-be is thinking that you'll be holed up in your home office, unfriendly and unwilling to engage with your fellow colleagues. Plus, you may think that you are sending a message that you don't like people and would prefer to work alone.

21) Would you tell us what you have read in the past two months? Why have you done this reading?

Why employers ask questions about the last book you read ? Employers often use this question to start the interview and get to know you better. Learning about a recent book you've read can give an interviewer insight into your individual characteristics, personal values or hobbies outside of work.
If you're applying for a position that requires you to read many books, such as a librarian or teacher, the interviewer may ask this question to determine your literacy and reading comprehension skills.

How to answer "What is the last book you read?"

Here are some steps to help you answer a question about the last book you read:

1. **Choose a book** Consider what book you could discuss in an interview. You can choose any book that you've read recently and feel comfortable reviewing for another person. Think about some books you've read in the past year and choose a title in advance.

2. **Take notes** After you've chosen which book to talk about, write some brief notes about the main plot, themes or general topic. Writing down some details can help you remember more about the book if an interviewer asks you this question. Try to review your notes before the interview to refresh your memory about the book.

3. **Briefly explain the book** If an interviewer asks you this question, start with the title of the book and a brief explanation. Describe either the premise of the book if it's nonfiction or a plot summary for a fiction story. This helps introduce the interviewer to the book and can allow them to understand the essence of what you've read.

4. **Mention why you like the book** After the summary, discuss the aspects of the book that you particularly liked. If it's a nonfiction book, mention why this topic appeals to you. For a fiction book, pick a thought-provoking element, such as the plot,

characters or theme and try to link this aspect to one of your personal characteristics.

5. **Relate the book to the job position** Talking about books that you've read can provide you with an opportunity to further demonstrate the skills and characteristics that make you a qualified candidate for the position.
When describing the book, try to apply its contents to the job position. For example, if you're applying for a surgeon job, you can say that a book about motorcycle repair helps you improve your motor skills and your ability to see how smaller pieces affect a larger machine.

QUESTIONS FOCUSED ON TECHNICAL SKILLS

1) How would you apply technology to enhance instruction and increase student learning and achievement?
Almost 90 years ago, an overhead projector was used to display images in a classroom for the first time. A few decades later, Texas Instruments invented the handheld calculator. In the 1980s, schools started introducing Apple Macintosh computers to the classroom.
The ratio of computers to students in U.S. schools at the time was 1-to-92. Today, technology is widespread among schools. Access to computers has become so ubiquitous that digital devices are replacing the use of pen and paper in many classrooms. While public opinion on the use of technology in schools has been divided, experts have found that technology has the ability to create profound changes in teaching and learning, creating opportunities for unprecedented collaboration, engagement, and support.
The key is knowing how to use technology in meaningful ways—a skill some education degree programs are bringing to the forefront of their curricula.

What Is Instructional Technology?

Instructional technology is the theory and practice of using technology for education. Encompassing the design, development, use, management, and evaluation of technology in education, instructional technology can take many forms. Anything from electronic whiteboards to online courses or even virtual reality classrooms can be considered instructional technology. While the applications and benefits of instructional technology vary widely, all instructional technology shares one main purpose: to create engaging and effective learning experiences. And many applications of instructional

technology have proved effective at achieving this goal. Experts widely agree that instructional technology provides many benefits to the education process, including better access to information, more opportunities for collaboration, and better capabilities for meeting diverse learners' needs.

The Role of Technology in Modern Classrooms
Just a couple of decades ago, teachers used very little (if any) technology in the classroom. Today, technology is a fundamental part of the education process.
A recent study conducted by MidAmerica Nazarene University reports that students complete less than 42% of their work, both in and out of the classroom, using paper and pencil. In addition, the study found that 73% of teachers said that their students use tablets or laptops every day.
The increasing prevalence of technology in the classroom reflects a broader cultural shift. As the modern world becomes more digitized, tech literacy is becoming increasingly important. Teachers who use technology to support learning in meaningful ways can help prepare students for success in the

digital era.

Uses of Instructional Technology According to the U.S. Department of Education, schools can use educational technology to support both teaching and learning by infusing the classroom with valuable digital tools, expanding course offerings, increasing student engagement, and accelerating learning. Instructional technology offers nearly endless applications, but experts have identified three key areas where integrating technology can have a significant impact.

Collaborative Learning Instructional technology provides unparalleled opportunities for collaborative learning. Advances in technology have made sharing information easier than ever before. Today, educators have access to digital tools that allow students to work collaboratively outside of the classroom, discussing ideas or completing projects remotely and eliminating constraints such as standard classroom hours or geographic location.

Instructional technology also provides opportunities for students to work collaboratively with teachers, discussing ideas or asking questions outside of the physical classroom. For example, teachers could hold digital office hours, making themselves available via instant messaging or video chat to support students as they tackle the day's homework.

Virtual Classrooms and Online Learning Virtual classrooms can be a useful tool at every level of education. One common challenge of the traditional

classroom environment is that students learn at their own pace, so teachers need to find a way to tailor their lesson plans to the average learner, rather than addressing each student's unique needs. Online courses level the playing field and provide students with the time and resources to develop the skills they need.

For example, students could listen to a lecture for a second time if they didn't immediately grasp the subject matter or move ahead to the next one if they grasp a particular subject quickly.

On top of this, online learning provides access to a wider array of topics, giving students opportunities to enrich their education by taking courses that their schools might not offer.

Real-Time Feedback Instructional technology provides better capabilities for gathering or providing feedback compared with more traditional methods.

Teachers can use a variety of digital tools to gauge where their students are in a particular lesson. For example, teachers might conduct an online survey of students' current understanding of a topic to gain insight into where they should focus the next lesson.

Or they might opt for using digital education software so they can provide immediate feedback to students on lessons and homework, which could help keep students on track with learning objectives.

Some schools have even been piloting virtual reality classrooms, where teachers can rehearse lessons or work through professional challenges in an artificial environment, helping them hone their abilities without negatively impacting real students.

How Technology Can Impact Student's Learning Even the best teachers deal with resistance from students either because the student cannot relate to the teacher or they cannot relate to the subject material. The best thing an educator can do for a student is to empower them to be responsible for their learning. Technology helps them do this with very little upfront training.

GoGuardian, a device management solution company for classrooms says, "With technology in hand, students suddenly become the builders of their own knowledge, and they experience a greater sense of independence and autonomy from using digital tools to augment their understanding."
Along with making learning more personalized to each student, technology is also helping teachers, students, and their families connect increasingly outside the classroom.

Students can reach out for extra help or resources when they need it, and families can work together with their child and their child's teacher for optimal learning.

Benefits of Integrating Technology into the Classroom

There are many ways to enhance a classroom with technology. Here are two examples of why using tech in the classroom gives students the extra learning edge.

Students Can Set Their Own Pace Joan Giblin, PhD, an assistant teaching professor in the Graduate School of Education at Northeastern University, explains that the use of technology has become common in the K-12 setting. "Students can work ahead or review content according to their needs," she says. "This allows students to proceed at their own pace and receive specific reinforcement on some content and access more challenging content as needed."

Connecting Students to the World with Social Media and Virtual Reality Imagine being a teacher based in Boston and teaching your class about Switzerland. Your lesson might fall a little flat with just a book's description and photos of the country.
Utilizing technology, your class can conduct a virtual chat and interview with a class in Switzerland. They might be able to write and send emails to a government official who is happy to answer questions about the country or even use virtual reality tech to take tours of landmarks and local museums.

Ways Teachers Integrate Technology to Improve Outcomes Gamification Makes Learning More Rewarding Most students naturally love games, whether video games or board games. Children especially are wired for fun, which can make sitting still in a classroom for several hours a day difficult. Not all gaming is bad, and Psychological Bulletin reported that 10 to 30 hours of select gameplay per week.

can improve a student's spatial cognition and multitasking ability. Teachers are using gamification strategies to drum up interest in a specific subject or to help young minds dive deeper into a topic without relying solely on books and lectures. For example, instead of another worksheet on vocabulary words, an app or game that features silly cartoon monsters can be used to help kindergartners have fun while learning basic phonics. Gamification doesn't always require

technology. A trivia game created from your history lesson on a dry erase board would be a form of gamifying, too. However, children are entering classrooms addicted to technology, so using the technology they are familiar with to teach them new subjects is a practical way to connect with the modern student.
Gamification can help with student's social and behavioral development as well. "I am particularly intrigued by the growing trend of creating games to assist students with developing socio-emotional regulation," Giblin says. "This has the ability to help students with difficulties in these areas gain mastery, allowing them to better engage with their academics."

Technology Allows Students to Do More A few decades ago, students were limited in project creation. For example, if a class wanted to collaborate to write a book, getting it published in a timely and affordable manner was not a possibility.

Similarly, recording any audio or video required expensive and specialized equipment. Now, many students have easier access to technology, making goals like these possible.
"Technology allows students to author and create their projects, moving them into higher-order learning," Giblin says. "Instead of reading about a topic, students can create and author learning experiences for themselves and others. For example, a middle school class discussing empathy may interview different people about their understanding of what it means to be empathetic." Giblin explains that through the use of technology, the students are able to detect patterns and non-verbal responses when they analyze the interviews. They are then able to create their own content based on what they learned to teach their classmates.

How Teachers Can Utilize Technology to Have a Greater Impact As an educator, you have access to millions of teachers worldwide at your fingertips. Use technology to connect with them and share ideas. Ideas and resources from others with different teaching styles, grade levels, and viewpoints are easily accessible. For example, you might learn a new strategy for teaching cultural awareness from a teacher overseas, or your unique idea on how to conduct collaborative screenwriting with a tablet might inspire a teacher across the country. Technology is never meant to replace a trained and caring teacher, though. Instead, technology-driven education can benefit both the educator and the student by allowing them to make the classroom experience unforgettable. Find out how you can learn more tech-centered ideas for the classroom through North eastern's Doctor of Education program. Students can complete their studies in

their own time, virtually. You will be learning real-world applications that you can start integrating into your classroom immediately.

2) Explain your skills using a computer – address classroom management (ex: grade book), instructional, etc.

I have a love and hate relationship with technology. Hate is probably too strong a word, but there are days that technology does not make my job easier. I am not talking about the multiple uses for it in the classroom,
I am talking about managing technology in general. Everyone of our students interacts with some sort of technology on a regular basis. We may like to kid ourselves about the use of technology, but the reality is, our students are growing up in a digital age.
They have more computing power in one cell phone

than the first moon launch did. ZME Science states that the I phone 6's clock is 32,600 times faster than the fastest computer used in the Apollo era computers and could perform instruction 120,000,000 times faster.

Used correctly, this is a powerful tool in the hands of our students. Used incorrectly, we look at pictures of chemistry cats and play video games. My issues with technology have less to do with the use of it and more to do with the management. With a background in physical and health education, I am not a fan of technology in the classroom. However, I have used it effectively in many ways. And yes, even I have had students pull a cell phoneout in the middle of an active game or activity to check messages, which has given me pause. Advancements in technology have made our lives significantly easier. I do like the appropriate use of technology. Classroom management software, educational software, curriculum software, and the vast array of good programs out there allow me to more effectively present information. If used properly it can be an amazing educational tool in your classroom. If we speak from a classroom management issue, it can become an absolute nightmare for a teacher. Students, and adults, are addicted to technology. We get that a hit of dopamine as we expect the reward of a social media message, text, or other "ping" from our device and we feel good about it.

We become dopamine addicted to social media and it eats up our time as is presented by Trevor Haynes a research technician in the Department of Neurobiology at Harvard University in a recent study.

We are in a struggle for time over technology in our classrooms. Our students are masters of using technology.

They know how to do the finger swipe from screen to screen to hide what they were seeing. They have multiple screens open at any one time.

These are the students who think they can multi-task but really are distracted by social media, games, music, video or any other form of programming they can access.

It is inhibiting their relationships and there is even good research being presented that suggests that the cell phone that is turned off and stowed is impacting the students learning.

As suggested in a recent article on Edutopia.org, students who split their time between learning tasks and cell phone or Facebook performed poorly when compared to students who did not split their time. With this information in mind, what can I do as a teacher to manage the technology use in the classroom?

This is an easy answer if you have a clear technology policy in place for the school. The school should have an agreed upon acceptable use policy for electronic devices in the school and classroom setting. With an acceptable use policy, the students, teachers, and administrators can identify key behaviors, times, and places that are acceptable within the school. In an era of cyber-bullying, online harassment, sharing of test information, and many other nefarious uses, this is not just prudent behavior for a school, it is necessary and even required.

These are just some examples, found through searches on the internet, of good quality acceptable technology usage. Are they perfect for every school? course not. You must address the individual issues within the school setting. With a clear policy in place, the school and the teacher have a strong foundation for addressing appropriate internet and technology usage.

As the administrator, you must ensure that the teachers, students, and the parents are aware of the policy and the enforcement of the policy within the school setting. You must ensure that teachers support his policy and fairly enforce it within the context of their setting. I say fairly rather than equally because the ultimate usage of technology is up to the teacher. Each teacher must make the decision of how they will manage technology in the classroom within the guidelines of the school.

As the administrator, you must ensure that the teachers, students, and the parents are aware of the policy and the enforcement of the policy within the school setting. You must ensure that teachers support his policy and fairly enforce it within the context of their setting.

I say fairly rather than equally because the ultimate usage of technology is up to the teacher. Each teacher must make the decision of how they will manage technology in the classroom within the guidelines of the school.

Focusing on acceptable use at the beginning of the year is the best time to resolve issues. This is where involvement and buy in with the students is critical. There are many methods a teacher could use to address the management of technology in the classroom. However, the most critical is the decision of the comfort level of the teacher with technology use in the class setting.

As the educator, you need to set clear expectations for the use of technology in the classroom. However, we must also recognize that students will find ways to work around the rules and expectations we set. This is especially true if we do not include them in the discussion and only dictate the rules to them.

Worse, if you outline one set of rules, and the teacher next door does something completely different, the students will be upset and work to disrupt the teacher who has set stricter expectations. However, if you involve the students in this discussion on what is acceptable use, they will support the class expectations that are set, especially if they believe that they are responsible for its development and the usage is fair to the class setting.

Students want to know why they must follow a direction or rule. Students are just like adults in that regard and knowing "why" is a fair request. Providing the explanation as more than "because the school policy says so" or worse "because I say so" is critical. So is allowing flexibility under the guidelines. Consider how we use technology in the school as an adult. We use it to communicate, check social media, email, set appointments, and many other uses. If we tell students to not do these things, then do them ourselves, we create a natural conflict. However, if we allow for appropriate use of technology in the classroom, we must teach the students what that looks like.

In addition to creating your own class expectation of technology and agreeing to it, one must also teach appropriate use. Ideally, this is a school-wide instruction on how to use technology appropriately. In this manner, consistent uses of technology can be shared school-wide. However, absent this expectation, the teacher must provide this instruction.

Regardless, the teacher must provide at least minimal instruction on what the expectations are, and look like, within the classroom. Model appropriate use. Discuss it in class. Allow them time to use technology appropriately. Reinforce appropriate behavior. And most importantly, respectfully address breaches of the class technology expectations.

This is not to say that we allow students free reign within our classroom to use technology as they see fit. We must identify that this would be a problem. Instead, it is to provide instruction and guidelines on technology use, especially as we technology in class or in professional settings.

The complex issues of cyber-bullying, online harassment, and abuse need direct instruction and clear guidelines. However, copying information from sites or even plagiarism or using copyrighted material are not clear. We must instruct on these topics, so our students understand rather than assuming what they know and finding ourselves addressing issues of academic honesty.

From a purely management standpoint, it is recommended that the teacher uses some form of a sign, non-verbal image or signal to alert students when they might use technology freely. Identify when students must use strict classroom expectations, and when they may have flexibility in its use. Realize one very important point though, unless you have the ability to fully control the electronics devices in the classroom, you do not have full control of the management of the devices. It is a hard reality, but a reality none the less.

Some teachers choose to require students to check in cell phones early in class and get them at the end. Some teachers have a holding area for technology where items are stored. Some teachers choose to allow students to use devices freely in class with minimal expectations. There is nothing wrong with any of these options. It depends on you, the educator or administrator, to determine acceptable levels of use.

As my background is in health and physical education, I cannot highly stress the importance of breaks from technology. Provide students with options to technology use or simply times for the students to have breaks. Students do need to disengage from technology and have discussions that do not require electronic devices. This is where a teacher can bring in Socratic Seminars or other discussion strategies to engage students without devices.

Finally, on can not address the issue of a technology use policy without addressing the consequences for violation of said policy within the school and classroom. These must be reasonable, enforceable, and appropriate for the environment. The students will need technology for use in their classrooms or simply for communication during the day. To simply take the electronic devices as a consequence, while effective, results in the teacher or administration being responsible for damage to the device. In addition, the student may have a legitimate need to use the device during the day and loss of it would create a hardship for the student and teachers. That being said, there should be a consequence for the student who continues to violate the technology use policy. That may mean checking the device into the office in the morning, or not bringing a laptop to school. The more creative a school can get with this, and the more the student is responsible for the consequence and re-education of the use of the device, the more effective the consequence will be. However, for this to be effective, consequences must be consistent and enforce the policy. The greatest challenge the administrator will face is inconsistency within the school in this regard.

3) Are you comfortable with the use of technology in the classroom?

Teachers' comfort with technology in the classroom can vary widely. Some teachers are very comfortable and adept at integrating technology into their teaching practices, using it to enhance student learning and engagement.
Others may be less comfortable or familiar with technology and may require more support and training to effectively incorporate it into their teaching. Support, training, and access to resources can play a significant role in helping teachers become more comfortable with using technology in the classroom.

Technology can be incredibly useful in teaching in several ways:

1. Enhanced Learning: Technology can provide interactive and multimedia experiences that enhance learning. For example, educational videos, simulations, and games can make complex concepts easier to understand.

2. Access to Information: The internet provides access to a vast amount of information, allowing students to research topics in depth and explore diverse perspectives.

3. Communication and Collaboration: Technology enables communication and collaboration among students and teachers, breaking down barriers of time and space. Tools like email, discussion forums, and collaborative documents facilitate communication and teamwork.

4. Personalized Learning: Technology can be used to personalize learning experiences based on students' individual needs and learning styles. Adaptive learning software, for example, can adjust the pace and content of instruction to match each student's abilities.

5. Efficiency: Technology can streamline administrative tasks for teachers, such as grading, attendance, and lesson planning, allowing them to focus more on teaching and student interaction.

6. Preparation for the Future: In today's digital world, it is essential for students to be familiar with technology. Using technology in the classroom helps prepare students for the future workforce, where digital skills are often required.

Overall, technology has the potential to greatly enhance teaching and learning, making education more engaging, accessible, and effective.

4) What are some ways you and students will use technology in your classroom? Describe your experience and skills in terms of applying technology.

Although many technology-based teaching methods and resources effectively engage students and build their skills, many educators encounter difficulties when using technology in the classroom. Maybe a specific platform is too hard to introduce. Or maybe it won't run on your devices.

Despite the challenges, you likely want to enjoy the benefits that education technology can deliver.

Using the ones that best apply to you and your students, consider these 25 easy ways to use technology in the classroom:

Delivering Content

1. Run a Virtual Field Trip If a location is out of reach due to logistical issues, you can simulate a virtual trip by buying a Google Cardboard for less than $15. There are apps you can use to explore famous buildings, such as the Empire State Building, and natural phenomena, such as the Great Barrier Reef.

You may ask: "How will this connect with a learning objective?" You could visit a foreign landmark, holding a mock conversation in that country's language. Or, you could study the area itself from a geographic perspective. This can add a new, engaging element to your lessons.

2. Preview Field Trips Virtually Similarly, you can use Google Earth to explore locations before actually visiting them. Let's say your class is set to go to the Zoo.
Find the location, traveling through it using Street View to see which exhibits pique the most student interest.

You can quickly discuss what they're looking forward to, boosting excitement levels for the trip. Popular field trip destinations will also have websites filled with visual media you can use to complement the preview. All it takes is a device connected to a projector or large screen.

3. Quiet a Noisy Classroom To make it easier to give lessons and presentations, use a tool that tracks and displays classroom noise. For example, Too Noisy is an accurate noise meter. You'll likely find that — without having to tell them — students will become quiet when the meter spikes. This means most of them won't be as disruptive when you give a lesson or run an independent work activity. They may even shush each other. In turn, you'll have an easier time presenting content.

4. Use Videos for Mini-Lessons You can bolster your lesson plans by using videos as stand-alone overviews for some topics. Also available as skill reviews and previews, there are many websites that host teacher-made video content.

Teacher Tube is an example of an education-only version of YouTube, covering core school subjects. You can search for a specific topic or browse by category, quickly finding relevant videos.

For example, searching for "middle school algebra" will load a results page containing study guides, specific lessons and exam reviews. This easy way to use technology in the classroom adds a multimedia element to your lessons, which can effectively resonate with visual learners.

Research has shown that the use of animated videos can positively impact a child's development in several competence areas including memory, creativity, critical thinking, and problem solving.

5. Co-ordinate Live Video You don't have to limit yourself to pre-recorded videos, as conferencing technology can allow subject matter experts to deliver lessons. Whether it's a contact from another school or a seasoned lecturer you reach out to, bringing an expert into your classroom will expose your students to new ideas and can lighten your workload. You can add the person as a contact on Zoom, Microsoft Teams or whichever platform your school users! Ask your students to prepare questions, helping them enjoy — and fulling participate in — this modern take on traditional lessons.

6. Play Podcasts Playing relevant podcasts for kids can not only supplement your lessons, but engage auditory learners and act as a learning station. Made by groups ranging from media giants to ordinary people passionate about a particular subject, you can find podcasts that are:

• Interviews with the author of a book your students are reading
• Lessons about studying techniques and strategies
• Explorations of a curriculum-related topic
• Lectures from professors for a high school course, you may want to design a project that allows students to create and play their own podcasts. This is one of the easiest ways to use technology in your classroom — you just need a device with strong speakers.

7. Add Multimedia Elements to Presentations Whereas slideshow presentations entirely made up of text can disengage students, ones with multimedia elements can effectively hold their attention by varying content delivery.

When applicable, try to include:
• Images
• Graphs
• Pictographs
• Podcast clips
• Sound effects
• Short video lessons
• News, movie and television show clips

You don't have to scour the Internet to find relevant graphs and pictographs — you can make them yourself. There are free online tools that take you through steps to input data, adjust labels and modify your design. It's likely that slideshow presentations already play a part in your lessons, and adding different kinds of media can make them more engaging.

8. Send Adaptive Content If each of your students has a smartphone and is always on it, why not use the situation to your advantage by delivering content through the phones? There are adaptive learning programs that students can access through tablets and smartphones.

For example, ClassK12 offers a mix of adaptive math and English exercises for students. It's made up of mobile apps that students can download onto their personal devices.

As a teacher, you can create virtual classrooms, deliver assignments and run reports. Delivering appropriate content through such programs may seem difficult, but the process is usually intuitive and automated.

9. Share an Online Class Calendar To keep students informed regarding the content they'll be tackling, create and share a class calendar that details lessons and highlights important dates. You can use a program such as Google Calendar, emailing your calendar's hyperlink to your students or their parents.

This not only keeps them informed, but helps you stay organized — you'll quickly see if you've set too many due dates in a short period. And by keeping students in the loop, you'll help them come prepared for each class.

Helping Students Process Content

10. Use Virtual Manipulatives When teaching and reinforcing some math concepts, students can use virtual manipulatives in more ways than physical ones. For example, a 6th grade geometry activity from the National Library of Virtual Manipulatives involves using geoboards to illustrate area, perimeter and rational concepts.

Although there are a few websites that provide these manipulatives, many teachers regard the National Library of Virtual Manipulatives as the most versatile and engaging. The website is made up of tasks targeted to students from pre-kindergarten to 12th grade. So, there should be something for your class.

This method of using technology in the classroom is not only easy to run, but appeals to hands-on learners.

11. Run Learning Stations Learning stations are a method of both delivering a range of content and giving students different ways to process it. With a device at each station, you can provide videos, podcasts, slideshows and other digital media. Students can then solve challenges to build understanding of the material.

This can involve: • Using virtual manipulatives • Solving relevant problems in a computer game • Recording their thoughts about, and responses to, a podcast • Contributing notes to a group Wiki page, which this guide explains in a later section One of the best parts of this approach? It works for classes without one-to-one device use, as students can group together at each station.

12. Provide Online Activities for Students Who Complete Work Early Similarly, you can set up stations for students to use when they complete work early, giving them engaging ways to further process content.

Set up a few devices that have videos, websites and educational games open.

Take time to ensure that this material is aligned with your lesson, allowing students to delve into relevant topics.

By doing so, you'll encourage them to wisely use every bit of class time. Even those few minutes before the bell rings.

13. Save Time for Exit Tickets Saving ten minutes at the end of class for exit tickets opens the door for easy technology use. Exit tickets can take the form of: • Online Journal Entries — Using an online notepad, students can write a journal entry to summarize what they learned.
• Slideshow Comments — Sharing copies of slideshows from the day's lesson, students can make comments through PowerPoint or Google Slides to review and expand on important points.
• Tweets — In 280 characters or less, students can summarize the most important point they learned in class. You can easily see what they wrote by asking them to use a class-exclusive hashtag.

Exit tickets are not only quick from a student perspective, but you should find them easy to introduce and oversee.

14. Use Twitter Hashtags to Take Questions Just as you can use a class-exclusive hashtag for exit tickets, you can use it to take questions throughout the day.

By inputting the hashtag in Twitter's search bar, you can display the feed on a screen during class or check it periodically on your device.

You can choose to answer all the questions at once, or as they pop up. Either way, you don't want to see an empty feed. Encourage students to ask inquiry questions, as well as specific ones related to lessons, presentations, homework and more. This use of technology can be especially beneficial for introverts, who may not be comfortable asking questions in front of the class.

15. Study, Review and Critique Content on Web Pages Here's a technology-focused spin on notetaking: Find a web page with content reflecting or related to your lessons, and get students to make notes directly on the page. Using a program such as Bounce, you can create an interactive screenshot of any page just by inputting its URL. When students open the screenshot, they'll see commands to create notes, feedback and other edits. In classrooms with one-to-one device use, students can do this individually. In classrooms without one-to-one device use, you can make it a group activity. Ask each group to make notes and feedback aimed at improving the web page's content.

Once each group is done, compare the edits to see which group improved the page the most. Who knew writing notes could be so engaging?

16. Use Online Mind Maps for Class Brainstorms A digital take on brainstorming, there are websites you can use to create clear and detailed mind maps faster than written ones. For example, many teachers use Mind Meister, as its features are designed for students and educators. Put the program on a screen that everyone can see. Work with your students to brainstorm ideas as a way to reinforce lessons or launch a problem-based learning exercise. It should only take a few minutes to set up this kind of classroom technology.

17. Gather Student Feedback To encourage student input about content-processing activities, create and distribute surveys. In a few minutes, you can create forms and polls using applications such as:
• Socrative
• Google Forms
• SurveyMonkey
• Poll Everywhere Students can give responses through personal or classroom devices, giving you insight about the activities they prefer. Based on the results, you may find an easy way to improve lessons.
This could even involve using new technologies in the classroom.

Allowing Students to Create Products

18. Launch a Wiki Page for a Collaborative Assignment Collaboration doesn't have to take place face-to-face, as you can give group assignments focused on creating a wiki page. There are many programs you can use to create wiki pages, which are web pages that different people can edit. As a project, students can create one about a relevant topic. This process inherently encourages collaboration — students must contribute their own content to the page, editing and refining each other's work. This version of a group paper may also prove to be more engaging than its classic counterpart.

19. Set Up Student Blogs Blogging can be a creative outlet for students, lending itself especially well to language arts classes and other writing-heavy subjects. There are free templates and comprehensive privacy settings on platforms such as WordPress, which you can use to host each student's blog.
As for the products they can create? Some popular options are:
• Poems

• Short essays
• Diary entries from the perspective of a historical figure or character from a novel Blogging takes some time to set up, but — once you're rolling — it's one of the easiest ways to introduce and use technology in the classroom.

20. Offer Open-Ended Projects When it comes time to start a new project, give students a list of options to choose from. This way, you can appeal to their distinct learning styles and they can effectively demonstrate their knowledge.
The projects can involve:
• Designing web content
• Putting together e-books
• Creating original artwork
• Composing musical tunes
• Crafting multimedia products

Students can use widely-accessible software to complete these projects, which you may want to provide on classroom devices. This way, you can dedicate in-class time to project work while giving students some autonomy over how they use technology in school.

21. Use Online Sign-Ups When it comes time for students to deliver presentations, using digital signup forms is an easy way to incorporate technology. Like sharing a class calendar, send students a link to a survey. It should just contain a list of dates to choose from, so they can schedule a presentation time that works for them. They'll likely be happy to complete the project on their own paces.

22. Base Assignments on Technology-Focused Subjects Worried that students will find it too hard to use specific technologies when creating products? Instead, you can base assignments on subjects related to software and other technology. For example, students can write guides explaining how to use their favorite computer programs.
For a greater challenge, they can investigate and report how certain technologies have impacted history, politics or any other subject. They may develop a new appreciation for the technologies in question.

Offering a Unique Learning Experience

23. Introduce a Game-Based Learning Platform An ambitious way to use technology in the classroom is to introduce a game-based learning platform. Most are designed to engage students, enlivening difficult topics and subjects. Research backs up other benefits, too.

For example, video games stimulate an increase in midbrain dopamine to help store and recall information, according to a 2014 article in the journal of Learning, Media and Technology. Prodigy Education offers adaptive game-based learning through Prodigy Math and Prodigy English. Teachers can create classrooms, track student progress and deliver custom questions through plans and assignments.

24. Play Simulations Geared to solo and group use, online simulation games can add context and real world applicability to your lessons. Most simulations deal with subjects such as business and economics, which require the player to have math skills higher than the elementary level. But it is possible to find ones that appeal to younger students.
Regardless, as simulation programs become more advanced, they grow more engaging by teaching students how to apply their knowledge in a greater range of scenarios. And, because many of these programs work on most devices, you'll have an easy time testing and using them.

25. Participate in a WebQuest WebQuests encourage students to find and process information in engaging contexts, adding an interesting spin to the research process.
These free online adventures could, for example, place students in the role of a detective. To solve a specific case, they may have to collect clues — and information — related to a curriculum topic by scouring certain sources and web pages.
You can create your own adventure, but you should find WebQuests through some Google searches. By the end of it, your students will be surprised by how much research they did.

5) What do you believe distinguishes a good teacher from a great teacher (values, skills, knowledge)?

Distinguishing between a good teacher and a great teacher can be subjective and can vary depending on individual perspectives. However, there are some common traits and characteristics that are often associated with great teachers:

1. Passion for Teaching: Great teachers are passionate about their subject matter and about teaching itself. Their enthusiasm is contagious and inspires students to learn.

2. Effective Communication: Great teachers are able to communicate complex ideas in a clear and

understandable way. They listen actively to their students and provide constructive feedback.

3. Empathy and Understanding: Great teachers are empathetic and understanding, and they genuinely care about their students' well-being. They are able to connect with students on a personal level, which helps create a positive learning environment.

4. Adaptability: Great teachers are flexible and adaptable, able to adjust their teaching methods to meet the needs of individual students or changing circumstances.

5. Commitment to Continuous Improvement: Great teachers are always looking for ways to improve their teaching practice. They are open to feedback and are willing to try new approaches to enhance student learning.

6. High Expectations: Great teachers have high expectations for their students and motivate them to achieve their full potential. They provide the support and encouragement needed to help students succeed.

7. Lifelong Learners: Great teachers are lifelong learners themselves, continuously seeking to expand their knowledge and skills.

In terms of values, great teachers often value the importance of education, the empowerment of students, and the impact they can have on their students' lives.
They prioritize creating a positive and inclusive learning environment where all students feel valued and supported.

In summary, while good teachers possess many of the same skills, knowledge, and values as great teachers, what often distinguishes a great teacher is their passion, empathy, adaptability, commitment to improvement, high expectations, and dedication to lifelong learning.

6) Discuss the processes of assessment and documentation of student learning in your classroom (rubrics, portfolios, student-involved assessment, standards-based assessment, assessment of and for learning, quantitative/qualitative).

Assessment and Evaluation Assessment is the process of objectively understanding the state or condition of a thing, by observation and measurement. Assessment of teaching means taking a measure of its effectiveness. Assessment is the

systematic process of documenting and using empirical data on the knowledge, skills, attitudes and beliefs. By taking the assessment, teachers try to improve student learning. "Formative" assessment is measurement for the purpose of improving it. "Summative" assessment is what we normally call "evaluation."

Evaluation is the process of observing and measuring a thing for the purpose of judging it and of determining its "value," either by comparison to similar things, or to a standard. Evaluation of teaching means passing judgment on it as part of an administrative process. Evaluation focuses on grades and may reflect classroom components other than course content and mastery level.

Evaluation is a final review on your instruction to gauge the quality. It's product-oriented. This means that the main question is: "What's been learned?".

Finally, evaluation is judgmental. Ideally, a fair and comprehensive plan to evaluate training would incorporate many data points drawn from a broad array of teaching dimensions.

Such a plan would include not only student surveys, but also self-assessments, documentation of instructional planning and design, evidence of scholarly activity to improve teaching, and most importantly, evidence of student learning outcomes. But that is not all. A comprehensive evaluation of training would necessarily include various types of peer assessment, more commonly referred to as "peer observation."

Types of Assessment We can consider three main types of Learning Assessment: Diagnostic Assessment Formative Assessment Summative Assessment Diagnostic Assessment is a form of pre-assessment that allows a trainer to determine a student's individual strengths, weaknesses, knowledge, and skills prior to training. Its main benefits include: guides efficient and meaningful lessons and curriculum planning, provides information to individualize instruction, and creates a baseline for assessing future learning.

Formative Assessment is an ongoing assessment that helps to understand learners' progress and their level of understanding during training.

In contrast to assessment OF learning, formative assessment is known as assessment FOR learning because this information can help adjusting training during the unit to help learners.

Its main benefits are: facilitates modifying instruction based on the learning of the students, learners can receive feedback about their learning in order to identify strengths and weaknesses, learners are challenged to self-evaluate what and how they've learned and their level of understanding.

Summative Assessment is used to evaluate learning as well as serve as comparisons for standards. It measures a student's achievement at the end of a learning process. The goal of summative assessment is to evaluate student learning at the end of an instructional unit by comparing it against some standard. Information from summative assessments can be used formatively by learners of trainers to guide their efforts and activities in subsequent courses.

Research in education has focused on these three types of assessment:
1. Assessment for learning;
2. Assessment as learning;
3. Assessment of learning.

These three types of assessment might be described as follows:

1. Assessment for learning is designed to give trainers information to modify and differentiate training and learning activities. It acknowledges that individual students learn in idiosyncratic ways, but it also recognizes that there are predictable patterns and pathways that many students follow. It requires careful design on the part of trainers so that they use the resulting information not only to determine what students know, but also to gain insights into how, when, and whether students apply what they know. Trainers can also use this information to streamline and target instruction and resources, and to provide feedback to students to help them advance their learning.

2. Assessment as learning is a process of developing and supporting metacognition for students. Assessment as learning focuses on the role of the student as the critical connector between assessment and learning. When students are active, engaged, and critical assessors, they make sense of information, relate it to prior knowledge, and use it for new learning. This is the regulatory process in metacognition. It occurs when students monitor their own learning and use the feedback from this monitoring to make adjustments, adaptations, and even major changes in what they understand. It requires that trainers help students develop, practice, and become comfortable with reflection, and with a critical analysis of their own learning.

3. Assessment of learning is summative in nature and is used to confirm what students know and can do, to demonstrate whether they have achieved the curriculum outcomes, and, occasionally, to show how they are placed in relation to others. Trainers concentrate on ensuring that they have used assessment to provide accurate and sound statements of students' proficiency, so that the recipients of the information can use the

information to make reasonable and defensible decisions. This document focuses on assessment for learning as the tool that enables trainers to systematically develop the knowledge of their students that they need to provide personalized, precise instruction and assessment. It incorporates strategies to engage students and support assessment as learning as an integral part of the process.

The Benefits of Assessment for Learning Studies have shown that the use of assessment for learning contributes significantly to improving student achievement, and that improvement is greatest among lower achieving students.

Assessment for learning is the process of gathering evidence about a student's learning from a variety of sources, using a variety of approaches, or "assessment tools", and interpreting that evidence to enable both the trainer and the learner to determine: - where the learner is in his or her learning; - where the learner needs to go; and - how best to get there. Trainers can adjust instructional strategies, resources, and environments effectively to help all students learn only if they have accurate and reliable information about what their students know and are able to do at any given time, and about how they learn best. Ongoing assessment for learning provides that critical information; it provides the foundation for differentiated instruction.

Components of Assessment for Learning Assessment for learning includes diagnostic assessment and formative assessment: Diagnostic assessment can include both classroom (educational) assessments and professional assessments (i.e., speech and language, medical, and psychological assessments providing information and/or diagnosis of specific conditions that affect learning).

Diagnostic assessments are conducted before instruction begins and provide trainers with information about students' readiness to learn, and about their interests and attitudes. This information establishes the starting point for new learning, and helps trainers and students set appropriate learning goals. It enables trainers to plan instruction and assessments that are differentiated and personalized to meet students' learning strengths, needs, interests, and learning preferences. Diagnostic assessment helps identify what the student brings to his or her learning, in general or with respect to a specific subject. Information can be gathered from various sources – from the student, the student's previous trainers, and the student's companies, etc. The information gathered provides a baseline that informs further assessment, the

results of which can be used in developing a student profile and/or a class profile. Examples of diagnostic assessment tools are: reviews of recent reports, consultation with previous trainers, companies, classroom observation (e.g. anecdotal notes), classroom assessment (pre-test, assessment of prior knowledge, etc.), commonly used assessments as well as assessments of achievement of alternative learning expectations (e.g. those relating to daily living, social skills, etc.), professional assessment, reviews of any existing transition plans, etc.

Formative assessment is conducted frequently and in an ongoing manner during learning and is intended to give trainers and students precise and timely information .so that instruction can be adjusted in response to individual students' strengths and needs, and students can adjust their learning strategies or set different goals. This use of assessment differs from assessment of learning in that the information gathered is used for the specific purpose of helping students improve while they are still gaining knowledge and practicing skills. When assessment is viewed as integral to learning, students are engaged as collaborative partners in the learning process. Formative assessment is used to provide benchmarks to confirm the suitability of instructional strategies and specific interventions for individual students as well as groups of students. A gap analysis can be performed on the basis of these benchmarks to guide reflection on past practice and aid in making sound decisions about future instruction.

Examples of formative assessment tools are: classroom assessments of various types, using various modes and media that best suit students' strengths and needs, learning styles and preferences, interests, readiness to learn; provision of descriptive feedback to students; use of assessment results to guide further training; assessment results to guide ongoing assessment and monitoring students learning; etc.

The reliability of assessment for learning depends on: - the identification, clarification, and sharing of learning goals in student friendly language; - the student's understanding of the success criteria of these goals in specific terms – what successful attainment of the learning goals looks like; - descriptive feedback that helps students consolidate new learning by providing information about what is being done well, what needs improvement, and how to take steps towards improvement; and- self-assessment that motivates students to work more carefully and recognize their own learning needs, so that they can become effective advocates for how

they learn best. Assessment for learning involves collaboration among trainers, companies and students, and enables students to experience the successes that come with timely intervention and with instructional approaches and resources that are suited to the ways they learn best. Both factors help build students' confidence and provide them with the incentive and encouragement they need to become interested in and focused on their own learning. Planning Assessment and Instruction Knowing Your Students Education is moving away from a model based on the transmission of information in one direction – from trainer to student – and towards a reciprocal model that ensures students are listened to, valued, respected for who they are, and recognized as partners in their education. Greater student involvement in their own learning and learning choices leads to greater student engagement and improved achievement.

Planning Assessment and Instruction - Knowing Your Students

Education is moving away from a model based on the transmission of information in one direction – from trainer to student – and towards a reciprocal model that ensures students are listened to, valued, respected for who they are, and recognized as partners in their education.

Greater student involvement in their own learning and learning choices leads to greater student engagement and improved achievement.

Involving students as partners in the learning and teaching process calls for educators to:

-See the student as a whole person;
-know about various dimensions of every student's learning process, and not just about the student's performance;
-support every student in playing a more active role in his or her learning;
-take students' strengths, needs, interests, and views into account in planning & learning opportunities.

An emphasis on knowing your students as the starting point for effective planning of assessment and instruction is consistent with this approach. The following steps are part of the process of getting to know all the students in the class:
- gathering information about the students;
- engaging students and companies during the course of information gathering;
- processing and synthesizing information in order to develop an understanding of each student's strengths, learning style(s), preferences, needs, interests, and readiness to learn;

- selecting and/or developing, and implementing, appropriate and productive combinations of assessment and instructional strategies, activities, groupings, and resources to address the diverse needs of the students. Two highly effective tools that can assist trainers in getting to know their students and in planning effective instruction and assessment are the class profile and the individual student profile. The class profile is an information-gathering tool, a reference tool, and a tracking tool, all in one. It helps trainers plan effective assessment and instruction for all the students in the class, monitor student progress, and provide timely interventions when needed. The class profile provides a snapshot of the strengths and needs, interests, and readiness of the students in the class. It is a resource for planning that conveys a great deal of critical information at a glance, serving as an inventory of accumulated data.

It is a living document, in that it is both a reference tool for planning assessment and instruction at the beginning of the year, semesters or term, and a tracking tool for monitoring progress, recording changes, adjusting instructional strategies, planning subsequent instruction or interventions, and sharing information with other educators and organizations. The class profile can be developed at the beginning of the training, as trainers embark on the process of assessment for learning. It serves as a tool for recording and summarizing information gathered through diagnostic assessment prior to instruction and through formative assessment during instruction.

A class profile can be updated as the training process progresses. It enables trainers to identify patterns among their students in terms of:

- their learning styles and preferences (often referred to as a "learning profile");
- their current place in the learning, or "readiness to learn", with respect to the expectations of the particular subject and grade or course, as well as their learning strengths and areas in need of improvement; - their interests and talents;
- their socio-affective characteristics;
- the challenges involved in meeting their learning needs, and the supports that are required to address those needs.

The class profile assists in:
- sorting, categorizing, and summarizing classroom data;
- detecting patterns of similarities and differences among the students that will help guide the planning of assessment and instruction;
- engaging in evidence-based trainer inquiry centered on student learning;
- using data to design differentiated instruction

- forming flexible groupings; - monitoring student progress by noting results of ongoing assessments; - making adjustments in response to assessment results to better focus instruction; - sharing information among fellow trainers and company.

The profile provides an at-a-glance summary of the strengths and needs of all the students in the class and can serve as a quick reference for daily planning.

The student profile gives detailed, in-depth information about the learning strengths and needs of the individual student. It supplements the class profile as a tool for planning precise and personalized assessment and instruction for students who need extra attention and support in particular areas of learning.

The individual student profile provides detailed information about the student to guide the selection of assessment tools, instructional strategies, and, where appropriate, individualized supports that are best suited to that student's learning style, preferences, strengths, needs, interests, and readiness.

A student profile provides the detail trainers need in order to devise assessment and instruction that take into account the student's particular needs while capitalizing on his or her particular strengths. One of the key pieces of information detailed in the individual student profile is the student's current instructional level in the area (or areas) that present challenges for the student.

Essentially, the student profile facilitates the "gap analysis" that needs to be performed in order to determine where the student's abilities are relative to the stage of development in particular areas of learning.

On the basis of this analysis, instruction can be provided that directly targets the critical skills that the student needs to develop.

Assessment Tools Observation Observation is a method of gathering data by watching an individual's behavior in their natural setting. It entails simple watching and noting a person's behavior, for example after a training course to determine if they are able to perform the intended objectives. This method allows many aspects to be captured, including the physical environment, the person's own behaviors, and his or her interactions with others. Among the main benefits of using observation

as an assessment tool we find: Inexpensive method. It only requires observers' time. Easy to complete. Gathers information on actual behaviors rather than reported behaviors. Allows observer to directly see what people do rather than relying on what people say they do. Non-verbal language can provide valuable information.

Able to collect information as the learning is being applied. Does not rely on people's willingness or ability to provide information.

We should also take into consideration its main disadvantages: Can be time-consuming.

It assesses one person at a time Validity and reliability of the data may be affected since people usually perform better when they know they are being observed Difficult to assess preferences, opinions, or thought process Is open to misinterpretation Does not increase understanding of why a person behaves as they do Can be considered intrusive Susceptible to observer's bias (partiality, prejudice).

Interview Interviews are a data collection method aimed at gathering both facts and opinions. They involve asking open-ended questions where the respondent can answer the questions in as much detail as her or she wishes to.

Interviews can provide valuable insight into the behaviors, attitudes, opinions and mindsets.

There are different ways to conduct interviews including face-to-face, by telephone, or online.

The main benefits of using interview as an assessment tool are:

Flexible. Can provide valuable insight into individual perspectives.

Can ask follow questions to clarification. Can research deeper into potential issues.

Can be recorded to provide information for closer review at a later time (i.e. assess body language).

There are also disadvantages we should consider:

Can be time-consuming to administer

Not the most cost effective since you typically only interview one person at a time

No direct evidence a person can perform specific behaviors How to prepare an Appraisal Interview

PREPARATION - Arrange with enough time - Time and privacy - Assessment of performance

DEVELOPMENT - Review of assessment- Exploration of internal/external factors - Consensus and determination of objectives

FOLLOW-UP - Support - Reviews

Personal aspects in the interview Communication Listening Motivation Time Management Feedback Assertiveness Security Control of Emotions (EI) Objectivity.

"As a Physics teacher's crucial role in education"

1. Foundation of Science: Physics is often considered the foundation of all natural sciences. A physics teacher helps students understand fundamental concepts such as motion, forces, energy, and matter, which form the basis for understanding other scientific disciplines.

2. Problem-Solving Skills: Physics teaches critical thinking and problem-solving skills. A physics teacher helps students develop these skills, which are valuable in many areas of life, not just science.

3. Technology and Innovation: Many technological advancements are rooted in physics principles. A physics teacher can inspire students to pursue careers in fields such as engineering, technology, and research, driving innovation and progress.

4. Global Challenges: Physics plays a crucial role in addressing global challenges such as climate change, energy production, and healthcare. Physics teachers can educate students about these challenges and inspire them to contribute to solutions.

5. STEM Education: Physics is a key component of STEM (science, technology, engineering, and mathematics) education. Physics teachers help prepare students for careers in these high-demand fields.

They play a vital role in shaping the future of science and technology by inspiring the next generation of innovators and problem solvers.

*****************the end*****************

www.ingramcontent.com/pod-product-compliance
Lightning Source LLC
Chambersburg PA
CBHW081005180426
43194CB00044B/2808